The Clarinet

The Clarinet

Edited by Jane Ellsworth

UNIVERSITY OF ROCHESTER PRESS

First published 2021

University of Rochester Press
668 Mt. Hope Avenue, Rochester, NY 14620, USA
www.urpress.com
and Boydell & Brewer Limited
PO Box 9, Woodbridge, Suffolk IP12 3DF, UK
www.boydellandbrewer.com

ISBN-13: 978-1-64825-017-0
ISSN: 1071-9989 , v. 179

Library of Congress Cataloging-in-Publication Data:

Names: Ellsworth, Jane, author.
Title: The clarinet / edited by Jane Ellsworth.
Description: Rochester : University of Rochester Press, 2021. | Series: Eastman studies in music, 1071-9989 ; 179 | Includes bibliographical references and index.
Identifiers: LCCN 2020056218 | ISBN 9781648250170 (hardback)
Subjects: LCSH: Clarinet. | Clarinet–History.
Classification: LCC ML945 .C53 2021 | DDC 788.6/2–dc23
LC record available at https://lccn.loc.gov/2020056218

This publication is printed on acid-free paper.

Printed in the United States of America.

CONTENTS

NOTE TO THE READER

Pitch Notation

The method of designating pitches in this book is scientific pitch notation, which has been adopted for its visual clarity and ease of use. In this system, C^4 = middle C on the piano keyboard. The standard written range of most clarinets thus begins at E^3 (E below middle C), and extends upward to C^7 and beyond. Clarinets with extended low ranges reach down as far as C^3. Since most clarinets are transposing instruments, the pitches given are written rather than sounding pitches. For an explanation of this, see the Introduction.

Source References

Articles in *Grove Music Online* (*Oxford Music Online*, Oxford University Press) may be found at the following URL (a subscription-based resource): https://www.oxfordmusiconline.com/grovemusic

The abbreviation *MGG* refers to *Musik in Geschichte und Gegenwart*, also now available online by subscription: https://www.mgg-online.com

ACKNOWLEDGMENTS

It has been my great pleasure to work with the authors who have contributed to this book, all of whom are experts in multiple facets of the clarinet and its history. Some—Eric Hoeprich, Colin Lawson, Ingrid Pearson, and Al Rice—are longtime friends and colleagues. But I am glad to have also made new friends in the process, in Julian Rushton, David Schneider, Marie Sumner Lott, and Fred Starr. All of these distinguished scholars and performers are also first-rate human beings.

I am grateful to Ralph Locke, senior editor of the University of Rochester Press's Eastman Studies in Music series, for asking me to serve as editor of this book, and for his cheerful support and patience; and to my dear friend and mentor Charles Atkinson, who recommended me to Ralph. I thank Julia Cook, Rio Hartwell, and many other individuals at Boydell & Brewer for helping this book into publication.

Lastly, my love and thanks go to my husband, Bill Conable, who helped in the areas of feedback, proofreading, music typesetting, and all-around spousal support.

INTRODUCTION

Jane Ellsworth

The clarinet has been part of European musical life for a little more than 300 years. This makes it rather new by comparison with many other instruments. Yet, once established, it was adopted for use in military bands, orchestras, and popular music of many different types. Today it is a familiar instrument played by both professionals and amateurs, heard in settings ranging from school bands to world-renowned orchestras, from community musical theater productions to Broadway, and in genres from klezmer and Brazilian choros to symphonic music and jazz. From simple beginnings around 1700, the clarinet has developed into a sophisticated and versatile instrument.

Numerous excellent English-language books have been written about the clarinet, starting with F. Geoffrey Rendall's monograph of 1954 and continuing through recent works by Rice, Lawson, Hoeprich, and others.[1] These provide excellent comprehensive surveys of the instrument's history. Why, then, another book? The answer is at least twofold. In the first place, previous writings have been aimed

---

1 F. Geoffrey Rendall's *The Clarinet: Some Notes upon Its History and Construction* (London: Williams and Norgate, 1954) was the earliest book-length history of the clarinet. Albert Rice has written a series of books on the clarinet: *The Baroque Clarinet* (Oxford: Clarendon Press, 1992, soon to be released in a second edition), *The Clarinet in the Classical Period* (Oxford: Oxford University Press, 2003), and *From the Clarinet d'Amour to the Contra Bass: A History of Large Size Clarinets, 1740–1860* (New York: Oxford University Press, 2009). Colin Lawson edited the very useful *The Cambridge Companion to the Clarinet* (Cambridge: Cambridge University Press, 1995), and wrote *The Early Clarinet: A Practical Guide* (Cambridge: Cambridge University Press, 2000) as well as several important volumes on clarinet repertoire in the series Cambridge Music Handbooks. Most recently, Eric Hoeprich has contributed an extensive volume to the Yale series with *The Clarinet* (New Haven, CT: Yale University Press, 2008).

at readers with a rather specialized knowledge, insiders with a working understanding of the clarinet's technical, mechanical, and musical intricacies. The present book, on the other hand, has a more varied readership in mind. As part of a set of volumes on musical instruments within the series Eastman Studies in Music, its rationale is to appeal to a broad spectrum of readers: not only those engaged as professionals or students in the field of music, but also musically informed amateurs, concert-goers, recording collectors, and the like.[2] Secondly, rather than attempting exhaustive coverage of the entire history and development of a given instrument, the volumes in this set focus on selected topics related to repertoire, style, and other matters that are manifestly central to the history of the instrument and its uses in musical life, yet in many cases are not covered extensively elsewhere in the literature. The chapter authors are leading musicologists, historians, and performing musicians (many occupy more than one of these roles), who present unique perspectives reflecting wide experience in their disciplines.

The emphasis in this book is therefore not so much on the clarinet as an object as on the way it has been used, by various types of composers and players in different kinds of music, over the span of more than three centuries. A number of the essays also consider the clarinet's socio-cultural position during the period of its existence, ranging from its presence in court and theater orchestras patronized by the eighteenth-century aristocracy to its appearance in jazz bands and other types of popular music in our own time. Eric Hoeprich's opening chapter on clarinet iconography, which draws upon his large collection of graphic depictions of the instrument, allows us literally to see the many different types of people who have played the clarinet over the course of its history, and the varied contexts in which they have done so.

Because of its late appearance relative to other woodwinds, the clarinet's repertoire is somewhat more circumscribed than that of, say, the flute or the oboe. Baroque music for the clarinet, as well as for its slightly older relative the chalumeau, does exist in ample supply, however, as Albert R. Rice demonstrates in his chapter on the pre-Mozart repertoire and its players. Rice surveys this repertoire, including some recently uncovered works, and introduces the reader to a few of the earliest performers.

---

2   The first book in the set, on the violin, is already published: Robert Riggs, ed., *The Violin* (Rochester, NY: University of Rochester Press, 2016)._

As the clarinet became more firmly established its repertoire grew apace, and by the later eighteenth century it had taken hold as a regular solo instrument in concertos and chamber music and as a semi-regular member of the orchestra. In theater and court or concert orchestras, composers found the clarinet to be an important addition to the orchestra's color palette; it could be used to express particular effects and to portray or accompany specific types of characters. Three chapters on the clarinet in the orchestra explore these ideas. My own chapter on the clarinet in the concert orchestra is a historical survey of the ways in which composers have used the clarinet in abstract and programmatic music. The chapters by Ingrid E. Pearson and Julian Rushton on the clarinet in the opera orchestra add valuable insights to this rarely studied subject. Pearson has rediscovered a large repertoire of eighteenth- and early nineteenth-century music from the major operatic centers of Paris, London, Naples, and Vienna that gives an important role to the clarinet. Rushton, in discussing the more well-known operas of the later nineteenth century, reminds us that composers made the clarinet as much a "singer" as the divas themselves.

At the same time as the clarinet began to appear more frequently in orchestras, the age of the clarinet virtuoso was beginning. For much of the eighteenth century it was possible (indeed, it was common practice) for the clarinet to be played by a jack-of-all-trades woodwind player, who might carry an oboe and flute with him as well. As the instrument developed mechanically and the technical demands placed upon it grew, however, it became increasingly necessary to employ specialist players. Starting in about 1770, numerous individuals emerge as early celebrities in the history of the clarinet. The lives of these performers are as important to the history of the instrument as is the music that was written for them, and their biographies have been traced by historians such as Pamela Weston, whose three volumes on clarinetists of yesteryear and today have become staples of the literature.[3] The music played by these virtuoso clarinetists is examined in chapters on the concerto (David E. Schneider) and chamber music (Marie Sumner Lott). Schneider's chapter looks at the "golden age" of the clarinet concerto, from 1800 to 1830, and examines how works by Spohr, Weber, Crusell, and others helped to shape the formal and dramatic conventions of the genre in the nineteenth century. Sumner Lott discusses the clarinet quintet, examining four examples

---

3   *Clarinet Virtuosi of the Past* (Denham Green, UK: the author, 1971), *More Clarinet Virtuosi of the Past* (London: the author, 1977), and *Yesterday's Clarinettists* (Ampleforth, UK: Emerson Edition, 2002).

by Mozart, Weber, Meyerbeer, and Brahms to show how the genre developed, and how particular clarinetists influenced those composers. My chapter on clarinetists since 1900 considers a selection of the important virtuoso clarinetists of the twentieth and early twenty-first centuries and suggests some ways in which the profession is changing to become more inclusive.

It is intriguing to imagine how music from the earlier periods of the clarinet's history might have sounded in its own time, played on instruments with key mechanisms and other attributes quite unlike those that now exist. Arguably the most important movement in classical music performance in the second half of the twentieth century has been the approach now known as historically informed performance—HIP, for short—embracing both stylistic practices and the use of period instruments. Colin Lawson's chapter on the history of the HIP clarinet, written from the perspective of someone centrally involved as both a performer and a scholar, offers an appraisal of the ways in which this movement has touched clarinetists, and the conceptual and technical demands it has placed on them.

One of the most striking features of the clarinet, and perhaps the source of its lasting appeal, is its tremendous adaptability. Certainly, no other woodwind instrument has been used as successfully in as wide a variety of musical styles. The clarinet has found a comfortable home in classical music, as this book demonstrates in some detail, but also in American jazz and in many ethnic popular traditions. The expansive chapter by S. Frederick Starr illuminates the fascinating ways in which the clarinet entered some of this "vernacular" repertoire, exploring the roots of these diverse traditions and taking us from Austria to Eastern Europe (for Balkan wedding music and klezmer), and from Mexico and Haiti to Cuba and the United States (for Latin dance styles and early jazz).

Lay readers may find it helpful to have a brief overview of the main types of clarinets in use, along with an introduction to some common terminology, and the following section provides that.[4] Readers proficient in the terminology may wish to proceed to the book's main chapters.

---

4   Further definitions of clarinet-related terminology may be found in Jane Ellsworth, *A Dictionary for the Modern Clarinetist* (Lanham, MD: Rowman and Littlefield, 2015).

Terminology

Like many instrument families, the clarinet family is divided into categories based on vocal ranges: soprano, alto, tenor, and bass. To these may be added a category higher than soprano (sopranino), and a category lower than bass (contrabass). The clarinet most frequently encountered by the public is the soprano clarinet, although the prefix is rarely used. All clarinets share more or less the same written playing range, which is quite large, extending from E^3 on the low end to C^7 and above on the high end; but the written pitches are generally not the sounding pitches (see more about this below).[5] Instruments with the prefix "**basset**" (from the Italian *bassetto*, meaning "little bass")—namely the basset clarinet and the basset horn—have an extended low range that reaches down below the ordinary range of the clarinet to written C^3. The **basset horn** appeared around 1760 as a way of filling the tenor range. During its heyday, up until the 1840s, it acquired a substantial repertoire as a solo and chamber music instrument, as well as being used in orchestras (especially opera orchestras).[6]

The **basset clarinet**, on the other hand, was a soprano clarinet with an extended lower range. First appearing around 1775, it was most famously used by the clarinet virtuoso Anton Stadler (1753–1812), for whom Mozart wrote his Clarinet Concerto K. 622 and other works. The basset clarinet has relatively little repertoire, and the continued production of historical replicas as well as modern basset clarinets serves mainly to facilitate the performance of Mozart's works using the instrument.[7] Most modern **bass** and **contrabass clarinets** also extend

---

5   This book uses scientific pitch notation for the designation of pitches. In this system, middle C is C^4, and the octaves above and below are numbered accordingly.

6   For more information on the basset horn and other low clarinets, see Rice, *From the Clarinet d'Amour to the Contra Bass*; John Newhill, *The Basset-Horn & Its Music*, 3rd ed. (Sale, Cheshire, UK: the author, 2003); and Thomas Grass and Dietrich Demus, *Das Bassetthorn: Seine Entwicklung und seine Musik*, 2nd ed. (Norderstedt: Books on Demand, 2004).

7   More information about the basset clarinet and its repertoire can be found in Albert Rice, "The Basset Clarinet: Instruments, Designs, and Patents," in *Instrumental Odyssey: A Tribute to Herbert Heyde*, ed. Laurence Libin (Hillsdale, NY: Pendragon Press, 2016), 157–78; Colin Lawson, *Mozart: Clarinet Concerto*, Cambridge Music Handbooks (Cambridge: Cambridge University Press, 1996); and Pamela Poulin,

downward to at least written Eb^3, and bass clarinets with extensions to written C^3 are common.

The discussion above refers to "written" pitches because most clarinets are **transposing instruments**; that is, the written pitch (i.e., the pitch fingered by the player) is not the sounding pitch. As an example, the common (soprano) clarinet, used today in school and community bands and the like, is pitched in B-flat. This designation is sometimes made explicit in its name, "B-flat clarinet," and for that reason B-flat is said to be its **nominal pitch**. In this case, this means that the sounding pitch is one whole-step lower than the written/fingered pitch: if the clarinetist fingers C, the sounding pitch is Bb; if the clarinetist fingers G, the sounding pitch is F. Clarinets in other nominal pitches also exist, and their transpositions may be larger than a whole step in relation to C. For example, a soprano clarinet in A sounds a minor third lower than the written/fingered pitch; a sopranino clarinet in E-flat sounds a minor third higher than the written/fingered pitch; a bass clarinet in B-flat sounds a major ninth lower than the written/fingered pitch. While perhaps confusing in theory, in practice this transposition need not bother the clarinetist, who simply plays what is written on the page.[8]

Table I.1 shows the generally accepted categories of modern clarinets (with the most commonly used in bold type) and their nominal pitches. This is by no means a comprehensive listing, but it will serve to orient the reader to the main clarinets referred to in this book and will allow for comparison when other types of historical clarinets are mentioned.

"Anton Stadler's Basset Clarinet: Recent Discoveries in Riga," *Journal of the American Musical Instrument Society* 22 (1996): 110–27.

8   In other words, it is the responsibility of the composer and publisher to make sure the written notes correspond to the required sounding notes—that music is correctly transposed before it reaches the performer. It should be noted that there are some occasions in the orchestral literature where a part written for a clarinet in a particular nominal pitch must be played on a clarinet of a different nominal pitch, for reasons of convenience (a passage is easier to finger on one clarinet versus another) or necessity (the composer has requested a change to a different clarinet, but hasn't left enough time for the performer to switch instruments). In these cases, the clarinetist must either transpose at sight, or go to the trouble of writing out the part in the transposed key. It should also be noted that clarinets in the nominal pitch of C—that is, requiring no transposition—were not uncommon in the eighteenth and nineteenth centuries.

Table I.1. Main types of modern clarinets

Sopranino	Soprano	Alto/Tenor	Bass/Contrabass
Clarinet in A-flat	Clarinet in C	Clarinet in G	**Bass Clarinet in B-flat**
Clarinet in G	**Clarinet in B-flat**	Alto clarinet in F	Contrabass clarinet in E-flat
Clarinet in D	**Clarinet in A**	Basset horn in F	Contrabass clarinet in B-flat
Clarinet in E-flat	Basset clarinet in A		

The most commonly used types are shown in bold.

The inventor of the clarinet was the Nuremberg woodwind maker Johann Christoph Denner (1655–1707). Documentary evidence indicates that he had developed the instrument by about 1700. The typical early eighteenth-century clarinet had two or three keys; by the late eighteenth century the usual number was five. Makers continued to add keys, and in the first half of the nineteenth century innovative key mechanisms were invented by Iwan Müller (1786–1854) and the partnership of Louis-Auguste Buffet (1789–1864) and Hyacinthe Klosé (1808–80). These inventions (with numerous intervening stages in the case of Müller's mechanism) were the source of the two differing **fingering systems** in use today: the German Oehler system and the French Boehm system, respectively.[9]

For ease of manufacture, the clarinet is divided into separate segments, or **joints**. The exact segmentation has varied in different historical periods, but today the standard number of joints is five: the **mouthpiece**, to which a single **reed** is attached by a **ligature** to generate sound; the **barrel** (or a curved **neck** on lower instruments), connecting the mouthpiece to the main body of the clarinet and serving as a tuning slide of sorts; the **upper and lower joints**, which bear the keys operated by the left and right hands, respectively; and the **bell**, which flares outward to add resonance to the notes produced when all the tone holes are closed and the instrument is sounding at its full length.

The clarinet differs acoustically from other woodwind instruments in its combination of closed pipe and cylindrical bore. This

---

9   A useful narrative of these nineteenth-century developments is found in Hoeprich, *The Clarinet* (New Haven, CT: Yale University Press, 2008), chapters. 7 ("1800 to 1843: Astounding Innovation and Breathtaking Virtuosity") and 8 ("1844 to 1900: The Clarinet Joins the Establishment").

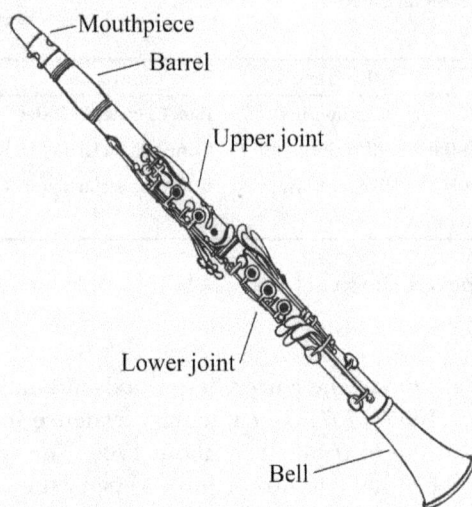

Figure I.1. Soprano clarinet (Boehm system) with parts labeled.

causes the first (i.e., the lowest, or **fundamental**) register and the second (or **overblown**) register to be in a relationship of a twelfth, rather
than an octave as it is on the oboe, flute, bassoon, and saxophone.
For example, when a clarinetist fingers written C^4 in the fundamental register, then adds the so-called **register** (or **speaker**) **key** to obtain
the overblown note, the resulting pitch is written G^5. It was in part
Denner's relocation of the hole covered by the speaker key to produce
a true overblown register that marked the difference between the clarinet and its older cousin, the chalumeau (which, practically speaking,
played only in its fundamental register). The other main difference
was the clarinet's flaring bell, as distinct from the chalumeau's cylindri-
cally bored foot joint.[10]

---

10 Readers interested in knowing more about clarinet acoustics may
    wish to consult Murray Campbell and Clive Greated, *The Musician's
    Guide to Acoustics* (Oxford: Oxford University Press, 1987); and O. Lee
    Gibson, *Clarinet Acoustics* (Bloomington and Indianapolis: Indiana
    University Press, 1994). Also useful is the Clarinet Acoustics website
    of the University of New South Wales (Australia): http://newt.phys.
    unsw.edu.au/jw/clarinetacoustics.html.

Each of the individual registers within the clarinet's range has its own tonal characteristics and nomenclature. The lowest is called the **chalumeau register** (E^3 to F^4), in reference to the precursor of the clarinet. Overblowing these pitches with the aid of the register key produces the **clarion register** (B^4 to C^6). Because the clarinet overblows twelfths rather than octaves, there is a short connecting register between the chalumeau and clarion, called the **throat register** ($F\#^4$ to Bb^4). The highest notes on the clarinet belong to the **altissimo register** (above C^6). A particular challenge for clarinetists is achieving a smooth connection at the point where the throat tones transition to the clarion register (i.e., from Bb^4 to B^4), a point known as the **break**.

Of course, none of these pitches can be produced without the aid of a **reed**, a small, specially shaved piece from the *Arundo donax* plant (informally referred to as **cane**) that is bound to the mouthpiece with a ligature and set in vibration by the player's air stream. The clarinet is an example of a **single-reed instrument** (as opposed to the double-reed oboe and bassoon). Some ancient single-reed instruments, such as the Egyptian *memet*, and folk single-reed instruments like the Middle Eastern *mijwiz*, make use of an **idioglot** reed, meaning that the reed is not a separate component that is attached to a mouthpiece (as on a modern clarinet), but is integral to the body of the instrument itself. The modern clarinet, in contrast, uses a **heteroglot** reed, a separate piece of shaved cane which is either fashioned by the player from scratch, or, more commonly, purchased in ready-made form.

With this basic background in hand, readers will be equipped to understand concepts and terminology used in the chapters that follow, and to enjoy the fascinating story of the clarinet and its repertoire presented in this book.

1

CLARINET ICONOGRAPHY

Eric Hoeprich

Context is everything in any iconographical study. In the case of the clarinet, images can provide essential clues about the instrument's origin, development, and amazingly diverse role in the history of musical life. Initially an anomaly, Johann Christoph Denner's prototypes from circa 1700 seem practically to have appeared out of thin air, notwithstanding slight and ambiguous connections with various folk instruments, organ pipes, and bagpipe drones, as well as the more established woodwinds. Early images of clarinetists start to bring the instrument into focus in a unique and informative way, providing details and context for this nascent stage. Prior to Denner's invention, an engraving by the Dutch artist Gerrit Clausz Bleker (1592–1656) shows a cowherd blowing on some sort of pipe, very possibly a single-reed instrument (fig. 1.1). Such simple, idioglot instruments had already made their way into Mersenne's highly regarded *Harmonie universelle* (Paris, 1636), albeit somewhat dismissively referred to as "a shepherd's pipe."[1] In this description, these Dutch and French depictions find common ground.

By the early 1700s, we are on firmer footing, and perhaps no image better illustrates this than Johann Christoph Weigel's iconic "Clarinetist" from his *Musikalisches Theatrum* (fig. 1.2). The elegantly attired player stands in an impressive room, and the caption suggests a noble, if not military, context.

---

1 Marin Mersenne, *Harmonie universelle* (Paris: Sebastien Cromoisy, 1636).

Figure 1.1. Gerrit Clausz Bleker, *Der Kuhhirte* (1638). With kind permission of the Boston Museum of Fine Arts.

When the trumpet call is all too loud,
The clarinet knows how to please
Eschewing both the high and the lowest sound,
It varies gracefully; and thus attains the prize.
Wherefore the noble spirit, enamored of this reed,
Instruction craves and plays assiduously.

Similarly, Martin Engelbrecht's patrician (amateur?) musician, posed next to a table replete with woodwind instruments, entitled "Flöten, Hautbois, Flachinett, Fagot und Clarinett, &c." (Augsburg, ca. 1725), shows the clarinet as an equal among its woodwind peers, again in a refined setting.[2] And although they are quite pretty, the more utilitarian fingering charts from J. F. B. C. Majer (*Museum Musicum*, Schwäbisch Hall, 1732; fig. 1.3) and J. P. Eisel (*Musicus Autodidaktos*, Erfurt, 1738) do not go much beyond the merely informative. The

---

2   Martin Engelbrecht (ca. 1720–30). New York Public Library, New York; see Albert R. Rice, *The Baroque Clarinet and Chalumeau*, 2nd ed. (Oxford: Oxford University Press, 2020), 193. Rice also includes an anonymous illustration of a "Baroque" clarinetist from this period on p. 196.

CLARINETT.

*Wañ der Trompeten-Schall will allzulaut erthönen,
so dient das Clarinet auf angenehme weiß
es darff den hohen Thon auch niedern nicht entlehnen
und wechselt lieblich um; Ihm bleibt hierdurch der preiß.
Darum manch Edler Geist, dem dieses werck beliebet
Sich Lehr-begierig zeigt und emßig dariñ übet.*

Figure 1.2. Clarinetist from Johann Christoph Weigel's *Musikalisches Theatrum* (Nuremberg, ca. 1722).

relative importance of their being included in these important volumes at all should not be underestimated; a presence among the more ubiquitous and well-established woodwinds envisages a bright future for this new instrument.

The clarinet's association with the horn is well-documented both in print and in depictions of the pair. Ancelet, in his *Observations sur la musique* ... (1757), noted, "The horns please me still more when they

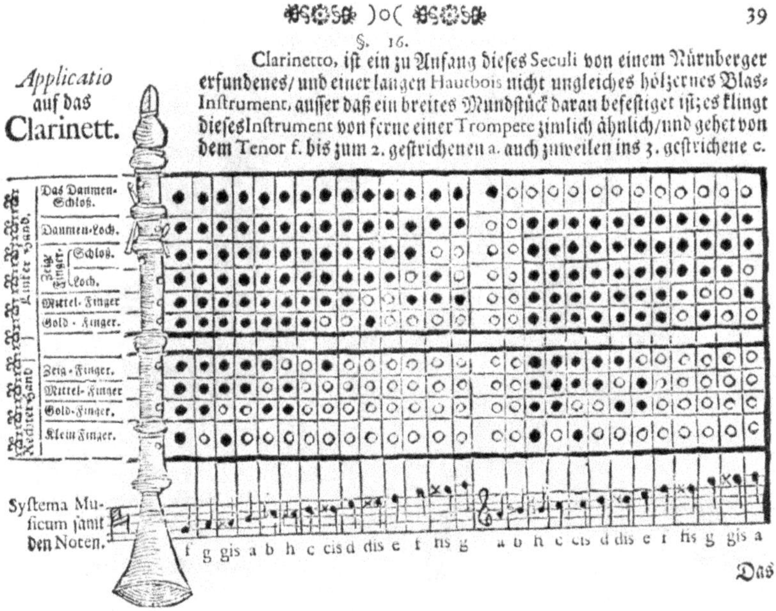

Figure 1.3. Fingering chart from J. F. B. C Majer's *Museum Musicum* (Schwäbisch Hall, 1732).

accompany clarinets," a point well supported in the operas of Jean-Philippe Rameau.[3] A depiction of two *commedia dell'arte* musicians from circa 1720 shows them with these two instruments; the clarinet appears slightly conical.[4] This combination can be seen in other early eighteenth-century images such as the festive sleigh ride in a Dutch engraving from Leiden, created in commemoration of the treaty of Utrecht and the founding of Leiden University (fig. 1.4). F. A. P. de Garsault's drawing of a two-key clarinet in high F, in his *Notionaire, ou mémorial raisonné* (Paris, 1761), appears together with a horn.[5] Like Ancelet,

---

3   As noted in other chapters of this volume, Rameau's operas with clarinets include *Zoroastre* (1749), *Acante et Céphise* (1751) and *Les Boréades* (1764).

4   Illustrated in Albert R. Rice, *The Baroque Clarinet* (Oxford: Clarendon Press, 1992), 150.

5   P. Lescat and J. Saint-Arroman, eds., *Clarinette: méthodes et traités-dictionnaires* (Courlay: Éditions J. M. Fuzeau, 2000), 12.

Figure 1.4. Nicolaas van der Worm, engraving of clarinetists and horn players, after drawings by Abraham Delfos (Leiden, ca. 1775). Private collection, used with permission.

Garsault notes that the clarinet is "merry & sonorous, & blends well in concerts with hunting horns."

In several mid-century images, the circumstances in which the clarinet could be found seem to increase. A clarinetist beautifully depicted by Johann Elias Ridinger appears "solo" in a pastoral setting somewhere in the Low Countries, suggestive of the folk music idiom, even though both the clothing and instrument hint at relative sophistication.[6] And while Guillaume Voiriot's Perceval family (shown at the Paris *Salon* in 1767) represent the *haute-bourgeoisie*, the child playing the clarinet is dressed up to depict a street musician of the lowest order—a *savoyard* (fig. 1.5).[7]

---

6   Cover illustration for Rice, *The Baroque Clarinet*.

7   *Les deux petits savoyards* (1789) from this period was an extremely popular comic opera by the French composer Nicolas Dalayrac; sophisticated Parisians felt a certain empathy with the "simple life" of the Savoyards.

Figure 1.5. Guillaume Voiriot, *The Perceval Family* (Paris, 1767). Private collection, used with permission.

In the 1740s Gabriel Weiss decorated the choir loft of the Pfarrkirche St. Magnus in Bad Schussenried, where he included two angels playing the clarinet.[8] While at this time the clarinet did not play a significant role in sacred music, its inclusion represents a step up from street music. We note with interest the difference in hand positions in the Weiss painting, which suggests that at this date the issue had not yet been settled.[9] The proximity of Bad Schussenried to Nuremberg makes it probable that these instruments came from the Denner workshop.

Clearly a multiplicity of roles in musical life appears to have been characteristic of the clarinet from the start: it was welcome at court, in the military, on stage, in church, on city streets, and in the countryside.

---

8   Cover illustration for Eric Hoeprich, *The Clarinet* (New Haven, CT: Yale University Press, 2008).

9   It was not until instruments included a key (or keys) for the left little finger that hand position was "locked in," with the right hand below the left.

Given its relatively late appearance on the musical scene, such diversity certainly helped guarantee survival. Competing with several other perfectly good and well-established woodwind instruments, the clarinet was initially, it could be argued, surplus to requirements. However, this is belied by an increase in the number of players and a growing interest on the part of composers already in the early eighteenth century.[10]

Iconographical evidence usually shows a certain bias. Particularly at the earliest stage, most interesting information pertains to details of the setting: ensemble/solo, outside/indoors, technique (reed position, hand position), type of instrument ("up-to-date" or anachronistic), and the social status of the player. Examination of the *musical* context of the clarinet in the late eighteenth century unavoidably invites comparison with the other woodwind instruments. In wind band culture, the flute, more or less useless out of doors, leaves the piccolo as the only viable cross-blown alternative. The oboe, also somewhat feeble, would have been confined to more rarified settings. The bassoon hardly competes with the clarinet in range and sonority, offering instead the perfect partner as a bass instrument. Together with the horn, a novel and most satisfactory combination of clarinets, bassoons, and horns is achieved, typically in pairs—a logical progression from the quartet of clarinets and horns discussed above. This provides a key to the instrument's success in finally becoming part of established woodwind culture.

Valentin Roeser's *Gamme de la clarinette* (Paris, ca.1760) shows a clarinet with four keys, set up to be played with the reed above.[11] Published a few years later, his *Essai d'instruction … pour la clarinette et le cor* (Paris, 1764) provides useful instruction for the wind sextet at the earliest stage, an ensemble formation that had already been employed by Jean-Philippe Rameau, Johann Stamitz, and by the end of the century many others, including Johann Christian Bach, W. A. Mozart (K. 375), and even the young Beethoven (op. 71). A well-known and evocative pastiche of silhouettes from the Oettingen-Wallerstein court (1791) shows all of the wind instruments, including (at least) two clarinets, circa 1791.[12]

---

10 As discussed in Chapter 2 of this volume, in addition to Rameau, important composers such as Vivaldi and Telemann composed several works for the "new" instrument.

11 Lescat and Saint-Arroman, *Clarinette: méthodes et traités-dictionnaires*, 5.

12 Collection of the Oettingen-Wallersteinsche Bibliothek, Universitätsbibliothek, Augsburg; illustrated in Hoeprich, *The Clarinet,*

The encyclopedists Diderot and d'Alembert illustrated a truly anachronistic two-key clarinet in their *Encyclopédie* in 1756, followed by an equally outdated instrument with only four keys in 1799. Even by the earlier date we expect to see a clarinet with five keys. Presumably the scope of their Enlightenment project created significant delays resulting in "old news," albeit not without interest to us today. The two-key clarinet shows the reed on the lower side, whereas the chalumeau from the same volume has it positioned above. Occasionally iconographic evidence is simply out of step with the evolution on the ground.[13]

Relatively few portraits from this early "Classical" period have survived. Joseph Beer (1744–1811), the first clarinet virtuoso of true international standing, may possibly be the player depicted in an anonymous engraving from circa 1780 (fig. 1.6). His clarinet has five keys, and the music appears to be a concerto—perhaps one of Beer's own? During the heyday of the Concert Spirituel in Paris, clarinet soloists were in constant demand, and Beer appeared on more than twenty occasions. Such portraits of purported soloists lend some color to this eighteenth-century world. A French player, identified only as Villement, is nicely rendered in the painting shown in figure 1.7, quite unexpectedly with the reed below, contrary to French custom. From the same period, a well-known silhouette of Mozart's clarinetist, Anton Stadler, communicates a stolid assurance in the well-known engraving from Vienna.[14] To these can be added two images of what appear to be itinerant virtuosi. Similar in their audacious posture, both convey comprehensive and self-assured mastery of their art (fig. 1.8). Indeed, the "greatest clarionet player" (possibly Valentin Roeser) claims also to have been a director of music. The player depicted by the Swiss artist Hieronymous Hess (fig. 1.8b) appeared in a series portraying some thirteen different musicians.[15]

By the dawn of the nineteenth century the clarinet was ubiquitous and was popular in a variety of settings. When the Paris Conservatoire opened its doors in 1795, the faculty included more than thirteen

86.

13 Denis Diderot and Jean Le Rond d'Alembert, *Encyclopédie* (Paris: Briasson, David, Le Breton, 1751–65), vol. 5, *Recueil de planches*, plate 8. Reproduced in Rice, *The Baroque Clarinet* (1992), 45.

14 Gesellschaft der Musikfreunde, Vienna. Illustrated in Pamela Weston, *Clarinet Virtuosi of the Past* (London: Robert Hale, 1971), plate 4.

15 Such was their popularity that several (including this one) were made into ceramic figurines by Anton Sohn in Germany.

Figure 1.6. Anonymous engraving of a clarinetist from the Classical era (French?, ca. 1780). With kind permission of the New York Public Library.

Figure 1.7. Anonymous engravings of a clarinetist, "Villement" (French, ca. 1780). Private collection, used with permission.

Figure 1.8. a) Anonymous hand-colored engraving of a clarinetist (French?, ca. 1790). With kind permission of the British Library; b) Hieronymous Hess, portrait of a clarinetist (Basel, ca. 1828). With kind permission of the Gemeentemuseum, The Hague.

clarinet teachers, including Jean Xavier Lefèvre, author of the first truly thorough instruction book, his *Méthode de clarinette* (Paris, 1802), while in Germany, Franz Joseph Fröhlich's *Vollständige theo-retische-praktische Musikschule* appeared in 1810–11. Drawing to a large extent on Lefèvre's work, Fröhlich too recommends the reed-above position. J. G. H. Backofen, Lefèvre's pupil, suggests in his *Anweisung zur Clarinette* (1803) that habit and comfort are the main factors in determining reed position, although he himself played with the reed above. We are drawn to these sources for practical information about the instruments and playing techniques. Lefèvre's clarinetist appears quite natural with the reed above, and is not playing at an exaggerat-edly obtuse angle (fig. 1.9).[16]

---

16 Three sources help to identify this essential playing technique: clari-net methods, images of clarinet players, and mouthpieces from the period with an instrument maker's mark. If the maker has stamped the mouthpiece on the same side as the reed, we can assume the instrument was mean to be played with the reed above, and vice versa.

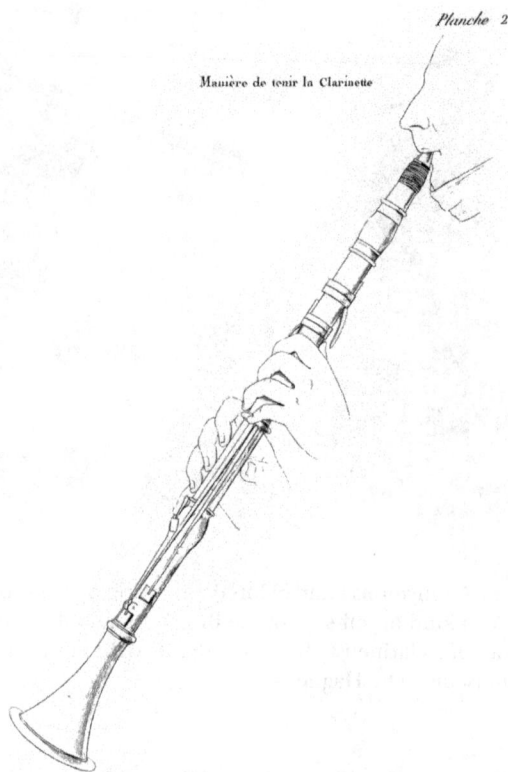

Planche 2

Manière de tenir la Clarinette

Figure 1.9. Clarinetist from Jean Xavier Lefèvre's *Méthode de clarinette* (Paris, 1802).

In this era of virtuosi, the most prominent soloists had their portraits painted with flair. Baermann, Hermstedt, and Crusell make a handsome trio, and while disappointment sets in at not seeing any of them holding an instrument, it is nonetheless reassuring that they are worthy of such fine artistic effort.[17] A portrait of Johann Gottlieb Kotte (1797–1857), on the other hand, shows the artist holding his clarinet (fig. 1.10). A member of the Dresden *Hofkapelle*, he was associated with composers such as Mendelssohn, Wagner, and Schumann. Identifying his clarinet as the work of the Dresden instrument maker Carl

---

By the early 1800s, most players played with the reed below, as clarinetists do today.

17 Illustrated in Hoeprich, *The Clarinet*, 148.

Figure 1.10. Schaeffer, portrait of Johann Gottlieb Kotte (1823–57), clarinetist of the royal Saxon court orchestra, lithograph after E. B. Kietz (Dresden, ca. 1830). With kind permission of the Sächsische Landesbibliothek-Staats- und Universitätsbibliothek, Dresden.

Gottlob Bormann reminds us of the importance of iconography in the practical sense.[18] During February 1849 Kotte, a frequent visitor in Schumann household, appeared at exactly the time Schumann composed the *Fantasiestücke* op. 73.

As the clarinet became ubiquitous, so too did its various roles proliferate. Outside more established musical centers such as the court and

---

18 Certain characteristics visible in the portrait point to Bormann, such as double holes for L3 and a side key for f/c. Also, there are several extant Bormann clarinets stamped with "K. S. C." indicating ownership by the Königlich Sächsische Capelle (royal Saxon court orchestra), where Kotte was employed.

the military, clarinetists could be found plying their trade in an array of less-organized venues such as taverns and private parties, or out on the street. The poor, itinerant, quasi-beggar clarinetist is depicted with increasing frequency throughout the nineteenth century. The French were among the first to create expressive caricatures, and few were the equal of Jean-Ignace Isidore Gérard (1803–47), known as "J. J. Grandville." Grandville developed a special skill for creating portraits of men with animal heads, imbuing his images with highly expressive features that communicate immediately with the viewer (fig. 1.11). As with any caricature, there is always a subtext; in this instance, the poor quality of the clothing (patched in several places) and a rickety duet stand, along with a nearly empty glass of wine and perhaps a few too many bottles waiting in a basket on the floor. The instrument appears to be a five-key clarinet in C, made of boxwood and ivory (possibly by Amlingue or Prudent), a bit out of date for circa 1840. We are drawn to the player's head, clearly that of a duck, or *canard*—also the French word for a "squeak"—two of which we can see escaping from the bell. So we have a *canard* playing a *canard* during an Andante con variazione from *Duos pour deux clarinettes* (possibly by Michel Yost or Amand Vanderhagen), but sadly his duet partner is absent.[19]

From Grandville it is a short step to another Parisian artist: the great Honoré Daumier (1808–79), who depicted clarinetists in dozens of his editorial-style engravings for Parisian newspapers such as *Le charivari*. Reading between the lines, it appears that Daumier did not think much of the instrument, or perhaps more to the point, its players, who were usually only slightly better off than beggars and frequently trying to pull off some sort of stunt. Surely in the French capital he would have enjoyed first-rate clarinet playing at the Paris Opéra or in concerts, but perhaps there was no fun in ridiculing legitimate musicians (fig. 1.12). We can add to these some highly amusing caricatures from a series by Charles Joseph Traviès de Villers (1804–59, signed "CJT"), such as the "Nazillard," which appeared in *Le charivari* in 1832 (fig. 1.13). Such images possessed a far deeper meaning than might be suggested. Here the victim was an influential politician, "Mr d'Argot," or Antoine Maurice Apollinaire, Comte d'Argout (1782–1858), a peer and governor of the Bank of France.

The "amateur" was frequently the subject of many images, probably because there simply have always been so many amateur clarinet players. Traviès de Villers's depiction of the *amateur* is more benign

---

19 Many much later images show clarinets being played by a variety of animals, often to advertise a product. See below.

Figure 1.11. J. J. Grandville, *Le canard* (Paris, ca. 1840). Bibliothèque de Nancy, fonds Thiéry-Solet.

Figure 1.12. Honoré Daumier, lithograph from *Le charivari* (Paris, ca. 1840). Private collection, used with permission.

Figure 1.13. Charles Joseph Traviès de Villers, "Nazillard," from *Le charivari* (Paris, 1832). Private collection, used with permission.

than that of d'Argout, although no less amusing, and his "Jean Canardin" again refers to the squeak, this time presumably only a small one (fig.1.14).

Plying his painterly trade in countless Bavarian taverns, the artist Peter Kraemer (1823–1907) produced portraits of itinerant buskers satisfied with earning a handful of coins for a day's work. Playing five-key clarinets made of the usual boxwood, Kraemer's musicians clearly have the reed above and generally favor the C clarinet, perhaps because of its brightness and volume: it is undoubtedly much more

Figure 1.14. Charles Joseph Traviès de Villers, "Jean Canardin," from *Le charivari* (Paris, ca. 1830). Private collection, used with permission.

audible in a crowded space. Meanwhile, in Poland, an engraving based on a painting by Hugo Kötschenreiter (1854–1908) offers a similar view of clarinet culture (fig. 1.15).

Not too distant from such scenarios, there was room for the clarinetist as a general nuisance. A French cartoon by Paul Gavarni neatly points out the difference between the flageolet and the clarinet, while also depicting the player as apparently clueless (fig. 1.16a). And the vagabond "caricature" in a British cartoon suggests that poor clarinet playing might be used to one's advantage (fig. 1.16b). Back in

Figure 1.15. Clarinetist in an engraving based on a painting by Hugo Kötschenreiter (Munich, ca. 1880). Private collection, used with permission.

long-haired France, the maestro cannot believe what he is hearing, and the player's only defense is a non-sequitur: he needs the work to support his family (fig. 1.16c).

Post-Müller-system instruments, made of dark wood (cocus, blackwood) and fitted with improved keywork (German silver with countersunk holes), would have been nearly indestructible in comparison with the other woodwinds. By the turn of the twentieth century, clarinets were on offer in a variety of systems and materials, and factory manufacture in large numbers made them affordable. The "Henry Ford"-style production in large factories made it by far the

Figure 1.16a. Paul Gavarni, engraving of a musician (Paris, ca. 1840). The caption reads, "It's been three hours, neighbor, three hours that you've been playing that flageolet to us, and you'll allow me to point out to you that …" "But how was I to guess that you would prefer the clarinet?" Private collection, used with permission.

"There's threepence for you, and Master wishes you'd move on."
"Threepence indeed!! I never moves on under sixpence—d'ye think
I does n't know the walley o peace and quietness?"

Figure 1.16b. Anonymous hand-colored cartoon (British, ca. 1850). Private collection, used with permission.

Figure 1.16c. Abel Faivre, cartoon (Paris, ca. 1920). The caption reads, "But that's abominable! Have you no ear?" "Oh! Sir! I am the father of three children." Private collection, used with permission.

most popular woodwind instrument; the clarinet had not only survived, it had arrived. A catalogue like that of Boston's Cundy-Bettoney Company from circa 1900 overwhelms with the surfeit of styles and options (fig. 1.17).

Playing technique, however, remained inconsistent. For example, nineteenth-century methods from Naples by Ferdinando Sebastiani and Gaetano Labanchi feature up-to-date instruments being played in the old-fashioned manner, with the reed against the upper lip.[20] Despite the pleas of important and influential teacher-players like

---

20 Ferdinando Sebastiani, *Metodo per clarinetto* (1855); Gaetano Labanchi, *Metodo progressive per il clarinetto* (Naples: Calcografia Cali, Partenopeo, 1868).

THE STYLES OF BUFFET CLARINETS.

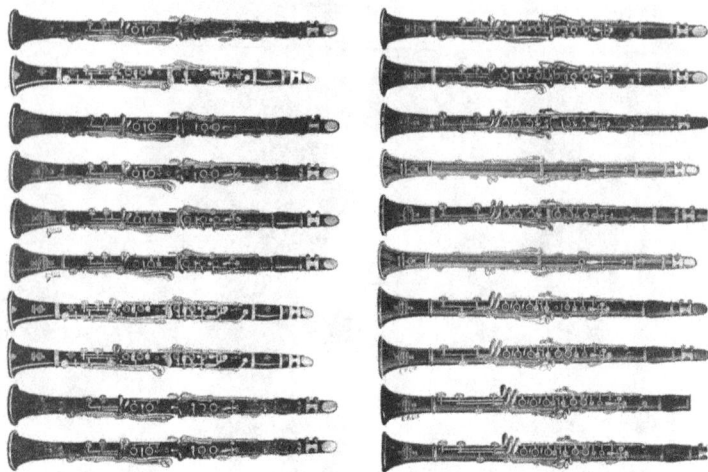

Figure 1.17. Buffet clarinets from the Cundy-Bettoney Company catalogue (Boston, ca. 1900).

Joseph Berr, professor at the Paris Conservatoire, this reed position persisted, especially in southern countries.

The dawn of jazz in the late nineteenth century brought the clarinet to the front of the band, where it would remain for decades. By this time, photography had begun to displace hand-made images. Music was the medium, but the "show" was a big part of the Vaudeville era, making it common for clarinetists to dance and clown around while playing. Johnny Dodds, a member of the eponymous band, was among the first to gain prominence in New Orleans and later, Chicago. Meanwhile, at the St. Louis Cotton Club, an apparently distraught clarinetist impaled himself (fig. 1.18). The well-known caricaturist Al Hirschfeld created portraits of Benny Goodman on at least three occasions. The image shown in figure 1.19 shows a possible secret to the "King of Swing's" considerable success: a double set of fingers![21] Several players experimented with playing two, or even three, clarinets at the same time, as seen in an 1940s photograph of Rudy Gaehler from New York City (fig. 1.20). (Wilbur Sweatman was possibly the first to try this trick, some years earlier.)

---

21 Note the appearance of Hirschfeld's daughter's name, Nina, just above Goodman's ear.

Figure 1.18. Musicians performing at the St. Louis Cotton Club, ca. 1925. Photo from the Block Brothers Studio, with kind permission of the Missouri History Museum.

The clarinet had by now become sufficiently commonplace that several great painters incorporated the instrument into their works. Still-life paintings by both Pablo Picasso and Georges Braque in 1911–12 featured titles like *Man with a Clarinet* (Picasso) and *Clarinet and Bottle of Rum on a Mantelpiece* (Braque), en route to launching the artists into a new orbit: Cubism. Sculpting in stone a few years later, Jacques Lipchitz created his *Seated Man with Clarinet* (1920), where the instrument emerges incorporated into the player's body. On the cover of this book, Roy Lichtenstein's homage to Matisse moves beyond Cubism with a clarinetist representing *The Musician* (1948).

Back over in Europe, the tiny clarinet in G, called the *picksüßes Hölzl* (sickly-sweet little stick) in the Viennese dialect, was a mainstay of so-called *Schrammelmusik*, created and popularized by the Schrammelquartett at the end of the nineteenth century. In a truly iconic portrait of the Schrammel brothers with the clarinetist Georg Dänzer and the contra-guitarist Anton Strohmayer, we see the ensemble at its peak in the 1880s (fig. 1.21). Not far away, in Eastern Europe and Russia, the

Figure 1.19. Al Hirschfeld, caricature of Benny Goodman (New York City, 1957). With kind permission of the Yale University Art Gallery, Irving S. Gilmore Music Library Transfer.

Figure 1.20. Anonymous photograph of Rudy Gaehler at a CBS broadcast (New York City, 1940s). Private collection, used with permission.

Figure 1.21. The Schrammelquartett (Vienna, ca. 1886). With kind permission of the Museum der Stadt Wien.

music of the klezmorim was the top choice for celebrations like weddings and parties.

Initially most clarinet players tended to be men, but as women began to take up the instrument they too became subjects of iconographical interest. As usual, the French were among the first with a caricature, as in the amusing vignette of a shapely clarinetist helping out a blind, angelic orphan shown in figure 1.22. Given her questionable hand positions, the similarly attired "cigarette girl" next door appears to need lessons. And although most advertising campaigns for actual instruments tended to refer to well-known soloists, this advertisement for Buffet suggested another route to "top performance." .

Figure 1.22. Anonymous, "Vieux dicton—l'amour est aveugle" (Old saying—love is blind); (Paris, ca. 1900); clarinetist from a cigarette advertisement for W. Duke & Sons (New York, ca. 1900); advertisements for Buffet and Selmer clarinets, ca. 1950. Private collection, used with permission.

In a return to the clarinetist as a nuisance, other humorous images stem from two types of players, children and animals, where the clarinet usually serves merely as a prop. Figure 1.23 shows holiday greeting cards in German and French with cute, furry creatures "playing" the clarinet, while "A la place Clichy" appears funny in and of itself; the oversize instruments make the children look truly *mignon*. The exact purpose of La Maison Rouge's band of monkeys in selling fabric is somewhat puzzling . In any case, the clarinet player has had enough!

Various psychological studies suggest that learning a musical instrument at an early age can help with getting on in life. Typically, a young person's introduction to the clarinet has involved playing in a local band, although hopefully not one quite as dreary as this *Orchesterprobe* (orchestra rehearsal) seems to be (fig. 1.24). From here, the clarinet found a welcome home in the military, where it was rivaled only by the brass instruments. Much of the impetus for the founding of the Paris Conservatoire and music academies elsewhere came from the effort to produce musicians to play in military bands like the

Figure 1.23. "Herzlichen Glückwünsche zum Geburtstag" (Hearty congratulations on your birthday), ca. 1900; Easter greetings, ca. 1900; "À la place Clichy" (Paris, ca. 1900); "La Maison Rouge," advertisement for textile products (Paris, ca. 1900). Private collection, used with permission.

Orchesterprobe der Musiklehrlinge.
Nach dem Gemälde von D. Bilz.

Figure 1.24. *Orchesterprobe der Musiklehrlinge* (Orchestra rehearsal with music students), after a painting by D. Bilz, ca. 1880. Private collection, used with permission.

post-revolutionary Garde Nationale and Garde Républicaine—ensembles which still thrive today. Initial training may have been minimal, but many nineteenth-century images communicate considerable order and consummate discipline. We also often see the traditional combination of clarinets with horn and bassoon at the heart of wind music and as the key to instrument's success.

This account allows for but a fraction of the visual evidence pertaining to the diverse role of the clarinet over the past three centuries. Although we experience any instrument through its sound, most of these images manage to "speak" to us from an era that is otherwise mute. Occasionally useful information can be extracted, such as the type of instrument (key configuration, mouthpiece, ligature) and details of actual performance practice. Often, the atmosphere conjured by an image provides the imagination with a glimpse into an era that is otherwise lost to us.

THE CHALUMEAU AND CLARINET
BEFORE MOZART

Albert R. Rice

The history of the clarinet is closely linked to that of the chalumeau. Both have a distinct origin and development, beginning in 1694 for the chalumeau and 1710 for the clarinet. Both use a single-reed mouthpiece and have a cylindrical bore and were quickly adopted by musicians for their unique tone qualities and a playing technique similar to that of the recorder. As the chalumeau and clarinet spread throughout Europe, a repertoire for these instruments began to develop. This chapter summarizes chalumeau and clarinet music to 1770, showing how each instrument became treasured and valued even before Mozart and his clarinet masterpieces appeared. Briefly described are chalumeau instruments, the earliest performances on the chalumeau and clarinet, and some evidence concerning orchestral and solo players.[1]

A complete chalumeau family consists of five sizes: soprano, alto, tenor, bass, and *basson de chalumeau* (a chalumeau with an extended low range).[2] Not all these instruments were available to composers at one location. Compositions for the chalumeau written between 1694

---

1   The author thanks his wife, Eleanor Montague, and Jane Ellsworth for editing the manuscript; Geoffrey Burgess for preparing musical examples; and for copies of music and advice Jóhannes Ágústsson, Bruce Alan Brown, Michael Finkelman, Franz Gratl, Colin Lawson, Luca Luchetta, Luigi Magistrelli, Kjartan Óskarsson, and Ernst Schlader.
2   The lowest instrument is also listed in scores as a basso chalumeau or bassone.

and 1780 reflect a musical style similar to that of compositions for the recorder. Baroque clarinets with two or three keys appeared in various tonalities, and in stylistic contrast to the chalumeau, clarinet compositions from 1715 to 1760 featured triadic themes and repeated notes similar to music for the trumpet, or diatonic themes similar to music for the oboe. Beginning about 1760, professional and amateur musicians played Classical-period four-, five-, and six-key clarinets made in Paris, London, and German cities. Clarinets were primarily constructed in C, B-flat, and A, making them popular and useful to composers. Clarinets with two or three keys continued to be made and played by beginners and professional musicians as late as the early nineteenth century. Indeed, some clarinetists, such as the Swedish/Finnish soloist Bernhard Henrik Crusell (1775–1838), learned to play on a two-key clarinet.

Chalumeau Instruments

Musicians in the late seventeenth century and eighteenth century trained on several wind and stringed instruments, which made them versatile performers for towns and for noblemen. The late seventeenth-century single-reed chalumeau first appeared about thirteen years before the two-key clarinet, in a 1687 instrument invoice from Nuremberg for the Duke of Römhild-Sachsen, as "Ein Chor Chalimo von 4. Stücken" (a four-part chalumeau choir).[3] Seventeenth-century chalumeaux are not extant, but they may have been similar to the keyless soprano chalumeau engraved in Diderot and d'Alembert's *Encyclopédie* (1767, fig. 2.1), with seven finger holes (without keys), one thumb hole, and a separate single-reed mouthpiece.[4]

A similar instrument called the mock trumpet was made during the late seventeenth and early eighteenth centuries. Four instruction books were published from 1698 onward in London,[5] of which only the *Fourth Compleat Book for the Mock Trumpet* (ca. 1706–08) is extant. It includes a

---

3   The Römhilder Kammerrechnungen are now in the Staatsarchiv, Meiningen, according to correspondence from Herbert Heyde; Albert R. Rice, *The Baroque Clarinet* (Oxford: Clarendon Press, 1992), 15.

4   Illustrated in Colin Lawson, *The Chalumeau in Eighteenth-Century Music* (Ann Arbor, MI; UMI Research Press, 1981), 19, plate 4.

5   William C. Smith, *Bibliography of the Musical Works Published by John Walsh during the Years 1695–1720* (London: Bibliographical Society, 1948), 6, no. 1; 8–9, no. 21; 41, no. 137.

Figure 2.1. Denis Diderot and Jean Le Rond d'Alembert, eds., *Encyclopédie, ou dictionnaire raisonné des sciences, des arts et des métiers par un société de gens de lettres*, vol. 5, *Recueil de planches* (Paris: Briasson, David, Le Breton, 1767), "Lutherie, suite des instruments à vent," plate. 8.

fingering chart with a compass of one octave, G^3 to G^4 (fig. 2.2), along with basic music theory instruction, directions for playing, and solos and duos.[6] The music's style, in imitation of the natural trumpet, made the mock trumpet a popular instrument for amateur players, but it was not used in art music, and was initially sold as a musical toy.[7]

Various early eighteenth-century writers on music describe the chalumeau, both in the simple version described above (e.g., Buonanni, 1722, who calls it a *scialumò*) and in a slightly more sophisticated version with two keys (called a *calandrone* by Buonanni).[8] An example perhaps similar to Buonanni's *scialumò* survives in the collection of the Sacro Convento (Sacred Convent) in Assisi; it is an incomplete main body section with six finger holes and one thumb hole, lacking a mouthpiece and bell.[9] The German writer Johann Gottfried Walther (*Musicalisches Lexicon*, 1732) also described both types of chalumeau; the simpler one had a range of F^3 to A^4, and the keyed type a range of F^3 to A^4 and Bb^4 (possibly also reaching B^4 and C^5).[10] Another German, Joseph Majer (1732), provided further details, noting that there were soprano, alto or quart, tenor, and bass chalumeaux, and maintaining that since the

6   Smith, *Bibliography of the Musical Works Published by John Walsh*, xxvi.

7   Anthony Baines, *European and American Musical Instruments* (New York: The Viking Press, 1966), 112.

8   Filippo Buonanni, *Gabinetto armonico pieno d'istromenti sonori indicate, e spiegati* (Rome: G. Placho, 1722), 68.

9   Laura Pontecorvo, "La collezione di strumenti musicali e la prassi strumentale nel Sacro convento di San Francesco ad Assisi durante il Seicento," *Recercare* 24, nos. 1–2 (2012), 63–92, especially 88–91. Because of the missing parts, the instrument's identity as a *scialumò* or recorder is unclear; however, it is covered in black leather similar to a mock trumpet. The author thanks Laura Pontecorvo for a photograph of this instrument.

10   Johann Gottfried Walther, *Musicalisches Lexicon oder musicalisches Bibliothek* (1732; repr., Kassel: Bärenreiter, 1953), 153.

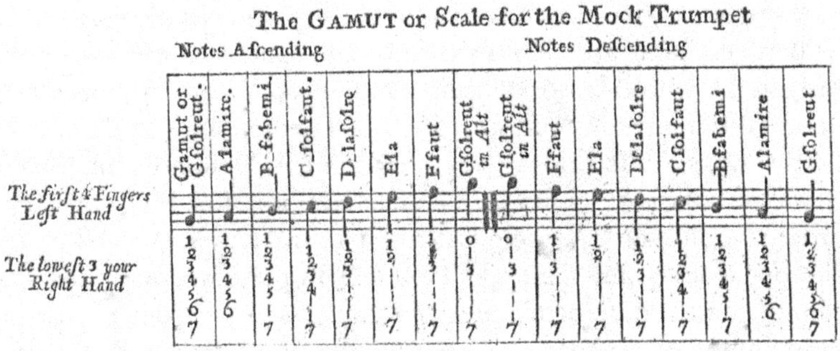

Figure 2.2. "The Gamut or Scale for the Mock Trumpet," in *The Fourth Compleat Book for the Mock Trumpet* (London: I. Walsh, I. Hare, and P. Randall, ca. 1706–08), [iii]. By permission of The University of Glasgow Library, Special Collections, Sp. Coll B.e.19.

fingerings corresponded closely with the recorder, one could perform easily on the chalumeau.[11] Only ten chalumeaux survive today.[12]

Chalumeau Music, 1694–1780

The chalumeau repertoire is substantial, including 260 vocal works and 76 purely instrumental. The earliest extant published chalumeau music is two volumes called *Fanfares pour les chalumeaux & trompette propres aussi à joüer sur les flûtes, violons, & haubois*, 1st ed. (Amsterdam: Roger, 1703–04), by the Dutch composer Jacques Philippe Dreux (ca. 1670–1722).[13] Dreux's third edition of *Fanfares*, published in 1712–15, is extant.[14]

---

11 Joseph Friedrich Bernhard Caspar Majer, *Museum Musicum Theoretico Practicum, das ist Neu-eröffneter theoretisch-und practicum Music-Saal* (Schwäbisch Hall, 1732; repr., Kassel: Bärenreiter, 1954), 32.

12 More detail on these surviving instruments may be found in Albert R. Rice, *The Baroque Clarinet and Chalumeau*, 2nd ed. (Oxford: Oxford University Press, 2020), appendix 1.

13 François Lesure, *Bibliographie des éditions musicales publiées par Estienne Roger et Michel-Charles Le Cène (Amsterdam, 1696–1743)* (Paris: Société Française de Musicologie, 1969), 66.

14 Herzog-August Library, Wolfenbüttel, 28.1 Musica div.; Lesure, *Bibliographie*, 66.

These works are in a style appropriate to the keyless chalumeau or trumpet.[15] Roger's 1716 catalogue lists additional chalumeau music.

Between 1705 and 1740, soprano, alto, and *basson de chalumeau* were often featured in works at the Viennese court; by 1773 forty-three operas and twenty-four oratorios had been written for Vienna by composers such as Attilio Ariosti, G. B. Bononcini, A. M. Bononcini, Johann Joseph Fux, Marc'Antonio Ziani, Francesco Conti, Johann Georg Reinhardt, Antonio Lotti, Antonio Caldara, Nicola Matteis, Georg Reutter, Giuseppe Bonno, and Giuseppe Porsile.[16] In these works the soprano chalumeau is used in the manner of an expressive recorder, portraying sentiments that are "pastoral, charmingly melancholy, sad, longing, pleading, and tragic."[17]

Of all these Viennese composers, Fux (1660–1741) was the most productive for the chalumeau, with ten operas and nine oratorios written between 1707 and 1728.[18] Also important was Agostino Steffani (1654–1728) who, besides working in Vienna, held positions at various German courts. In the 1709 revision of his opera *Il turno* (1693–97) under the name *Amor vien dal destino* at the Hannover court, chalumeaux are incorporated prominently. The sweet tone of the soprano chalumeau is used to personify the dream of a faun in the scene 2 aria "Oh mia progenie" (ex. 2.1); in another scene, the aria "I gran fatti" uses alto and tenor chalumeaux along with *basson de chalumeau*.[19]

---

15 Angela Maria Owen, "The Chalumeau and Its Music," *The American Recorder* 8, no. 1 (1967): 8; Lawson, *The Chalumeau in Eighteenth-Century Music*, 34–36.

16 Dagmar Glüxam, "Das Chalumeau in der Oper und im Oratorium am Wiener Hof zwischen 1705 und 1740," in *Geschichte, Bauweise und Repertoire der Klarinetteninstrumente*, Michaelsteiner Konferenzberichte 77 (Augsburg: Wißner, 2014), 64–67; Ernst Kubitschek, "Block- und Querflöte im Umkreis von Johann Joseph Fux: Versuch einer Übersicht," in *Johann Joseph Fux und die Barocke Bläsertradition: Kongreßbericht 1985*, ed. B. Habla (Tutzing: H. Schneider, 1987), 110; and Eleanor Selfridge-Field, "The Viennese Court Orchestra in the Time of Caldara," in *Antonio Caldara: Essays on His Life and Times*, ed. B. W. Pritchard (Aldershot: Scolar Press, 1987), 115–52.

17 Glüxam, "Das Chalumeau in der Oper und im Oratorium," 43.

18 Ibid., 64–67; Glüxam, *Instrumentarium und Instrumentalstil in der Wiener Hofoper zwischen 1705 und 1740* (Tutzing: H. Schneider, 2006), 462. Arias by Fux and others are beautifully recorded by the Calamus Consort on *Un dolce affanno*, Passacaille PAS 986, 2012, compact disc.

19 Colin Timms, *Polymath of the Baroque: Agostino Steffani and His Music* (New York: Oxford University Press, 2003), 97. Score prepared by

Example 2.1. Agostino Steffani, *Amor vien dal destino* (1709), "Oh mia progenie."

The Fauno must be accompanied by an entire consort of chalumeaux during this scene, by two bassoons behind the stage wings, and by two theoboes in the orchestra that play chords when marked

Soprano
Chalumeau I

Alto
Chalumeau II

Fagotto I & Tenor
Chalumeau III*

Bass
FAUNO

Basset Bass
Chalumeau IV,
Fagotto II,
2 Teorbe*

* Chalumeaux III and IV sound an octave higher than written.

Oh   mia pro - ge - ni - e   oh di gran gen - te e-

let - to   pa - dre La - ti - no,   il di cui no - me   il mi - o   s'in - al - ze-

—(*continued*)

Example 2.1—*concluded*

Of great importance to the history of the chalumeau was Antonio Vivaldi (1678–1741). He wrote six chalumeau works, which range from sonatas and concertos that incorporate the instrument among others in a semi-soloistic manner to oratorios and other vocal works with religious texts that use the chalumeau as an important obbligato instrument.[20] For example, the soprano aria "Veni, veni me sequere" in the oratorio *Juditha triumphans* RV 644 (1716), features a highly ornate soprano chalumeau obbligato in dotted eighth and sixteenth notes imitating a turtle dove's cooing. In the fourth movement of *Nisi Dominus* RV 803 (1739), "For he has granted rest to those he loves" based on Psalm 126, a tenor chalumeau provides a rich obbligato tone with solo voice, violin, and organ. The idiomatic and flowing chalumeau part evokes sleep.

Ernst Schlader with the help of Colin Timms and Detlef Giese; see Ernst Schlader, "Neu entdeckt: Chalumeaux in einer Oper von Agostino Steffani," *Rohrblatt* 31, no. 2 (June 2016): 55, 57. A modern premiere occurred on April 23, 2016 at the Schiller Theater with members of the Staatsoper Berlin conducted by René Jacobs and the Akademie für Alte Musik Berlin.

20 Lawson, *The Chalumeau in Eighteenth-Century Music*, 162; Michael Talbot, "Recovering Vivaldi's Lost Psalm," *Eighteenth-Century Music* 1, no. 1 (2004): 66–68, 72–73, 76–77; *Antonio Vivaldi: Thematisch-systematisches Verzeichnis seiner Werke*, ed. Peter Ryom (Wiesbaden: Breitkopf & Härtel, 2007). See the list of extant chalumeau music in Rice, *The Baroque Clarinet and Chalumeau*, 2nd ed., appendix 3.

Like Vivaldi, Georg Phillip Telemann (1681–1767) was a well-known composer who made extensive use of the chalumeau; he also seems to have played the instrument, among many others, according to a 1740 biographical sketch.[21] Telemann held important positions in a number of large German cities. Although some of his chalumeau works were written in Frankfurt, where he worked from 1712 to 1721, most were composed during his time in Hamburg (1721–67). Telemann used the chalumeau in twenty-five works, including cantatas, operas, oratorios, secular and sacred vocal compositions, concertos, chamber music, and orchestral works. His Concerto for two chalumeaux TWV 52:d1 (ca. 1724) is written for alto and tenor chalumeaux, and is important for its intimate and sensitive writing, highlighting the dark chalumeau timbre in introspective and virtuosic displays. The *Concerto à 9 parties* TWV 50:1 (ca. 1765) is a late work, unusual in scoring for alto chalumeau, oboe, flute (or piccolo), violins, viola, first and second contrabass, and basso continuo. The first movement uses repeated rapid notes to humorously depict crickets chirping.[22]

A good example of a work using three sizes of chalumeaux (two sopranos, bass, and basset bass chalumeau) is *Parthie à 4* (1716) by the little-known composer Johannes Conradus Melchior Pichler (1695–ca. 1780), who was a court composer in Liechtenstein and later in Cracow. This unusual work may have been performed at Göttweig Abbey. It is charming and well written, and very effective in combining the tone colors and broad range of the chalumeau family (ex. 2.2).[23]

Johann Christoph Graupner (1683–1760) was primarily active in Darmstadt, where he became Vice-Kapellmeister in 1709 and Kapellmeister in 1712. He was the most prolific chalumeau composer,

---

21 Johann Mattheson, *Grundlage einer Ehren-Pforte* (1740; repr., Kassel: Bärenreiter, 1969), 357; Heinz Becker, "Das Chalumeau bei Telemann," in *Konferenzbericht der 2. Magdeburger Telemann-Festtage* (Magdeburg: Deutsche Kulturband, 1969), 69.

22 Peter Thalheimer in the foreword to Georg Philipp Telemann, *Grillen-Symphonie*, ed. P. Thalheimer (Stuttgart: Hänssler, 1978), 3. For lists of Telemann's extant chalumeau music see Rice, *The Baroque Clarinet and Chalumeau*, 2nd ed., appendix 3; Werner Menke, *Thematisches Verzichnis der Vokalwerke von Georg Philipp Telemann*, vols. 1 and 2 (Frankfurt: V. Klostermann, 1988, 1995); *Georg Philipp Telemann: Autographe und Abchriften: Katalog* (Munich: G. Henle, 1993).

23 "Parthie à 4: Chalemaux 2, Taillie 1 et Basso fagotto" in Göttweig Abbey, Austria, 2873. The author thanks Ernst Schlader for a transcription and arrangement of the score.

Example 2.2. Johannes Conradus Melchior Pichler, *Parthie à 4 chalumeaux* (1716), mvt. 2, Allemande.

writing almost eighty chalumeau parts in his cantatas between 1734 and 1753.[24] Other chalumeau works by Graupner include concertos, *ouverture*-suites, and trios. Graupner's student Johann Friedrich Fasch (1688–1758) was Kapellmeister at Anhalt-Zerbst from 1722. In 1724 two chalumeaux had been purchased from Dresden for the court;[25] perhaps as a result of becoming familiar with these, as well as having contact with the musician Johann Christian Klotsch (see below), Fasch wrote a concerto for soprano chalumeau between 1727 and 1734.[26] Because of its importance in the repertoire, this concerto is often performed today and has been recorded several times.[27]

A number of other important composers wrote chamber and orchestral works using the chalumeau, including Johann Melchior Molter (1696–1765), Joseph Starzer (1726–87), and Jan Dismas Zelenka (1679–1745). In Molter's two *Harmonie* or wind band works with the modern title of Concertino for two chalumeaux (alto and tenor), two F horns, and bassoon, the two chalumeaux are given leading and interesting melodic parts.[28] Lawson suggests they date from Molter's later

---

24 Lawson, *The Chalumeau in Eighteenth-Century Music*, 92.
25 Kammerrechnungen 1723/24, 168, nos. 1335 and 1336, Stadtarchiv Bibliothek, Eisenach; Hermann Wäschke, "Die Zerbster Hofkapelle," *Zerbst Jahrbuch* 2 (1906): 52, quoted by Barbara M. Reul, "The Court of Anhalt-Zerbst," in *Music at German Courts, 1715–1760: Changing Artistic Priorities*, ed. S. Owens, B. M. Reul, and J. B. Stockigt (Woodbridge: Boydell Press, 2011), 267.
26 Gottfried Küntzel, "Die Instrumentalkonzerte von Johann Friedrich Fasch" (PhD diss., University of Frankfurt am Main), 1965, 39, quoted by Lawson, *The Chalumeau in Eighteenth-Century Music*, 156. The manuscript is in the Sächsische Landesbibliothek, Dresden, MS 2423/0/12; a modern edition is Johann Friedrich Fasch, *Concerto in B flat for Chalumeau or Clarinet*, ed. R. Platt (London: Novello, 1992).
27 Fasch, *Concertos—Orchestral Suite*, with Colin Lawson (chalumeau) and the English Concert, conducted by Trevor Pinnock, Arkiv 449210, 1998, compact disc; *Fasch: Cantatas—Overture in D Minor—Concerto in B flat Minor for Chalumeau*, with Gili Rinot (chalumeau) and the Accademia Daniel, conducted by Shalev Ad-El, CPO 999674, 1999, compact disc; *Fasch: Concerti and Sinfoniae*, with Christian Leitherer (chalumeau) and the Main-Barockorchester Frankfurt, Aeolus 10017, 2005, compact disc.
28 Concertino à 5 in C (incomplete), MWV VIII/8, Mus. Hs. 675, and Concertino à 5 in F, MWV VIII/9, Mus. Hs. 508, Badische Landesbibliothek, Karlsruhe. See Klaus Häfner, "Verzeichnis der Werken von Johann Melchior Molter," in *Der badische Hofkapellmeister*

period, after 1747,[29] which make them early examples of *Harmoniemusik,* presaging the important role of the clarinet in this genre.

A few Classical-period composers wrote for the chalumeau, including Florian Leopold Gassmann (1729–74), Carl Ditters von Dittersdorf (1739–99), and the Esterházy composer Gregor Joseph Werner (1693–1766). The Mannheim composer Christian Cannabich (1731–98) is the only composer known to have written for both the chalumeau and the clarinet in a single work. His *Angélique et Médor, ou Roland furieux* (1768) includes *Chalmai primo* and *secondo* parts, and *Clarinetto Primo Ton C* and *Clarinetto Secondo in C* parts, presumably played by the same two players.[30] The last known chalumeau work is a concerto for chalumeau and orchestra (1770s) by Franz Anton Hoffmeister (1754–1812), in manuscript parts in Vienna's Gesellschaft der Musikfreunde.[31]

In summary, the music of the chalumeau was appreciated by amateur players in duets and played by church and professional musicians in operas, cantatas, chamber works, *Harmoniemusik,* and concertos. The majority of the thirty-eight known chalumeau composers were employed by courts. The instrument's greatest success occurred in Vienna in the 1730s, as shown by the large amount of surviving music there, but the instrument was also used in significant works by composers in Italy and Germany.

Chalumeau Players

The first known chalumeau player was the Prussian oboist Lodovico Ortoman (Ludwig Erdmann) (1683–1759), who joined the Venice Ospedale della Pietà in early 1706 as a *Maestro Professore di Salamuri.*[32]

Johann Melchior Molter (1696–1765) in seiner Zeit: Dokumente und Bilder zu Leben und Werk, ed. F. Rainer and K. Häffner (Karlsruhe: Badische Landesbibliothek Karlsruhe, 1996), 257.

29 Lawson, *The Chalumeau in Eighteenth-Century Music,* 152–54.

30 The cover of this work has a paper label with the date 1768, while the title page on the first page of the manuscript has the date 1773; thus the score was probably rewritten for a later performance in Mannheim. Mus. Ms. 216/0002, Universitäts- und Landesbibliothek Darmstadt.

31 Shelfmark VIII/1405; Lawson, *The Chalumeau in Eighteenth-Century Music,* 17.

32 Gastone Vio, "Precisazioni sui documenti della Pietà," in *Vivaldi: Veneziano Europeoe,* ed. Francesco DeGrada (Florence: Leo S. Olschki,

Various types of documentary evidence show his activities in procuring chalumeaux for the Pietà.[33] Erdmann was subsequently appointed oboist at the Tuscan court in Florence, and married one of the Pietà's *figlie di coro*, Madalena.[34] It may be that Erdmann was the inspiration for Vivaldi's use of the keyed chalumeau in the works mentioned above. Another musician with connections to the Pietà was Candida (ca. 1674/75–1757), who was a prominent *figlia di coro* there. She sang, played the chalumeau and viola, and performed on tenor chalumeau in Vivaldi's Sonata in C major for violin, oboe, organ, and optional tenor *salmoè*, RV 779 (ca. 1709).[35]

Chalumeau players have been identified in other places where important repertoire for the instrument was composed. In Vienna, the oboe, flute, and chalumeau player Joseph Ignaz Lorber was active in the imperial *Hofkapelle* from 1705 to 1724.[36] Andreas Wittmann was known as a virtuoso flutist and chalumeau player in 1721; he died in 1767.[37] Lawson notes that the oboist Daniel Franz Hartmann, who probably also played the chalumeau, was appointed to the Viennese court in 1721 and died in 1772.[38] In 1719 Johann Wilhelm Hugo (ca. 1689–1775) was a musician in the private chapel of August Christoph von Wackerbarth (1662–1734), field marshal, Imperial Count and Minister of State under August the Strong of Dresden, and in 1731 was hired for Dresden's court orchestra. Hugo became famous as a

---

1980), 105–6.

33 See Michael Talbot, *The Vivaldi Compendium* (Woodbridge: Boydell Press, 2011), 73–74, 139, and 159n30; and Federico Maria Sardelli, *Vivaldi's Music for Flute and Recorder*, trans. M. Talbot (Aldershot: Ashgate, 2007), 24–26.

34 Talbot, *The Vivaldi Compendium*, 75; Alfredo Bernardini, "The Oboe in the Venetian Republic, 1692–1797," *Early Music* 16, no. 3 (1988): 379; Geoffrey Burgess and Bruce Haynes, *The Oboe* (New Haven, CT: Yale University Press, 2004), 63–64.

35 Talbot, *The Vivaldi Compendium*, 39.

36 Glüxam, *Instrumentarium und Instrumentalstil*, 451; Ludwig Ritter von Köchel, *Johann Josef Fux, Hofcompositor und Hofkapellmeister der Kaiser Leopold I., Josef I. und Karl VI. von 1698 bis 1740* (Vienna: Alfred Hölder Beck'sche Universitäts Buchhandlung, 1872), 258, 384.

37 Köchel, *Johann Josef Fux*, 257, 389.

38 Colin Lawson, "The Chalumeau in the Works of Fux," in *Johann Joseph Fux and the Music of the Austro-Italian Baroque*, ed. Harry White (London: Routledge, 1992), 92.

chalumeau soloist by 1740, and several works were written for him by Zelenka, Heinichen, Fasch, and Ristori.[39]

In England, chalumeau concerto performances are noted from the 1720s, but the performers are unknown. In London in June 1722, *The Daily Post* announced, "RICHMOND-WELLS Will continue Open every Day during the Summer Season ... on Mondays will be a select Band of Musick from the Opera. ... N.B. There will be several Concerto's [*sic*] every Evening on a new Instrument from Germany, call'd *The Shalamo*, never play'd in Publick before."[40] England also enjoyed the activities of Mr. Charles, one of the most well-known performers during the first half of the eighteenth century, who performed on the chalumeau as well as other instruments between 1737 and 1757 (see below).[41]

Graupner's cantata *Seid barmherzig* (1734) is the first of his chalumeau works and includes an obbligato for the bass chalumeau. It may have been played at some point by Johann Christian Klotsch, a bassoon and chalumeau virtuoso, who left Zerbst to join the Hesse-Darmstadt court in 1735.[42] At this time it is probable that Graupner was

---

39 Janice B. Stockigt and Jóhannes Ágústsson, "Reflections and Recent Findings on the Life and Music of Jan Dismas Zelenka (1679–1745)," in *Jan Dismas Zelenka's Life and Music Reconsidered (Zelenka Conference Prague 2015)*, ed. J. K. Koupa, 14, 25, 37, accessed July 12, 2019, http://www.acecs.cz/media/cu_2015_04.pdf. For Heinichen's and Ristori's chalumeau works see Rice, *The Baroque Clarinet and Chalumeau*, 2nd ed., appendix 4.

40 Burney Collection of Newspapers, vol. 220B, British Library; quoted by Jennifer Beakes, "The Horn Parts in Handel's Operas and Oratorios and the Horn Players who Performed in These Works" (DMA diss., City University of New York, 2007), 413–14.

41 A listing of concerts and a discussion of Charles's career, with a focus on the horn, may be found in Beakes, "The Horn Parts in Handel's Operas and Oratorios," 405–12. Two other detailed accounts of Charles's career are Elizabeth Chevill, "Music Societies and Musical Life in Old Foundation Cathedral Cities 1700–60" (PhD diss., University of London, 1993), 158–59; and Elizabeth Chevill, "Clergy, Music Societies and the Development of a Musical Tradition: A Study of Music Societies in Hereford, 1690–1760," in *Concert Life in Eighteenth-Century Britain*, ed. S. Wollenberg and S. McVeigh (Aldershot: Ashgate, 2004), 49–50.

42 Colin Lawson, "Graupner and the Chalumeau," *Early Music* 11, no. 2 (1983): 209; Elisabeth Noack, *Musikgeschichte Darmstadts vom Mittlealter bis zur Goethezeit* (Mainz: B. Schott's Söhne, 1967), 215.

inspired to write instrumental bassoon compositions, and later works for the chalumeau. Klotsch and two other chalumeau players at Darmstadt—Jacob Führer (Klotsch's student) and Jacob Friedrich Stoltz (newly appointed oboist and chalumeau player)—may have been the performers of a new work for three chalumeaux by Graupner in 1738, referred to in a letter of that year as "Nacht-musique."[43]

As chalumeau music appeared, musicians taught themselves to play the instrument in addition to their other woodwinds. Their abilities and experience were skillfully used by court composers in the surviving music. The eventual replacement of the chalumeau in favor of the clarinet occurred during the 1760s for a variety of reasons, including the development of the four-, five-, and six-key clarinet; greater interest in composing for the clarinet after 1760; the wide clarinet compass used by composers for concertos and solo works; the use of the clarinet in military bands in England, France, and Germany; and the adoption of the clarinet in many court orchestras.

The Clarinet and Its Music, 1715–1770

There are 142 extant works by fifty-seven composers that use the clarinet, dating from about 1715 to 1770. Eighty-four are vocal works (operas, oratorios, cantatas, serenatas, various types of sacred works, and others), and fifty-seven are instrumental (chamber works, wind band music, concertos, and other orchestral music). Composers were often quick to write for the clarinet, when available, to take advantage of its wide compass and distinctive timbre. Clarinets were probably available in 1700 from Johann Christoph Denner (1655–1707) in Nuremberg, but the first documentation of clarinets ordered from Nuremberg is in 1710, probably from his son, Jacob Denner (1681–1735; see below). The earliest music with clarinet (now lost) was *Festivmusik* performed in January 1712 to celebrate the crowning of Kaiser Karl VI. Jointly composed by Maximilian Zeidler and Johann Jacob de Neufville, the first and third sections (by Zeidler) used two clarinets.[44]

---

43 Ursula Kramer, "The Court of Hesse-Darmstadt" in Owens, Reul, and Stockigt, *Music at German Courts*, 348–49, 358. The work may have been the *Ouverture* in C for three chalumeaux GWV 401; Lawson, "Graupner and the Chalumeau," 209.

44 Staatarchiv, Nuremberg, Rep. 67, Nr. 45, Akte 413, quoted by Ekkehart Nickel, *Der Holzblasinstrumentenbau in der Freien Reichsstadt Nürnberg* (Munich: Katzbichler, 1971), 245, 462n1428.

The clarinet was used by professional musicians in courts, churches, and theaters, and by amateurs. The earliest known representation of a clarinetist shows a well-dressed man playing a two-key clarinet in a luxurious room in what could be a wealthy residence. It is an engraving by the Nuremberg artist Johann Christoph Weigel in the collection *Musikalisches Theatrum* of circa 1722 (see fig. 1.2). The engraving's poetic first two lines describe the clarinet's sound: "When the trumpet would be too loud, the clarinet can replace it pleasantly."[45] Indeed clarinets, when available, were occasionally substituted for trumpets in some works, and much of the Baroque clarinet's music up to 1754 was in the overblown register, producing a sound that has a distinct resemblance to the natural trumpet. Its musical use was different from that of the contemporary chalumeau. Composers who wrote clarinet parts appropriate for the natural trumpet, and at times substituted the clarinet for difficult high trumpet parts, included Caldara, Telemann, Rathgeber, and Chinzer. After 1755 many clarinets had four or five keys, and composers began writing melodic and diatonic parts similar to flute and oboe parts.

Clarinet Concertos

The earliest extant concerto was written by Vivaldi in Venice: *Concerto per la Solennità di San Lorenzo*, RV 556 (ca. 1715). Two C clarinets primarily double two oboes in the first and third movements, with occasional short solos in the clarion or upper register, while in the second movement the clarinets play the continuo's bass part. In a revised version, Vivaldi suppressed the clarinet parts, distributing their notes in the outer movements as cues in other parts.[46]

Vivaldi's next works, with much more assured clarinet writing, are two concertos for two oboes, two C clarinets, strings, and basso continuo, RV 559 (ex. 2.3) and RV 560 (1720–24). In these concertos each clarinet's range is F^3 or G^3 to C^6. The clarion register has a distinctive trumpet-like character. In the chalumeau or lower register, Vivaldi uses diatonic writing with minor-key inflections, emphasizing the difference in timbre between the two registers. He employs a bass clef for

---

45 "Wann der Trompeten-Schall will allzulaut erthönen, so dient das Clarinet auf angenehme weiß." Johann Christoph Weigel, *Musikalisches Theatrum* (Nuremberg, ca. 1722, facsimile ed., ed. A. Berner, Kassel: Bärenreiter, 1961), sheet 14.
46 Michael Talbot, "Vivaldi's Instrumentation," in "Correspondence," *Early Music* 7, no. 4 (1979): 561.

Example 2.3. Antonio Vivaldi, Concerto RV 559 (1720–24), mvt. 1, Larghetto–Allegro. The two parts for clarinet in C are the top two staves.

the clarinet parts in the chalumeau register, although the sounding notes are an octave higher.

A concerto written by Giovanni Chinzer (1698–1749), a composer probably active in Florence, is found in the same manuscript collection as a similar anonymous double concerto. The editor of both concertos' modern editions suggests dates of 1725–30 on stylistic grounds.[47] These two works are similar to Vivaldi's in their employment of clarion and chalumeau registers to achieve timbre differences. Two concertos by Johann Valentin Rathgeber (1682–1750), a Benedictine priest and choirmaster at Banz near Coburg in southern Germany, are the earliest known for solo clarinet and orchestra that can be securely dated. They were part of a collection of twenty-four published works, *Chelys sonora* (Augsburg: J. J. Lotter, 1728). Rathgeber wrote for the C clarinet in an impressive trumpet or clarino style, with a compass restricted mostly to the clarion register (see ex. 2.4); the music is also appropriate for the natural trumpet.

---

47   Paul Everett, "Early Double Clarinet Concertos from Italy," *Clarinet & Saxophone* 24, no. 4 (Winter 1999): 18; Giovanni Chinzer, *Concerto in C Major* and Anonymous, *Concerto in F Major, Two Solo Clarinets, Strings and Basso Continuo* (Launton: Edition HH Ltd, 1999), iii–vi.

Example 2.4. Johann Valentin Rathgeber, *Chelys sonora*, Concerto no. 19 (1728), mvts. 1 and 2, *Clarineto vel Lituo* in C.

Four instrumental works for clarinet were written during the 1740s by the obscure composer Anton Bennegger (Antonio Benegger): "Sonata 1ma per clarineto solo ... for Mr. Carles D.5 Octor 1741," "Sinfonia Concertino per Clarineto Solo," "Concerto col Clarineto Solo," and "Concerto per un Clarineto Solo."[48] These works were possibly written for Mr. Charles, the touring musician previously mentioned (discussed further below). At present, they are in a private American collection, and not available for study.

Johann Melchior Molter's six concertos for D clarinet (ca. 1742–65) were written for the Karlsruhe court orchestra and consistently employ a very high tessitura, C^6 to G^6, with notes below C^5 usually treated in a triadic manner. They were probably written for and performed after 1750 by Jacob Hengel and Johann Reusch.[49] The elegant themes are in a *galant* style, which Molter developed after studying in Italy. These works are technically more demanding than earlier concertos, using wide leaps of more than one octave, triplet sixteenth-note figures, thirty-second and sixty-fourth-note flourishes, and many grace notes and trills. There are considerably more accidentals than found in works for the natural trumpet, and one concerto features leaps of more than two octaves from G^3. As seen in example 2.5, Molter's concertos illustrate a mature writing style for the two-key clarinet, with much greater technical challenges for the player than those seen in the Vivaldi and Rathgeber examples above.[50]

The apex of concerto writing for the Baroque clarinet is the *Concerto à 7 stromenti* or Clarinet Concerto GraS 313 written by Johann Stamitz (1717–57), probably during his stay at La Pouplinière's home near Paris during 1754–55. It is technically challenging but may be

---

48 Portions of the music are reproduced in *Printed and Manuscript Music, Auction, London, 7 December 2001* (London: Sotheby's, 2001), 32–33. An index of music of the Durlach court in Karlsruhe, ca. 1755, lists concertos and concertanti, including a work by Benneger. Rüdiger Thomsen-Fürst, "Die Musik am markgräflich badischen Hof in Karlsruhe (1715–1803)," in *Süddeutsche Hofkapellen im 18. Jahrhundert: Eine Bestandsaufnahme*, ed. S. Leopold and B. Pelker (Heidelberg: Heidelberger Akademie der Wissenschaften, 2014), 154.

49 Suggested by Simon Aldrich in his 2011 International Clarinet Association Presentation, Northridge, California, "The Clarinetist(s) That Inspired the Composition of the Six Clarinet Concerti of Johann Melchior Molter."

50 Rice, *The Baroque Clarinet* (1992), 109–14; Häfner, "Verzeichnis der Werken von Johann Melchior Molter," 243–62.

Example 2.5. Johann Melchior Molter, Concerto in A Major, MWV 6:41 (1742–65), mvt. 1, Allegro, clarinet in D.

played on a three-key B-flat clarinet, as suggested by Ernst Schlader. It is the earliest known concerto for the B-flat clarinet. The manuscript is marked only "Stamitz," but is attributed by Gradenwitz and Wolf to Johann Stamitz on the basis of several stylistic characteristics.[51] Its *galant* style has recurring phrases, refined texture, witty, highly ornamented melodies, simple harmony, and skillfully applied dissonance. The wide compass, E^3 to $F\#^6$, is larger than in previous clarinet concertos, incorporating frequent wide leaps, chromatic passages in the clarino register, and sixteenth and thirty-second notes. Newhill suggests that this concerto was written for Gaspard Procksch, clarinetist in La Pouplinière's orchestra and at the Paris Opéra from 1752 to 1762.[52]

Operas and Stage Works

The earliest opera with clarinets is Antonio Caldara's *Ifigenia in Aulide*, first written in 1718 and revived in 1723 in Vienna. The clarinets are paired with trumpets and timpani, which may have been prompted by their similar tone colors in the upper register.[53]

The clarinetists Jean (Johann) Schieffer and François (Franz) Raiffer were supplementary musicians for three rehearsals and twenty-five performances of Jean-Philippe Rameau's opera *Zoroastre* in 1749 and 1750.[54] However, the 1749 engraved score does not have separate clarinet parts, and since Rameau used clarinets in *Acante et Céphise*

---

51 Peter Gradenwitz, "The Beginnings of Clarinet Literature: Notes on a Clarinet Concerto by Joh. Stamitz," *Music & Letters* 17 (1936), 145–50; Eugene K. Wolf, "Johann Stamitz," §1 of the article "Stamitz Family," *Grove Music Online.*.

52 John Newhill, "The Contribution of the Mannheim School to Clarinet Literature," *Music Review* 40 (1979): 111–12.

53 Colin Lawson, "The Clarinet and Chalumeau Revisited," *Early Music* 14, no. 4 (1986), 554. Francesco Bartolomeo Conti was noted for a clarinet part in Rice, *The Baroque Clarinet* (1992, p. 85) in a manuscript of the opera *Don Chisciotte in Sierra Morena*, 1719. The score of the overture to this opera reproduced in *MGG* (vol. 2, 1642) includes "Clarinetti," but it was not written out by Conti, who also did not use the clarinet in later revivals of this opera. See Hermine Weigel Williams, *Francesco Bartolomeo Conti* (Aldershot: Ashgate, 1999) 102n5.

54 "Etat de Payments qui seront faits à plusieurs sujets cy-après nommez, employez à l'Opéra, par extraordinaire, depuis le 29 aoust 1749," Paris Opéra, archive, A. 19, *Emargements*, 1749–51, quoted by Lionel La Laurencie, "Rameau et les clarinettes," *Revue musicale* 9, no. 2 (February 1913): 27–28.

(1751), it is likely that the decision to use clarinets in *Zoroastre* was made after the engraving of the score started. The clarinetists, horn players, and trumpeters were paid only for the rehearsals and adequate time to learn the limited brass parts, suggesting that the clarinet parts were restricted to short sections or doubling of the violins and oboes.[55] Rameau's use of C, A, and D clarinets in twelve sections of *Acante et Céphise* is exceptional. It is one of the first musical works to reflect an orchestral conception in which each instrumental group plays a role adapted to its own timbre.[56] Especially noteworthy is Rameau's pairing of clarinets and horns; these figure prominently in act 2, including in the hunter's theme of "L'amour est heureux," and in the entr'acte between acts 2 and 3.[57]

Thomas Augustine Arne (1710–78) was the earliest British composer to write for the clarinet and may have known Rameau's use of clarinets in *Acante et Céphise*, which was performed in Paris through the 1750s. Arne's highly successful afterpiece *Thomas and Sally, or the Sailor's Return* (1760) prominently featured two C clarinets and two C horns at the beginning of the overture. The score includes precise directions for the timing and placement of the instruments; at the word "Enter" (m. 16), the first horn walks on stage while playing, followed by the second horn and the first and second clarinets. When the Squire enters singing the rousing song "The Echoing Horn," he is accompanied by clarinets and horns. Arne's writing is technically simple, and the horn and clarinet players could perform from memory while walking on stage. The clarinets' compass is mostly restricted to the upper or clarion register (see ex. 2.6).[58] A later work by Arne, *Artaxerxes* (1762), uses both C clarinets and C horns in act 2 in a melodic, stepwise manner that doubles the first and second violins. In act 3 he uses two C clarinets to double the violin melodically.

Johann Christian Bach (1735–82) was a champion of the clarinet, including them in parts in most of his works between 1763 and 1780. His first London opera performed at the prestigious King's Theatre

55 Jean-Philippe Rameau, *Zoroastre, version 1749*, ed. Graham Sadler, *Opera omnia Rameau*, ser. IV, vol. 19 (Paris: Gérard Billaudot, 1999), LIX.

56 Jean-Philippe Rameau, *Achante et Céphise ou la sympathie*, ed. Robert Fajon and Sylvie Bouissou, *Opera omnia Rameau*, ser. IV, vol. 21 (Paris: Gérard Billaudot, 1998), XXXVIII.

57 See Rice, *The Baroque Clarinet* (1992), 115–27.

58 Thomas Augustine Arne, *Thomas and Sally, or the Sailor's Return* (London: the author, 1761), 6.

Example 2.6. Thomas Augustine Arne, *Thomas and Sally, or the Sailor's Return* (1760, published 1761), act 1, scene 1, "The Echoing Horn."

was *Orione* (1763), where he uses D, C, and B-flat clarinets in an unusually full instrumentation with pairs of oboes, bassoons, and horns and, in selected numbers, flutes and "Tallie [*sic*]" (tenor oboes or English horns) in F.[59] Later works including clarinets are *Zanaida* (1763) with D clarinets; *Menalcas* (1764); *Adriano in Siria* (1765); *Carattaco* (1767); the ode *Happy Morn, Auspicious Rise* (1768–69); and the oratorio *Gioas, rè di Giuda* (1770).

Original stage works using clarinets continued to be written for the Paris Opéra after Rameau's death, by composers such as Pierre-Montan Berton, Bernard de Bury, Louis-Joseph Francoeur (1738–1804), and François-Joseph Gossec. In addition, from the 1760s through the 1780s many works from the late seventeenth and early eighteenth centuries were revived in heavily edited versions.[60] Some of these revisions included reorchestrations that added clarinet parts. For example, clarinet parts were added to Jean-Baptiste Lully's *Alceste*, *Persée*, and *Bellérophon*; to Henri Desmarets and André Campra's *Iphigenie en Tauride*; and to Rameau's *Castor et Pollux* and *Anacréon*.

Sacred Works

Joannes Adamus Josephus Faber (1692–1759) wrote a prominent C clarinet part in two sections of his *Missa Maria Assumpta* (1720). It is one of the earliest appearances of the clarinet and may have been played by Faber himself.[61] Georg Philipp Telemann wrote six cantatas

---

59   Parts at the Berkeley Music Library, University of California.

60   Lois Rosow, "From Destouches to Berton: Editorial Responsibility at the Paris Opéra," *Journal of the American Musicological Society* 40, no. 2 (1987): 285–86, 294–305. A detailed discussion of the reorchestration and additions to Lully's *Persée* for a performance in 1770 is in Benoît Dratwicki, "Le renouveau de l'orchestre français à l'âge classique (1760–1770): l'example du *Persée* Versallais de 1770," in *L'orchestre à cordes sous Louis XIV: instruments, repertoires, singularités*, ed. J. Duron and F. Gétreau ([Paris]: Librairie Philosophique J. Vrin, 2015), 376–97.

61   Albert R. Rice, "The Rediscovery of Faber's 1720 Mass and Recent Research on the Early 18th-Century Clarinet," *The Clarinet* 36, no. 4 (September 2009): 54–59; Eugeen Schreurs, "Church Music and Minstrel Music in the Southern Netherlands, with a Special Focus on Antwerp" in *Music and the City: Musical Cultures and Urban Societies in the Southern Netherlands and Beyond, c. 1760–1800*, ed. S. Berhein, B. Blondé, and E. Schreurs (Leuven: Leuven University Press, 2013), 103–26.

using a single D clarinet; in *Lobet den Herrn* TVWV 1:1061, three clarinets could substitute for three D trumpets.[62]

The composer Johann Zach (1699–1763) wrote a Requiem in G minor (ca. 1750) for the monastery at Bozen (Bolzano, South Tirol, Italy). It has two G clarinets (probably basset horns), one of the earliest known uses of this instrument.[63] Johann Wendelin Glaser, Wertheim court cantor and music director from 1743 to 1783, wrote for the clarinet in at least fifteen cantatas.[64] He was one of the earliest to feature clarinets and horns in a "hunting horn" style in his 1756 cantata *Alles was Odem hat, lobe den Herrn.*[65] The clarinet was employed in Austrian monasteries, initially by the priest and choirmaster Franz Sparry (1715–67), in the arias "Auf bedrängte Seelen," with two B-flat clarinets, and "Kommet her, Mariae Kinder," with two G clarinets (basset horns), both written around 1748–63 in Kremsmünster.[66] Georg Pasterwiz (1730–1803), a Kremsmünster priest and composer, was influenced by Sparry's clarinet writing in his motet *Sancta Maria* PW 8.42 (1756), which uses two A clarinets, the earliest known use of this instrument.[67] In the same year, Pasterwiz wrote music for the play *Floridus*, PW 10.18 (1756), with two parts for A and C clarinets written into the first and second horn parts, requiring the musicians to play three instruments.[68] Sacred music using clarinets was also written in France, England, and Slovenia.

---

62 Simon Rettelbach, *Trompeten, Hörner, und Klarinetten in der in Frankfurt am Main Überlieferten "Ordentlichen Kirchenmusik" Georg Philipp Telemanns* (Tutzing: H. Schneider, 2008), 56–66, 255–57, 271; Rice, *The Baroque Clarinet* (1992), 86.

63 Franz Gratl, "Original und Bearbeitung bei Johann Zach," *Wissenschaftliches Jahrbuch der Tiroler Landesmuseum* 7 (2014): 111, http://www.zobodat.at/pdf/WissJbTirolerLM_7_0103-0113.pdf.

64 Listed in *RISM*, www.rism.info.

65 96 *Johann Wendelin Glaser (1713–1783): Augewählte Kantaten*, ed. A. Traub and M. Jammermann, Denkmäler der Musik in Baden-Württemberg 6 (Munich: Straube, 1998), 300–303.

66 Ernst Schlader, "Kommet her Mariae Kinder," in *Musikland ob der Enns*, accessed August 14, 2016, www.musikland-ob-der-enns.at/werke/sparry.htm#.

67 Ernst Schlader, "Die Rezeption der Werke von Georg Pasterwiz (1730–1803) im Stift Kremsmünster: Kontinuität und Wandel," *Wissenschaftliches Jahrbuch der Tiroler Landesmuseum* 7 (2014): 62, www.zobodat.at/pdf/WissJbTirolerLM_7_0061-0071.pdf.

68 Ernst Schlader, *Georg Pasterwiz (1730–1803): Leben, Wirken, Werk* (Saarbrücken: Südwestdeutscher Verlag für Hochschulschriften,

Symphonies and Wind Band Works

The earliest symphonies including the clarinet were written for the Mannheim orchestra in 1758 by Johann Stamitz, and published in Paris by Venier as part of a six-work collection by various composers.[69] In Paris, Gossec included optional clarinet parts in his Symphonies op. 4 (1758), op. 5 (1761–62), and op. 8 (1765).[70] Composed in Oxford, William Herschel's Symphonies no. 18 in E-flat Major (1762), no. 19 in C Minor (1762), no. 20 in C Major (1762), and no. 22 in A Minor (1763) have clarinet parts in a later hand.[71] In Edinburgh, the Earl of Kelly included B-flat clarinets in his Periodical Overture no. 17 in E-flat (1766).[72] Players probably continued to use Baroque two- and three-key clarinets brought from Germany, as the earliest four-, five-, and six-key clarinets were made in London from about 1760.[73]

Music for a small wind band including pairs of oboes and/or clarinets, bassoons, and horns (in various combinations, sometimes with other instruments), known by the German term *Harmoniemusik*, was common from about the middle of the eighteenth century. Outside the opera house, one of the earliest known works with clarinets and horns is Johann Stamitz's *Quatuor à deux clarinettes et deux cors* (1755–56). This quartet, written in a Classical style, was printed in Valentin Roeser's 1764 instrumentation treatise *Essai d'instruction*, offering advice to composers on writing for a four-key clarinet.[74] Franz Joseph Ulbrecht (d. 1799) was active as a musician at the Rastatt court from

---

2011), 158, 309.

69   Eugene K. Wolf, *The Symphonies of Johann Stamitz* (The Hague: Nijhoff, 1981), 343n15.

70   Barry S. Brook, *La symphonie française dans la seconde moitié du XVIIIe siècle* (Paris: Institut de Musicologie de l'Université de Paris, 1962), 2:314–15.

71   Albert R. Rice, *The Clarinet in the Classical Period* (Oxford: Oxford University Press, 2003), 178; British Library, Archives and Manuscript catalogue finding aid, http://searcharchives.bl.uk. The author thanks Ingrid Pearson for sending photos of the parts and one score.

72   An advertisement appeared in *The Leeds Intelligencer*, June 9, 1767, for a "Benefit of Mr. Jobson"; listed on the program is a "Symphonia, by the Earl of Kelly, for Clarinets and French-Horns."

73   See Albert R. Rice, "Two Eighteenth-Century English Five-Key Clarinets: Their Characteristics and Importance," *Galpin Society Journal* 72 (2019): 148–50 and 163–73.

74   Valentin Roeser, *Essai d'instruction à l'usage de ceux qui composent pour la clarinette et le cor* (1764; repr., Geneva: Minkoff, 1972), 20–21.

1738 and wrote music for a larger wind band.[75] His *Musica à tavola*, scored for a septet of two B-flat clarinets, two E-flat horns, two E-flat trumpets, and bassoon, dates from 1756–66.[76] These are early examples of a *Harmoniemusik* repertoire that would eventually amount to thousands of works by the early nineteenth century.

In 1761, when Joseph Haydn (1732–1809) was Vice-Kapellmeister for Prince Paul Anton Esterházy, he wrote a five-movement Divertimento for a quartet of two C clarinets and two C horns.[77] The clarinet writing is conservative and limited to two octaves at its widest, from C^4 to C^6. Haydn wrote another work about 1764 for a larger ensemble of two C clarinets, two horns, two violins, two violas, and bass with the same conservative clarinet compass.[78]

Over the fifty-five-year period covered by this study, fifty-seven composers penned 142 clarinet works in more genres than were written for the chalumeau. By examining this music, one can trace the development of the instrument along with composers' abilities to write for it. From use of a limited compass and technical capacity in the early eighteenth century, a more mature style emerged in the 1750s, when composers began assigning leading musical roles to the clarinet and writing technically demanding music for instruments with four, five, or six keys.

Baroque Clarinets Made for Aristocrats and Churches

The aristocracy and churches were the first to use the clarinet. A 1710 invoice for Field Marshal Duke Johann Franz von Gronsfeld in Nuremberg mentions "4 [soprano] Chalimoú, 1 Alt Chalimoú, 1 Chalimoú

---

75 Rüdiger Thomsen-Fürst, "Die Hofkapelle der Markgrafen von Baden-Baden in Rastatt (1715–1771)," in Leopold and B. Pelker, *Süddeutsche Hofkapellen im 18. Jahrhundert*, 424.

76 Fürst, ibid., 419n56, states that the septet was written "presumably in 1758" for the *Harmonie* band.

77 There is some uncertainty about where Haydn wrote this work. Webster states that "a connection with the Esterházy court is possible." James Webster, "Joseph Haydn's Early Ensemble Divertimenti," in *Coll'astuzia, col giudizio: Essays in Honor of Neal Zaslaw*, ed. Cliff Eisen (Ann Arbor, MI: Steglein Publishing, 2009), 115–16.

78 Albert R. Rice, "The Clarinet in the Works of Joseph and Michael Haydn," *Eisenstädter Haydn-Berichte* 3 (2004): 29 and 38.

Basson, and 2 Clarinettes" (packed in a case).[79] A specific maker is not mentioned, but it seems likely it was Jacob Denner, Johann Christoph Denner's son. In the same year, six clarinets were brought to Eberbach Abbey in Mainz for the monks.[80] The earliest proof of Jacob Denner's activity as a maker is from 1711, when he delivered two pairs of clarinets to the Nuremberg Frauenkirche.[81] He provided two clarinets to the Sebalduskirche in 1714.[82] Another son of Johann Christoph Denner, Johann David Denner (1691–1764), continued to use his father's stamp until his death;[83] for this reason it was probably Johann David, rather than Johann Christoph, who produced two C clarinets mentioned in a 1775 musical instrument inventory of St. Michael's Church in Fürth as having been purchased in 1754.[84] Today there are three extant two-key clarinets by Jacob Denner, and one three-key C clarinet attributed to Johann David Denner.[85]

79 Staatsarchiv Nürnberg, Stadtrechnungsbeleg in Repertorium 54 a II, Nr. 1282, quoted by Nickel, *Der Holzblasinstrumentenbau*, 251–52.

80 Wiesbaden Haupt-Stadtarchiv, Archiv der geistlichen Institut, Abt. 22, Rechnungsbuch des Kloster Eberbach, Rheingau 1710, 39v; Adam Gottron, *Mainzer Musikgeschichte von 1500 bis 1800* (Mainz: Auslieferung durch die Stadtbibliothek, 1959), 115–16.

81 Rice, *The Baroque Clarinet* (1992), 41–42; Martin Kirnbauer, Peter Thalheimer, and Catherine Taylor, "Jacob Denner and the Development of the Flute in Germany," *Early Music* 23, no. 1 (1995): 96 and 100n66.

82 Landeskirchliche Archiv, Nuremberg, Kirchenrechnung Vereinigtes protestantisches Kirchenvermögen der Stadt Nürnberg 228, Nr. 5, 78; Nickel, *Der Holzblasinstrumentenbau*, 454n1246.

83 Nickel, *Der Holzblasinstrumentenbau*, 268; Herbert Heyde, "Maker's Marks on Wind Instruments," in William Waterhouse, *The New Langwill Index of Musical Wind Makers and Inventors* (London: T. Bingham, 1992), xviii; Martin Kirnbauer, "Überlegungen zu den Meisterzeichen Nürnberger 'Holzblasinstrumentenmacher' im 17. und 18. Jahrhunderts," *Tibia* 17 (1992): 17–18.

84 "Am 9. Januar 1754 wurden von dem Würdigen Gottes-Haus, zwei C-Clarinetten, von J. C. Denner, angeschaffet." Martin Kirnbauer, *Verzeichnis der Europäischen Musikinstrumente im Germanischen Nationalmuseum Nürnberg*, vol. 2, *Flöten- und Rohrblattinstrumente bis 1750: Beschreibender Katalog* (Wilhelmshaven: Florian Noetzel, 1994), 198.

85 Martin Kirnbauer and Heike Fricke, "Denner," in *The Grove Dictionary of Musical Instruments*, 2nd ed., ed. L. Libin (New York: Oxford University Press, 2014), 2:34.

The Württemberg-Stuttgart court was the first court to include the clarinet in its orchestra, where it was introduced in 1714 by the court composer Johann Christoph Pez (1664–1716). Three clarinetists, the earliest known by name, were Franz Anton Maximillian Pez (son of the composer), Georg Christoph Bleßner, and Antonio Meister. Pez also played the viola d'amore and viola da braccio; Bleßner played the oboe and flute; and Meister played violin and viola, sang descant parts, and copied music. They joined the court orchestra, which included flutes (two players) and oboes (four players).[86] A 1718 inventory of court instruments included only one clarinet.[87] Unfortunately, no Württemberg court music with clarinet has survived in the extant compositions now in the University Library in Rostock.

At the Rastatt court of Baden-Baden, Johann Caspar Ferdinand Fischer's stage work *Melagers Gelübd-mässiges Ehren-Feuer-Opffer* (1718) was written to celebrate the birth of Crown Prince Ludwig Georg Bernard Simpert. At least seven singers performed with a large orchestra that is not described, but the libretto mentions "Waldhörnern, Geigen and Flöten" (horns, violins, and flutes), and on the last page in the poetic aria "Chalmieu" (chalumeaux) and "Clarinetten."

To him sing glory and rejoicing
In his honour dance and spring
to chalumeaux and clarinets
Ludwig's name may soar up
to penetrate the stars
among thousands of fiery rockets.[88]

With the adoption of the clarinet in court orchestras during the second decade of the eighteenth century, musicians began to learn the

---

86 Samantha Kim Owens, "The Württemberg *Hofkapelle* c.1680–1721" (PhD diss., Victoria University of Wellington, 1995), 184–85, 445–46.

87 Ibid., 478; Samantha Owens, "Upgrading from Consorts to Orchestra at the Württemberg Court," in *From Renaissance to Baroque: Change in Instruments and Instrumental Music in the Seventeenth Century*, ed. J. Wainwright and P. Holman (Aldershot: Ashgate, 2005), 232.

88 "Diesem Ruhm / und Jubel singet: Dem zu Ehren tanßz und springet / Zu Chalmieu und Clarinetten: Ludwigs Nahme sich erschwinge / Bis hinauff zum Sternen tringe / Unter Tausend Feur=Ragetten." Johann Caspar Ferdinand Fischer, *Meleagers Gelübd-mässiges Ehren-Feuer-Opfer* (Rastadt: F. G. Tusch, 1718), 31, http://digi.u.b.uni-heidelberg. deglit/fischer1718/0003; translation by Thomas Reil. See also Thomsen-Fürst, "Die Musik am markgräflich badischen Hof," 418–19.

instrument and composers used it in various genres of music. Some performers became soloists, and this in turn contributed to the rise in the clarinet's popularity.

Clarinet Soloists

The Daily Courant reported the clarinet's London concert debut at Hickford's Great Room on March 24, 1726, when it was played by two Germans, August Freudenfeld and Francis Rosenberg. They gave two additional concerts on March 15 and April 19, 1727: a "Concert of Musick, with Two Clarinets" and "a Concerto for Two Clarinets."[89] These two German clarinetists are the earliest named soloists. On April 26, 1727, a vocal and instrumental benefit concert for the singer Miss Davies included "a Concerto for Two Clarinets"; Freudenfeld and Rosenberg probably played this concert even though they are not mentioned in the advertisement.[90]

Mr. Charles, mentioned above, toured the British Isles for a total of twenty-four years between 1733 and 1757, playing benefit concerts on the horn, clarinet, chalumeau, and oboe d'amore with his wife, son, and local musicians.[91] His first performance on the clarinet was at the Swan Tavern in London on April 1, 1735, and included "several new Pieces on the French Horn and Clarinet."[92] From that time forward he played clarinet and/or chalumeau in seventeen known concerts, and

---

89 *The Daily Courant*, March 24, 1726 and March 15, 1727; *Daily Journal*, April 19, 1727.

90 *Daily Courant*, April 26, 1727; *The London Stage, 1660–1800, Part 2: 1700–1729*, ed. E. L. Avery (Carbondale, IL: Southern Illinois University Press, 1960); *Part 3, 1729–1747*, ed. Arthur H. Scouten (Carbondale, IL: Southern Illinois University Press, 1961), 921–22.

91 It has been suggested by Beakes and Hiebert that Mr. Charles was Carlo (Charles) Vernsberg (Vernsburgh) (d. 1780), a member of the Royal Society of Musicians in 1739, 1742, 1744, and 1755. Beakes, "The Horn Parts in Handel's Operas and Oratorios," 114–15, 437–39; Thomas Hiebert, "Extraordinary Horn Writing in 'The Egerton Manuscript Collection': A Contribution to the History of the Horn in Mid-Eighteenth Century England," in *Jagd- und Waldhörner: Geschichte und musikalische Nutzung*, ed. Boje E. Hans Schmuhl and Monika Lustig (Augsburg: Wißner, 2006), 239–46.

92 *The London Stage, 1660–1800, Part 3: 1729–1747*, 475.

likely on many more that are not documented.[93] In June 1751, Charles became the proprietor of the New Vauxhall Theatre at Hotwells in Bristol, managing the concerts and performing on the horn with his son. This business venture lasted less than three years, however, and on March 30, 1754 Charles advertised for sale in Bath the "whole collection" of his music—which apparently was not sold, since he and his son continued to perform in provincial cities until 1757.[94]

Conclusion

This survey of chalumeau and clarinet music before 1770 indicates a widespread use of both instruments in dozens of operas and other stage works, in sacred music, and in instrumental works. Composers wrote for up to five chalumeaux in stage works to portray sentiments of a pastoral, melancholy, sad, and lovesick nature. Chalumeaux were also solo instruments in stage works, concertos, and small ensembles. Why was this instrument, with its distinctive tone color and ability to blend with wind and stringed instruments, obsolete by 1780? The chalumeau was never as successful as the clarinet because it was a softer instrument with a smaller compass. The crucial replacement period seems to have been around 1770, as is evident from the chalumeau's use in operas. For example, Christoph Willibald Gluck wrote for the chalumeau in his Viennese operas *Orfeo ed Euridice* (1763) and *Alceste* (1767), but later performances in Paris substituted the louder and already popular clarinet in his *Orphée et Eurydice* (1774) and *Alceste* (1776). It is also significant that several older works were reorchestrated with the addition of clarinets for performances at the Paris Opéra between 1760 and 1780. The instrument's dominance was cemented by the development of clarinets with more keys, which gave the instrument greater

---

93 The following sources provide dates and information for Mr. Charles's concerts: Elizabeth Cheville, "Music Societies and Musical Life in Old Foundation Cathedral Cities 1700–60" (PhD diss., University of London, 1993); Brian Boydell, *A Dublin Musical Calendar 1700–1760* (Dublin: Irish Academic Press, 1988); Donald Burrows and Rosemary Dunhill, *Music and Theatre in Handel's World: The Family Papers of James Harris 1732–1780* (Oxford: Oxford University Press, 2002); Pamela Weston, *Clarinet Virtuosi of the Past* (London: Robert Hale, 1971).

94 *Bath Journal*, June 12, 1751, June 24, 1751, and March 30, 1754; Kenneth Edward James, "Concert Life in Eighteenth-Century Bath" (PhD thesis, University of London, 1987), 535.

flexibility. This made it more attractive to composers, who then used its wide compass in concertos and other solo works. Also significant was the incorporation of the clarinet into official military bands in London and Paris and later America, thereby expanding the public's exposure to the instrument. From the 1760s onward many instruction books were published, bringing awareness of the clarinet's utility and versatile nature. The chalumeau was superseded, and the clarinet's popularity and future rapidly expanded.

FROM "LITTLE TRUMPET" TO UNIQUE VOICE

The Clarinet in the Concert Orchestra

Jane Ellsworth

The clarinet and the orchestra grew up, in a certain sense, togeth-er.[1] Granted, there had been early orchestras, some with wind instruments, prior to the invention of the clarinet around 1700. Lully in France and Corelli in Italy were both pioneers in directing and composing for orchestral ensembles in the second half of the seventeenth century. But the full concert or symphonic orchestra as we know it today—including multiple pairs of like wind instruments—was still in a formative stage in the first half of the eighteenth century, and

---

1 In this chapter, I base my definition of "orchestra" on ideas from Spitzer and Zaslaw: A relatively standardized ensemble consisting of a core of violin-family instruments, with several players per part, including sixteen-foot bass instruments, performing as a unified ensemble "under centralized control and discipline," with a distinct institutional identity and structure. It may or may not have a keyboard continuo and wind instruments depending on the time period; likewise, the wind players may or may not be specialists on their instruments. See John Spitzer and Neal Zaslaw, *The Birth of the Orchestra: History of an Institution, 1650–1815* (Oxford and New York: Oxford University Press, 2004), especially pp. 19–22.

its instrumentation continued to evolve at different rates in different places throughout that century.[2]

Likewise the clarinet. Like any new piece of technology, it experienced a time lag between its invention in the early eighteenth century and its general adoption some decades later. Although composers wrote concertos for it as early as the 1720s, it did not appear as a member of the concert orchestra (that is, in non-operatic "sinfonias" featuring the ensemble independently rather than as an accompaniment) on even an ad hoc basis until the 1750s, and was not a regular participant until the early nineteenth century. In the 1770s and 1780s, if you were of high enough social status to receive an invitation to an entertainment at a noble court that supported an orchestra, or wealthy enough to buy a ticket to one of the public concerts that were proliferating in places like Paris or London, you might—or might not—have seen and heard clarinets in the orchestra. If you did, they would probably have been played by the same performers who, in an earlier work on the program, had played oboe parts; even at this stage the clarinet was still too new to have acquired a cadre of specialist players.

The eighteenth century thus presents us with a web of new developments in instrumental combinations and musical genres, and we must follow the early history of the clarinet in the concert orchestra against this changing backdrop. By 1800, though, the orchestral woodwind section had attained a largely standardized instrumentation that included a pair of clarinets. In fact, this woodwind section remained stable for much of the nineteenth century, in spite of a few outliers like Berlioz and Liszt, whose orchestrational experiments were not uniformly adopted. The majority of nineteenth-century symphonies, certainly, include among the woodwinds just two clarinets.[3] What did change significantly in the nineteenth century was the clarinet itself. Through a series of mechanical developments—including several new strategies for the wholesale

---

2 I use the term "concert orchestra" to differentiate the type of ensemble I discuss in this chapter from the opera orchestra as discussed by Ingrid Pearson and Julian Rushton in chapters 4 and 5 of this volume, respectively. Concert and opera orchestras can be similar in instrumentation (depending on time period), but clearly they differ in function and repertoire.

3 This assertion can be checked using the database Daniels' Orchestral Music Online, https://daniels-orchestral.com/simple-search/, a convenient tool listing the instrumentation of thousands of orchestral works. The same assertion is not necessarily true for symphonic poems and other programmatic works, as will be shown.

redesign of the key system, as well as experiments with different materials, bore and tone hole sizes, and so on—the clarinet made considerable gains in technical facility, projection, and tonal color. Composers took advantage of these improvements in their orchestral writing, using the instrument as an individual expressive voice.

By 1900 the clarinet had become a very flexible instrument. It was, in many ways, the perfect vehicle for the stylistic eclecticism of twentieth-century art music. Early twentieth-century composers continued to explore the clarinet's ability to portray a wide range of affects, from sensuous (Debussy, Ravel) to plaintive (Sibelius) to cool and objective (Stravinsky). Composers who were interested in jazz (Milhaud, Gershwin, Copland) or national expression (Bartók, Kodály) found the instrument useful for evoking these styles. The list of twentieth-century composers who have written important clarinet parts in their orchestral works is long, including Strauss, Nielsen, Shostakovich, Prokofiev, and many others.

In this chapter, I aim to survey selectively the use of the soprano clarinet (also briefly mentioning the higher and lower members of the family) in what is conventionally termed the "symphonic literature," primarily the symphony and the symphonic poem. I will exclude concertos and other soloistic works, which are covered elsewhere in this volume, but I will include several works originally written for theatrical purposes—mainly ballets—that have since become known primarily in concert versions. This literature for concert orchestra encompasses all but the first few decades of the clarinet's history. I assume the reader will have a good working knowledge of the standard orchestral repertoire of the eighteenth and nineteenth centuries, and I have therefore chosen to highlight a few works that are perhaps less familiar, and to spend some extra time with the twentieth century. I encourage the reader to seek out recordings of the works mentioned, in order to bring the musical examples and descriptions to life.

The "Little Trumpet"

J. G. Walther, in his *Musicalisches Lexicon* of 1732, remarked that the clarinet, heard from far away, sounded "rather similar to a trumpet."[4] Other writers of the time echoed this idea, and the name of the

---

4   "… klingt von ferne einer Trompete ziemlich ähnlich … ." J. G. Walther, *Musicalisches Lexicon oder musicalisches Bibliothek* (Leipzig: Wolffgang Deer, 1732), 168. Translations in this chapter are mine unless otherwise noted.

instrument—a diminutive of the Italian *clarino*, the term used by Germans in the early eighteenth century to designate a high trumpet part—surely reflects the sound of its strong upper register.[5] This characteristic is apparent in surviving clarinets that are still playable, and in modern replicas. Most of the early music for clarinet, which features the instrument in a solo capacity, scarcely leaves this high register.

Yet this trumpet-like clarity is not the only timbre available on Baroque clarinets. The lower register is starkly contrasting, with a veiled tone quality and muted dynamic possibilities. While composers of brilliant, soloistic music might not have found this region of the instrument useful, it had a proponent in Antonio Vivaldi (1678–1741), who used both registers of the clarinet to great effect in three concerti grossi (RV 556, 559, and 560) probably written sometime between 1715 and 1725. Albert Rice has already mentioned these works in chapter 2 as the earliest concertos using the clarinet. They might with some justification appear also in this "symphonic" chapter, since they represent a species of ensemble concerto that, as the Vivaldi scholar Michael Talbot observes, "looks forward to the orchestration of the Classical symphony."[6] This is especially true of RV 556, in which the concertino comprises pairs of violins, recorders, oboes, and clarinets along with a single bassoon. While all of these are soloists, Vivaldi does not treat them equally; this is primarily a concerto for two violins. The winds are used in a way that, to an extent, foreshadows developments that would come to full fruition later in the century. They have a share of soloistic passages in the outer movements, to be sure (the recorders and oboes more than the clarinets, which emerge only briefly from their *ripieno* role), but one hears a hint of the tonal coloring and active dialogue

---

5   The word *clarino* as an appellation for a musical instrument has a complicated history. In the early eighteenth century, Italian musicians were more likely to use the word *tromba* for the trumpet, while "it was only in Spain and in Germanic countries (as well as in Poland, the Netherlands and Scandinavia) that the terms 'clarin' and 'clarino' were used during the 17th, 18th and early 19th centuries to denote a treble trumpet part." See Edward Tarr, "Clarino," *Grove Music Online*.

6   Talbot remarks on the "potential for giving the solo instruments (especially when wind instruments) independent or semi-independent parts in the tutti sections." See Arthur Hutchings et al., "Concerto," *Grove Music Online*.

among the instruments that would come to characterize orchestrational techniques in the 1780s and beyond.[7]

The *Galant* Clarinet

By the 1730s, a new style of music had emerged that was viewed at the time as lighter, more elegant, and more "natural" than the style that had prevailed in the previous decades. Like the new modes of dress, design, and social behavior that emerged in the wake of Louis XIV's death, this music was referred to by the French word *galant*—signifying all that was most chic and fashionable. There was a new focus on pleasing melody, with predictable phrasing and simplified harmonic and rhythmic structures. This style appeared first in Italian opera, which was also the source of what would arguably become the most important new instrumental genre of the eighteenth century: the symphony. Originating as an overture, or "sinfonia," of three short movements played as curtain-raiser to an opera, this type of piece was soon recognized for its potential as an independent composition, and composers began writing them in great numbers for use as concert works. Something upward of 16,000 eighteenth-century symphonies have so far been catalogued.[8]

The orchestra, now possessed of a musical genre that featured it as an independent ensemble rather than just as an accompaniment to soloists, grew in tandem. The earliest symphonies tended to be for the familiar four-part string ensemble with continuo. But as composers began to experiment with the new genre and its possibilities, wind instruments were soon included. The most common in the period were pairs of oboes and horns, and large numbers of symphonies "à 8" (that is, with eight separate parts, four for strings and four for winds) were written between about 1740 and 1770. Flutes and bassoons, singly or in pairs, sometimes made an appearance (the flute replacing the oboe—often the player was the same—and the bassoon doubling the cello), but use of the clarinet was relatively rare. The occasions when it does appear are, therefore, all the more noteworthy.

---

7   An excellent period instrument recording, demonstrating the both the clarinet's registral differences and the way it colors the sound of the wind section as a whole, is *Vivaldi: Concerti per vari strumenti* by Ensemble Zefiro with Lorenzo Coppola and Daniele Latini (clarinets), directed by Alfredo Bernardini, Naïve OP30409, 2005.

8   Jan LaRue, *A Catalogue of 18th-Century Symphonies*, vol. 1, *Thematic Identifier* (Bloomington: Indiana University Press, 1988), xii.

The earliest inclusion of the clarinet in a symphony was by the Mannheim composer Johann Stamitz (1717–57), in three symphonies published in the collection *La melodia germanica* (Paris, 1758). Although the wind parts for these works are labeled "per due violini, oboe, o flauti" (or sometimes "oboe o flauto" in the singular), the title page of the collection seems to suggest a preference for clarinets, stating that if clarinets are missing, the parts may be played by these alternative instruments.[9] Other composers in the 1760s and 1770s who wrote for clarinet in their symphonies were Gossec, Cannabich, J. C. Bach, Pokorny, Schacht, and Pichl, as well as numerous others who designated the clarinet an optional replacement for oboe or flute.[10] The technical demands of these parts are modest, and the clarinet writing does not particularly differ from that for the flute or oboe; in general the woodwinds in music of this period tend to spend a good deal of time sustaining harmonies and underpinning the strings in various ways. The clarinets do occasionally take a solo, however, as shown in ex. 3.1, from the Symphony in E-flat, op. 12, no. 5 by François-Joseph Gossec (1734–1829), published in 1769.

This example is typical of symphonic clarinet writing of this time: the clarinets are used as a pair, playing in sixths and thirds. Clearly the style of writing for the clarinet has changed since Vivaldi's time; the melodic orientation of the *galant* style has brought out the instrument's capacity to play a more cantabile line. This capacity would come to be a central focus in the nineteenth century, as we shall see. The addition of keys to the instrument and other technical developments helped to facilitate this shift, as well as allowing more technical flexibility. Fortunately, numerous orchestral pieces, including this symphony by Gossec, have now been recorded on period instruments. Hearing the sweet tone quality of the clarinets, so different from the sound of the more usual oboe pair, one better understands Mozart's famous comment from 1778 praising their "glorious effect" in symphonies.[11]

Gossec may have become acquainted with the clarinet as a member of the private orchestra of the wealthy tax farmer Alexandre-Jean-Joseph Le Riche de La Pouplinière. This orchestra, a kind of "musical

---

9   "Faute de Clarinettes, on peura les Exécuter avec deux Hautbois, Flutes ou Violons." *VI sinfonie a piu istrumenti intitolare la melodia germanica composte da vari autori* (Paris: Venier, 1758).

10 For an overview of these composers, see Albert Rice, *The Clarinet in the Classical Period* (Oxford: Oxford University Press, 2003), 174–79.

11 *The Letters of Mozart and His Family*, ed. Emily Anderson, 2nd ed. (London: Macmillan, 1966), 2:638.

Example 3.1. François-Joseph Gossec, Symphony in E-flat, op. 12, no. 5 (1769), mvt. 3, mm. 65–80, clarinets 1 and 2.

laboratory,"[12] was the earliest in France to employ clarinetists, beginning in 1750 or 1751 (under the direction of Rameau), and both Stamitz and Gossec were associated with it. La Pouplinière's clarinetists were Gaspard Procksch and Simon Flieger, who also played at the Concert Spirituel and the Opéra.[13] They may have inspired other composers such as Stamitz's fellow Mannheimer Christian Cannabich (1731–98), who visited Paris often during the 1760s and 1770s and wrote prominently for clarinets in some of his symphonies.

Haydn, Mozart, Beethoven

By the late eighteenth century clarinets were becoming more common, but even so, they were not always available. Mozart and Haydn wrote for them only occasionally, and conservatively, in their symphonies. Out of a total of forty-one symphonies, Mozart provided clarinet parts in just four, two of those in revised second versions. Haydn wrote for the clarinet in five late symphonies.[14] To a large extent these com-

---

12 The "musical laboratory" analogy is from Georges Cucuël, *Études sur un orchestre au XVIIIme siècle* (Paris: Librairie Fischbacher, 1913), 14.

13 Georges Cucuël, *La Pouplinière et la musique de chambre au XVIIIe siècle* (Paris, 1913; repr. New York: Da Capo Press, 1971), 331, 336–37, 339, 348, and 390–91. See also Pamela Weston, *More Clarinet Virtuosi of the Past* (London: the author, 1977), 102 and 199–200.

14 Mozart wrote for a pair of obbligato clarinets in K. 297 ("Paris," 1778–79) and K. 543 (1788), as well as in revised versions of K. 385

posers still utilized the clarinet as a doubling and reinforcing instrument, but they seem at least to have begun to show an awareness of the coloristic possibilities of the instrument's timbre. Mozart, especially, who used the clarinet to great advantage in the opera orchestra, may have recognized that something could be gained by transferring these colors to the symphony as well. In addition, he established the use of the clarinet in a particular "rustic" topos that would persist into the nineteenth century, as in the minuet movement of his Symphony in E-flat, K. 543. There, in the initial strain of the trio section, the first clarinet is featured in a folk-song-like melody while the second clarinet accompanies with a broken-chord (so-called Alberti) pattern.

With Beethoven the clarinet finally entered the orchestral mainstream in terms of both frequency and individuality of use. His symphonies contain clarinet parts with important solos that display the full range of the clarinet's registral colors and technical flexibility. Beethoven of course stretched the boundaries of all the woodwind instruments, requiring skilled players for his demanding parts; but, while oboists and flutists may have seen something approaching these challenges in Mozart and Haydn, for the orchestral clarinetist of the day it was a relatively steep learning curve. One could make the case that Beethoven's works finally forced the emergence of the true clarinet specialist in the orchestra, and the concomitant demise of the earlier woodwind "doubler" who picked up the clarinet when needed.

The Fourth Symphony (1806) provides a good example. The slow movement contains two lengthy, exposed solos for the first clarinet alone (rather than the pair of clarinets, as in earlier symphonies). In the first (mm. 26–34), the overall dynamic level is *piano*, with the expression marked "cantabile." The player must exercise careful control of breath and tone to achieve the delicate entrances and long phrases. The second solo (mm. 81–89) is a repeat of the first, but transposed up a fifth, with a top pitch of D^6, intensifying all of the aforementioned challenges. No previous symphony had made such demands on the orchestral clarinetist's control and endurance. In the final movement, dexterity of fingers and tongue comes to the fore. The solo with fast articulated sixteenth notes at measures 297–300 must have vexed Beethoven's original clarinetist (as it still does players today); surely

---

("Haffner," 1782, rev. 1783) and K. 550 (1788). Haydn's symphonic clarinet parts are found in Symphonies nos. 99–101 (1793–94) and 103–4 (1795). It should be noted that Haydn wrote somewhat more expansively for the clarinet in his two oratorios *The Creation* (1797–98) and *The Seasons* (1801).

the performer played with the reed situated on his bottom lip, as did most Austro-German players of the time. Elsewhere in the movement (mm. 39–43 and 215–21), both the first and second clarinet parts have extended passages of articulated triplet arpeggios in the lowest region of the chalumeau register, a type of passagework first used by Mozart and made characteristic by Beethoven.

Beethoven's Fourth Symphony was first performed in March 1807 at the house of his patron Prince Lobkowitz. The instruments used by the clarinetists in the orchestra could have had anywhere from five to twelve keys, depending on how up-to-date they were. Nine keys would not have been uncommon; an amateur player, who signs himself only as "M," recommended this number in his article on the clarinet in the *Allgemeine musikalische Zeitung* of March 1808, and several Viennese makers are known to have made instruments with at least this many keys.[15] Besides adding keys, clarinet makers were also experimenting with larger bore and tone-hole sizes, which resulted in improved intonation and greater projection.

By Beethoven's time composers had begun to write their orchestral works in ways that used each instrument for its particular "color" and "character," and authors began to describe these traits in treatises on aesthetics, and in pedagogical manuals on instrumentation—or, as it would later be called, orchestration.[16] In 1806 Daniel Schubart rhapsodically described the character of the clarinet as "a feeling melted by love—completely the sound of a sensitive heart. Whoever plays the clarinet as Reinecke does seems to make a declaration of love to the

---

15 *Allgemeine musikalische Zeitung* 10, nos. 24 and 25 (March 9 and 16, 1808), 369–75 and 385–91. The writer has been identified as Christian Friedrich Michaelis (1770–1834) by Thomas Gebhard (in *Rohrblatt* 3, 2003); quoted in Eric Hoeprich, "'Regarding the Clarinet': *Allgemeine musikalische Zeitung*, 1808," *Early Music* 37, no. 1 (2009): 99. Information about early nineteenth-century Viennese clarinet makers can be found in Rice, *The Clarinet in the Classical Period*, 51–55; see also Eric Hoeprich, *The Clarinet* (New Haven, CT: Yale University Press, 2008), 129.

16 See Emily I. Dolan, *The Orchestral Revolution: Haydn and the Technologies of Timbre* (Cambridge: Cambridge University Press, 2013). Several other useful writings on the history of orchestration are Kenneth Kreitner et al., "Instrumentation and Orchestration," *Grove Music Online*; Adam Carse, *The History of Orchestration* (London, 1925; rev. ed. New York: Dover Editions, 1964); and Julian Rushton, "The Art of Orchestration," in *The Cambridge Companion to the Orchestra*, ed. Colin Lawson (Cambridge: Cambridge University Press, 2003), 92–111.

whole human race."[17] The French clarinet maker Jacques François Simiot, in his *Tableau explicative des innovations et changements faits à la clarinette* (1808), noted the flexibility of the clarinet in range and tone quality, and stated that it "has all the characteristics which composers desire, and can play equally well the hymn of the warrior or the song of the shepherd."[18] Franz Joseph Fröhlich, writing in 1811 with the aim of providing "music directors, teachers, and amateurs" with information on "all the important instruments used in the orchestra," combines technical information about the clarinet with the following description:

> Among all the wind instruments, there is none that comes as near to a full, female soprano voice as the clarinet. The fullness of its tone, which can swell almost to the power of a trumpet on the one hand, and on the other to the pleasant gentleness that disappears into a scarcely audible breath, and gives the listener a deceptive imitation of a far-off echo; gives it the ability to portray every manner of expression that a composer gives it.
>
> With power and fullness it reigns as a solo instrument in the performance of the most brilliant passages, to which its innate gracefulness contrasts, while as an accompanying instrument it clings to every character, and in the orchestra it pairs a penetrating tone with richness and delicacy alike.[19]

Beethoven's new way of handling the clarinet in the orchestra reflects all of these contemporary descriptions, and points toward the way composers would treat the instrument in orchestral settings throughout much of the nineteenth century.

The Clarinet and the Epic-Lyrical Impulse

It is a commonplace to say that Beethoven's influence permeated much of European musical life for the rest of nineteenth century, at both practical and philosophical levels. Here is not the place for further discussion of this already much-explored topic; suffice it to say, at the very least, that composers approached the act of composition

---

17 Christian Friedrich Daniel Schubart, *Ideen zu einer Ästhetik der Tonkunst* [1784–85] (Vienna: J. V. Degen, 1806), 320.

18 Quoted in Hoeprich, *The Clarinet*, 123.

19 Franz Joseph Fröhlich, *Vollständige theoretisch-praktische Musikschule* (Bonn: Simrock, 1811), art 2, 7–8.

in a significantly different way because of him. They attempted works that were larger in scale, expressive range, and psychological scope. In the realm of orchestral music, Beethoven's symphonies changed the manner in which composers and listeners interacted with the genre, and with the orchestra itself. Monumentality and a sense of narrative, either literal (as in program music) or on an emotional level, were expected, and symphonies by Schubert, Schumann, Mendelssohn, Berlioz, Liszt, Brahms, Bruckner, Tchaikovsky, and many others met these expectations. In addition, the second half of the century saw the emergence of the symphonic poem as a significant new outlet for orchestral writing. With its extramusical (often literary) connections, the symphonic poem allowed composers to develop further the use of individual instruments to express a specific "character."

The *Grand traité d'instrumentation* (1844) of Hector Berlioz served to define the art of orchestration in a way that no previous treatise had. Besides providing the expected technical information, Berlioz also, and perhaps more importantly, made it a goal to delineate in some detail the effects and emotional states to which each instrument was best suited. Concerning the clarinet, he mentions the character of the different registers. The lowest register, he states, "is ideal for those icily menacing effects, those dark expressions of repressed fury which Weber ingeniously hit upon, especially in long held notes."[20] The clarion register (or intermediate register, as Berlioz calls it) is "marked by a certain haughtiness with intimations of tenderness and nobility." This, he says,

> equips it well for the expression of the most poetic thoughts and feelings. Only frivolity—and perhaps naïve joy too—seems to suit it not at all. The clarinet is not made for the *idyllic*, it is an instrument of the *epic*, like horns, trumpets, and trombones. Its voice is the voice of heroic love, and if the massed brass in large military bands bring to mind a regiment in shining armour marching to glory or death, massed clarinets in unison playing with them seem to evoke the loved ones, wives and sweethearts, whose proud eyes and earnest passions exult to the sound of arms, who sing as they enter the fray and who crown their conquering heroes or die with the defeated.[21]

Berlioz, like Fröhlich before him, goes on to praise the "feminine quality" of the clarinet, stating that there is "nothing so virginal or so pure

---

20 Hugh Macdonald, *Berlioz's Orchestration Treatise: A Translation and Commentary* (Cambridge: Cambridge University Press, 2002), 124. Here Berlioz refers to passages from Weber's *Der Freischütz*.

21 Ibid, 125.

as the shades of colour bestowed on certain melodies by the tone of the intermediate register of the clarinet in the hands of a skilful player."[22]

Indeed, between Beethoven's death and the middle of the century, when composers wrote for the clarinet prominently in symphonic works they often gave it just this type of "epic-lyrical" utterance.[23] Examples include solos in the second movement of Schubert's "Unfinished" Symphony, the slow movement of Mendelssohn's "Italian" Symphony, the "Scène aux champs" in Berlioz's *Symphonie fantastique*, and many others. One might also mention the early symphonies of the Danish composer Niels Gade (1817–90) which, while not often performed in concert today, were staples of the orchestral repertoire in the 1840s and 1850s (see ex. 3.2).

In these years, the clarinet underwent significant technical changes. One might argue that these changes were driven by increasing chromaticism and technical difficulty in the music of the time, but the clarinet's inability to play chromatic notes fluently had long been recognized, and simply adding more keys was no longer an adequate solution to the problem. It was time for a fundamental rethinking of the instrument's key system, a task undertaken in both France and Germany during the period from about 1840 to 1860. In the early 1840s the French clarinet virtuoso Hyacinthe Klosé (1808–80) and the woodwind maker Louis-Auguste Buffet (1789–1864) worked together to produce the so-called Boehm system, still the most widely used key system today. The principal changes included the adoption of the ring-key mechanism from the Boehm flute, and the addition of duplicate keys for the left and right little fingers. Around 1860 the Germans, through a similar collaboration between a player (Carl Baermann, 1810–85) and a maker (Georg Ottensteiner, 1815–79), developed a different solution to the same problems. Both the French and German efforts resulted in clarinets with a vastly improved capacity to play in all key signatures with technical facility and good intonation.[24]

---

22 Ibid.
23 I adapt this term from David Brodbeck, "The Symphony after Beethoven after Dalhaus," in *The Cambridge Companion to the Symphony*, ed. Julian Horton (Cambridge: Cambridge University Press, 2013), 70; he cites Siegfried Oechsle, *Symphonik nach Beethoven: Studien zu Schubert, Schumann, Mendelssohn und Gade* (Kassel: Bärenreiter, 1992).
24 Detailed information about these developments can be found in Hoeprich, *The Clarinet*, especially 170–205 (chap. 8, "1844–1900: The Clarinet Joins the Establishment").

Example 3.2. Niels Gade, Symphony no. 3 in A Minor, op. 15 (1847), mvt. 4, mm. 207–47, clarinets 1 and 2.

Clarinet writing in the orchestral repertoire from the second half of the nineteenth century takes advantage of these technical developments. The character traits attributed to the instrument by Berlioz were also sensed by symphonic composers such as Brahms and Dvořák, who mostly adopted the epic-lyrical approach to the clarinet. Their symphonies contain numerous noteworthy solos but demand more expressive refinement than technical prowess from the clarinetist. This statement, in fact, holds more or less true for most of the symphonies written in the second half of the century, including those by well-known composers such as Tchaikovsky as well as the many examples by composers whose symphonies are now more rarely heard, such as Franz Berwald, Joachim Raff, Anton Rubenstein, and Robert Fuchs. In symphonies by these composers, the clarinet is treated in solo passages as a voice of lyricism, nobility, and occasionally bucolic charm—the latter especially in the case of Dvořák, who had a penchant for using two clarinets playing in thirds and sixths to achieve this effect.

It was in the realm of program music that this essentially lyrical approach to clarinet writing was combined with technical virtuosity. Concert overtures, symphonic poems, programmatic symphonies, and works in related genres with prominent clarinet parts by Mendelssohn, Liszt, Smetana, Dvořák, Tchaikovsky, Mussorgsky, and a host of others constitute this large repertoire. Some of these works are part of today's standard orchestral programming, but many once-popular compositions are no longer fashionable. Among the repertoire still played, representative examples may be drawn from two works by Nikolai Rimsky-Korsakov (1844–1908) that every aspiring professional clarinetist studies. The first is *Capriccio espagnol* op. 34 (1887), where the clarinet executes brilliant roulades in the two *Alborada* movements as well as a cadenza in the *Scena e canto gitano.* The second is the symphonic suite *Scheherazade,* op. 35 (1888), inspired by the collection of Arabic folk tales *One Thousand and One Nights.* It contains numerous important clarinet solos, from the cantabile lines in the first movement to the rhapsodic cadenzas of the second and third movements and the knuckle-busting chromatic passages of the fourth. It is noteworthy that this type of virtuosic clarinet writing often appears in works that display national and "exotic" musical styles; composers seem to have recognized the clarinet's technical and expressive suitability for conveying Hungarian, Spanish, and "Arabian" character.

Stretching across the turn of the nineteenth century into the twentieth are two composers whose symphonic music transcends categorizations of epic-lyrical, national, or exotic: Gustav Mahler (1860–1911) in the realm of the symphony, and Richard Strauss (1864–1949) in that of the tone poem, as he called it. Both composers make colorful use of an expanded clarinet section that gradually came into use in the concert orchestra in the last quarter of the nineteenth century, including three or more clarinets of various nominal pitches and sizes: ordinary soprano clarinets in A, B-flat, and C, bass clarinets in B-flat and A, and sopranino clarinets in D and E-flat. Mahler, known for juxtaposing the sublime and the banal in his symphonies, used the instrument in contexts ranging from fanfares to bird calls to klezmer imitations, but rarely gave it long-phrased solos. Strauss, in his tone poems, wrote parts for all members of the clarinet family, including some of the most strenuous technical challenges players had faced up to that time—which still cause today's clarinetists no small amount of anxiety. A prime example is *Till Eulenspiegel's Merry Pranks.* The well-known solos for D clarinet (usually played on the E-flat instrument), representing the protagonist's execution toward the end of the work, are but one instance of several where some member of the clarinet section plays an exposed and important role in the narrative. The section as a whole is also used in noteworthy ways, as example 3.3 (leading into the scene where Till rampages through the marketplace) shows. Strauss's highly chromatic harmonic language and breakneck

Example 3.3. Richard Strauss, *Till Eulenspiegel's Merry Pranks* (1895), mm. 133–37, clarinet in D, clarinets 1 and 2, and bass clarinet.

tempi require much athleticism from the player in passages such as those shown in example 3.4. Strauss's technical demands set a precedent for later composers, whose music continued to raise the level of difficulty for orchestral clarinetists. Indeed, by the end of the nineteenth century the clarinet's capacity for both soaring, lyrical lines and acrobatic feats made it an indispensable tool in the composer's workbox.

Example 3.4. Richard Strauss, *Till Eulenspiegel's Merry Pranks*, mm. 491–98, clarinets 1 and 2 and bass clarinet.

The Twentieth Century through 1950

Scholars have noted that, after Mahler, many Austro-German composers stepped back from the genre of the large-scale symphony. The aesthetic upheaval and new expressive goals of the early twentieth century, underpinned by drastically changing societal and political circumstances, militated against the humanistic idealism and "community-building power" that had been associated with the symphony in the nineteenth century.[25] In addition the structural conventions of the genre, based as they were on traditional tonal harmonic procedures, were not aligned with the various ways in which tonality was being redefined, or in some cases rejected altogether. Instead, composers such as Arnold Schoenberg (1874–1951) channeled their urge to write for orchestral forces into other types of works; Schoenberg wrote a set of "orchestral pieces" (op. 16, 1909), as did his students Webern (op. 6, 1909–10, and op. 10, 1911–13) and Berg (op. 6, 1914–15).[26]

---

25 See David Fanning, "The Symphony since Mahler," in Horton, *The Cambridge Companion to the Symphony*, esp. 96–100. Fanning refers to the phrase *gemeinschaftsbildende Kraft* (community-building power), used by the German scholar Paul Bekker in 1918.

26 Works entitled "symphony" were written by Webern, Hindemith, Krenek, Zemlinsky, Weill, Hartmann, and many other Austro-Germans, of course. Many of these defy categorization as traditional

It was outside the Austro-German sphere that the large-scale symphony flourished, especially in Scandinavia (Sibelius, Nielsen), Russia (Shostakovich, Prokofiev), England (Vaughan Williams), and the United States (Ives, Copland), to name just a few of the more prominent writers of symphonies before and during World War II. Of particular note for their clarinet writing are the Scandinavians and Russians. For Jean Sibelius (1865–1957), the clarinet's dark tone played an important role in defining the overall sound of the wind section in his often-somber symphonic writing. The best-known of Sibelius's clarinet parts are found in his Symphony no. 1. The opening of this work is played by a solo clarinet, accompanied only by a timpani roll (and after a few measures completely alone), in a passage that seems to convey the very essence of a cold, bleak Finnish winter. Nielsen, in his Fifth Symphony, uses the clarinet extensively in a soloistic capacity, including long, lyrical solos, a lengthy cadenza at the end of the first movement, and technical passages in the fast fugue of the second movement that rival in difficulty the composer's Clarinet Concerto. Shostakovich's fifteen symphonies provide a veritable compendium of writing for all members of the orchestral clarinet family; for him the instruments provided a toolkit for the expression of the deepest tragedy as well as the sharpest satire. The entire range of his remarkable writing for clarinets can be found in his First, Fourth, Fifth, Sixth, Ninth, and Tenth Symphonies.

Non-symphonic orchestral works, including program music, continued to occupy the energy of many composers in the first decades of the twentieth century. (They included a number of important ballets that are now known primarily as concert works.) The sets of orchestral pieces by the "Second Viennese" composers have already been mentioned; here it is worth noting that in the first movement of his op. 16 Schoenberg further expands the clarinet section by one member: the contrabass clarinet (in A!), an addition that did not exert much influence on later composers. A list of other non-symphonic orchestral works with important clarinet parts would be a long one, and would include compositions by, among others, Debussy, Bartók, Gershwin, Holst, Kodály, Ravel, Respighi, Sibelius, and Stravinsky. Carrying on the nineteenth-century tradition of deploying the instrument to convey exotic or national flavors, Bartók (1881–1945) used it to portray the sinuous dancing of the prostitute in his 1926 ballet *The Miraculous*

---

symphonies in various ways, and only one (that of Webern) can be said to belong to the standard repertoire.

Mandarin; his Hungarian compatriot Zoltán Kodály (1882–1967) included a long clarinet solo in "Gypsy" style in the *Dances of Galánta* (1933). Stravinsky gives the entire clarinet section much to do in all three of his major early ballets (*The Firebird, Petrushka*, and *The Rite of Spring*, written between 1910 and 1913), as does Ravel in his ballet *Daphnis and Chloe* of 1912. The latter, usually heard in the form of two concert suites, includes famously difficult, harp-like arpeggios for the principal and second clarinets as well as blisteringly fast, chromatic sixteenth-note passages for all the clarinets (but especially the E-flat) in the final *Danse générale*. Darius Milhaud (1892–1974) became interested in jazz after a trip to the United States in 1922, and in 1923 wrote the ballet *La création du monde* (*The Creation of the World*), in which the clarinet plays several solos that display its suitability to the jazz idiom. Ottorino Respighi (1879–1936) composed a trilogy of tone poems (*Fountains of Rome, Pines of Rome*, and *Roman Festivals*, written between 1916 and 1928), all of which contain important clarinet solos. The section in *Pines of Rome* entitled "The Pines of the Janiculum" features a languid, three-phrase clarinet solo; at the end of the section, where a single phrase of the solo returns, it magically introduces the famous nightingale recording that Respighi asked to be played beneath the shimmering string trills. Also worth mentioning, although it is rarely performed, is the 1901 tone poem *Fifine at the Fair* by Granville Bantock (1868–1946), which features the clarinet in a lengthy cadenza (three minutes on the classic recording by the London Philharmonic under Beecham, with the clarinetist Jack Brymer).

By the 1930s the era of the symphonic/tone poem was waning, at least temporarily, although other types of non-symphonic orchestral works would continue to be written aplenty. The symphony remained a vital genre. In addition to the continued activity of some of the composers already mentioned, the 1930s and 1940s saw the appearance of symphonies by important composers such as Paul Hindemith in Germany; Arnold Bax, William Walton, and Michael Tippett in England; Olivier Messiaen, Arthur Honegger, and Milhaud in France; and Howard Hanson, Roy Harris, Aaron Copland, Samuel Barber, and Leonard Bernstein in the United States, among many others. All of these composers made use of the clarinet soloistically—often including bass clarinet, and sometimes including the E-flat instrument—though none used it in particularly novel ways. Some of their clarinet parts are nonetheless worth mentioning. Barber's single-movement First Symphony (1936) contains very fine (and difficult) writing for the whole clarinet section, including some important bass clarinet solos; Bernstein's Second Symphony ("The Age of Anxiety," 1949) begins with a two-minute duet by unaccompanied clarinets. Stravinsky, who famously voiced a preference for what he perceived as the less expressive sound of wind instruments, wrote lively parts for clarinets in his two neoclassical symphonies (Symphony in C, 1940, and Symphony in Three Movements, 1945).

Since 1950

The decades just after World War II saw the rise of avant-garde and experimentalist movements, such as total serialism, aleatory, and electronic music, and many composers in these styles were not inclined toward orchestral music, and especially not toward the symphony. As a noted scholar has observed, "to composers forging a brave new language in the aftermath of World War II the traditional preoccupations of symphonic writing—thematic development, tonal focus and unified architecture—seemed obsolete and irrelevant. And, as a result, many significant composers of the later (as of the earlier) 20th century chose to neglect the medium altogether."[27] There were notable exceptions; a list of symphony composers of consequence between 1950 and the early 1970s would include, among others, Shostakovich, Tippett, Hans Werner Henze, Henryk Górecki, Einojuhani Rautavaara, Arvo Pärt, Alfred Schnittke, Per Nørgård, Witold Lutosławski, and Vagn Holmboe. Some of these composers applied experimental principles to the symphony, while others hewed more closely to tradition. Outstanding among these for his clarinet writing is Holmboe (1909–96), author of thirteen symphonies and many other orchestral works. Holmboe's style was essentially neoclassical. All of his symphonies contain noteworthy solo writing for clarinet, including bass clarinet; his turbulent Symphony no. 8 ("Sinfonia boreale," 1951–52) is exemplary. This "northern" symphony begins with bass clarinet, which sets out the seed motive that will be subjected to Holmboe's process of "metamorphosis" as the work unfolds. In the slow movement the two soprano clarinets are used for a *fortissimo*, trumpet-like fanfare as well as for more lyrical material. Both soprano and bass clarinets are used prominently in the final movement as well.

---

27 Charles Wilson, "The Survival of the Symphony," §III.11 of the article "Symphony," *Grove Music Online*.

Since about 1980 there has been, among many composers, a return to tonal principles and audience accessibility (although composers like Holmboe never really abandoned them in the first place). A few composers, like Krzysztof Penderecki and Peter Maxwell Davies, returned to these principles later in life after beginning their careers as experimentalists. With this return to a tonal and accessible style came an increase in symphonic composition. Prolific Scandinavian symphonists such as Holmboe and Rautavaara continued their activity, joined by Kalevi Aho (b. 1949, seventeen symphonies so far), Aulis Sallinen (b. 1935, eight symphonies so far), and others. The Englishman Sir Peter Maxwell Davies (1934–2016) wrote ten, while the Pole Krzysztof Penderecki (1933–2020) has written eight so far. But it has been in the United States that symphonic composition has been taken up with the greatest enthusiasm. A list of prominent American composers who have written three or more symphonies since 1970 would include William Bolcom, John Corigliano, Richard Danielpour, Philip Glass, John Harbison, Stephen Hartke, Aaron Jay Kernis, Libby Larsen, Lowell Liebermann, Kevin Puts, Christopher Rouse, and Ellen Taafe Zwilich. Younger composers have also contributed to the genre. Several of these can be singled out for their use of the clarinet. The American composer John Harbison (b. 1938), in his Symphony no. 2 (1987), writes intricately for the entire clarinet section in the coda of the second movement, "Daylight" (ex. 3.5).

Penderecki's Third, Fourth, and Fifth Symphonies from the period between 1989 and 1995 contain excellent exposed clarinet writing, of both a lyrical and a technical nature, for soprano and bass clarinets. An early work by the British composer Thomas Adès (b. 1971), the Chamber Symphony op. 2 (1990), began as a concerto for basset clarinet; as composition proceeded, however, the composer decided to transform it into a work for small orchestra. The basset clarinet remained as part of the instrumentation, along with a bass clarinet, and both instruments are used prominently. The slow movement of the Second Symphony by Aaron Jay Kernis (b. 1960), written in 1991, begins with a long, mournful clarinet solo. Symphony no. 1 by Christopher Theofanidis (b. 1967), commissioned by the Atlanta Symphony and premiered by it in 2009, opens with a striking unison "call" in the clarinet section (assisted by the oboes), as shown in example 3.6.

The period since 1950 has also seen a profusion of non-symphonic orchestral works, some programmatic, others not. As in the nineteenth century, some of the most virtuosic clarinet parts are found in these works. For example, the *Variaciones concertantes* op. 23 (1953)

Example 3.5. John Harbison, Symphony no. 2, mvt. 2 ("Daylight"), mm.
171–78, all clarinets. Copyright © 1987 by Associated Music Publishers,
Inc. International Copyright Secured. All Rights Reserved. Reprinted by
permission.

—(*continued*)

by the Argentine composer Alberto Ginastera (1916–83) contains a
lengthy and notoriously difficult "Variazione in modo di Scherzo" for
solo clarinet. The part is written for clarinet in B-flat, but because of
its awkward key and extensive range (it contains a run that ends on
written C#[7]) performers often play it on the A or C clarinet, or even
have the second clarinetist switch briefly to E-flat clarinet to finish the

Example 3.5—*concluded*

run to the high note. The rarely played *Heliogabalus imperator* (1972) by Hans Werner Henze (1926–2012) contains extensive cadenzas for E-flat, B-flat, and bass clarinets, all including multiphonics. In *Blue Cathedral* (2000), the American composer Jennifer Higdon (b. 1962) uses the clarinet in several long solos to memorialize her brother, who played the instrument. Esa-Pekka Salonen (b. 1958), known as both a composer and conductor, has written marvelous lyrical solos for the clarinet in his tone poem *Nyx* (2011), depicting the mysterious Greek goddess of the night. Mason Bates (b. 1977), an imaginative American composer known for the incorporation of electronica and jazz/pop style into his orchestral works, features the clarinet section with interlocking arabesques in the "Nymphs" movement of his *Anthology of Fantastic Zoology* (2015).

Example 3.6. Christopher Theofanidis, Symphony no. 1, mm. 1–21, clarinets. Copyright © 2009 by Christopher Theofanidis (ASCAP). All Rights Reserved. Used by permission. Sole Agent: Bill Holab Music.

Of course, many other composers and works could be mentioned from the twentieth and early twenty-first centuries, or any of the other eras discussed in this chapter for that matter; in this brief space I have tried to be representative rather than comprehensive. Since the early days of the clarinet's use in the concert orchestra, composers have taken advantage of the instrument's characteristics in response to the stylistic priorities of their own times, and to the changing capabilities of the instrument as it evolved in mechanism and form. From the late eighteenth century onward, as the woodwind instruments were used less and less interchangeably and their individual expressive qualities were recognized, composers were attracted not only to the clarinet's dark tone quality relative to the flute and oboe, but also to its large pitch and dynamic range and its technical flexibility. In addition, even the modern clarinet retains some of the distinctive registral timbres that Berlioz prized, and this has continued to appeal to composers. In the twentieth century, the clarinet's immense versatility in a variety of styles, both classic and popular, has suited it to the stylistic eclecticism of the era. All of these characteristics have made the clarinet a vital member of the concert orchestra.

4

THE CLARINET IN OPERA BEFORE 1830

Instrument and Genre Come of Age

Ingrid E. Pearson

The years prior to 1830 were decisive for both the clarinet as an instrument in Western art music, as well as for the many sub-genres encompassed by the term "opera," including opera seria, opera buffa, *tragédie lyrique*, pasticcio, opéra comique, Singspiel, pantomime, grand opera, and others.[1] By using the clarinet as a lens through which to view opera we can begin to understand something of the diversity of music that dates from an era before the invention of the Boehm-system instrument so popular today. Though technology now allows us to access a great wealth of this music, an incredible amount of the rep-ertoire remains silent. No operagoer today will be ignorant of Mozart's works; history has not been so kind, however, to Henry Rowley Bishop, Nicolas Isouard, or Stefano Pavesi, even though they composed works much acclaimed and enjoyed by their contemporaries.[2]

---

1   Thanks to David Charlton, Michael Greenberg, Martin Harlow, Colin Lawson, Peter Linnitt, Michael Mullen, Michel Noiray, Albert Rice, Michael Robinson, Lois Rosow, Graham Sadler, and Richard Langham Smith for their help in obtaining materials for this study.

2   For further details of operas, readers should consult the various worklists at the end of the relevant composer articles in *Grove Music Online*.

We can now be certain that over 200 composers wrote for the clarinet in operatic contexts. Several factors make our appreciation of this music difficult. One of the largest obstacles is the fact that, until at least 1810, most opera scores were disseminated in manuscript rather than printed form. Librettos, which were almost always printed, survive in great numbers, but a composer's musical text for any given libretto could vary, since operas were routinely tailored for individual performances. This fact also complicates the establishment of a chronology for many operas. These features contrast with our present-day view of a complete, self-contained musical entity manifest in an authoritative score. In addition, the collaborative authorship of many pre-1830 operas runs counter to the value we currently place on originality. In embracing more components of flexibility than stability, opera was paradigmatic of European musical life at this time. The musicians themselves and the actual musical numbers were mobile, the former traveling in response to artistic and other opportunities, the latter enjoying substantial geographical reach in various guises and forms. This chapter focuses on Paris, London, Naples, and Vienna, in order for a manageable but still representative account of this vast repertoire to emerge.

Paris

From the middle of the eighteenth century until well into the nineteenth the political landscape of Paris, and France itself, was in a constant state of transformation. Under the Bourbon kings Louis XV (r. 1715–74) and Louis XVI (r. 1774–92) the Paris Opéra, or Académie Royale de Musique, was the city's most prestigious institution, "set apart from the almost total hegemony of Italian opera in Europe."[3] Other theaters received royal subsidies, including the Comédie-Française and Opéra-Comique.[4] Between 1791 and 1806, following the overthrow of the monarchy, regulatory emancipation dismantled the old hierarchy, fostering a growth in venues for opera and greater stylistic variety. In 1807 Napoleon re-established the Opéra's status amid a structure of primary and secondary theaters. By the end of the

---

3   David Charlton, *Opera in the Age of Rousseau: Music, Confrontation, Realism* (Cambridge: Cambridge University Press, 2015), 56.

4   Venues, company names, and genres were often intertwined; see David Charlton, John Trevitt, and Guy Gosselin, "Opera Companies, Theatres," §VI.3 of the article "Paris," *Grove Music Online*.

1820s the Opéra had a new home in the rue Le Peletier, and follow-ing a series of mergers, the Opéra-Comique continued to stage works combining music and spoken dialogue. The Théâtre Italien, fostered by Napoleon's love of Italian music, mounted original-language pro-ductions. Indeed, the story of opera in Paris at this time is one with both French and Italian flavors.

Three further features proved particularly significant for the clarinet in Parisian opera, beginning with the city's reputation as a leading center of woodwind-instrument making. Secondly, from 1770 Parisian music publishing entered a golden age. The technology that enabled full scores to be printed in an upright format, replacing the older, oblong, short-score format that did not specify full instru-mentation, was a development crucial to a clearer understanding of both instrument and genre. Between the years 1789 and 1810 Paris printed the highest number of opera scores in any European city, a factor which now greatly enhances our ability to understand the extent of the clarinet's use in this repertoire. Finally, with the estab-lishment of the Paris Conservatoire in 1795, clarinetists had access to rigorous training and education, a development which also signaled the emergence of specialist players.

The year 1749 was a landmark for the clarinet in Parisian opera: musical ensembles in the service of aristocrats were the first to include the instrument, and payment records show that it was used in the orchestra for Jean-Philippe Rameau's opera *Zoroastre*.[5] Rameau's *Acante et Céphise* (1751) is the earliest French opera with surviving clarinet parts. The works of Rameau were among motivating factors for Gluck's decision to turn his attention from Vienna to Paris. Seven of Gluck's

---

5   The earliest documentary evidence of the clarinet in France is a let-ter of February 11, 1749; see Jules Cousin, *Le comte de Clermont: sa cour et ses maîtresses; lettres et documents inédits*, vol. 1 (Paris: Académie des Bibliophiles, 1867), 13–14. Other aristocrats who employed clarinet-ists were Emmanuel-Félicité de Durfort, Duc de Duras (1715–89), and Jeanne-Louise Constance d'Aumont, Duchesse de Villeroy (1731–1816), as well as Alexandre-Jean-Joseph Le Riche de La Pouplinière (1693–1762) and Louis François de Bourbon, Prince de Conti (1717–76). While no clarinets parts survive for *Zoroastre*, documentary evi-dence confirms that the instrument was a part of the orchestra. See Lionel de la Laurencie, "Rameau et les clarinettes," *Mercure musicale* 9 (1913): 27–28; and Graham Sadler, "Preface," in Jean-Philippe Rameau, *Zoroastre, version 1749*, ed. Graham Sadler, *Opera omnia Rameau*, ser. IV, vol. 19 (Paris: Gérard Billaudot, 1999), XLV.

works for the Opéra composed between 1774 and 1779 include clarinet, a testimony to that institution's continuous tradition of employing the instrument. Indeed, the clarinet had been a more permanent member of the Opéra orchestra since 1769, a situation of which Johann Christian Bach also took advantage in *Amadis de Gaule*.[6] In the years following Gluck's triumph at the Opéra, Piccinni, Sacchini, Antonio Salieri, and Niccolò Antonio Zingarelli made effective use of the clarinet. Salieri's three operas for Paris continued Gluck's orchestrational legacy, among which the chorus "Quel charme inconnu nous attire" in the prologue of *Tarare* (1787) combines clarinet with muted strings perfectly to personify the moment when the spirits come to life.

At other Parisian theaters until the late 1780s the clarinet was still something of a luxury, although its infrequent appearances demonstrate an innovative use of the instrument. For example, in 1774 Jean-Paul-Egide Martini's use of clarinet within the context of military music in the lyric drama *Henri IV* necessitated hiring extra players for the Comédie-Italienne. Arsame's ariette from act 2, scene 1 of Étienne Joseph Floquet's lyric tragedy *Hellé* (1779) features two obbligato clarinets, supported by horns and strings. The clarinets combine melodic fluency and accompanying Alberti figurations, anticipating, imitating, and supporting the vocal line. This is an important early example of the instrument's personification of heroic love, a characteristic noted by Hector Berlioz in his 1844 orchestration treatise.[7]

At the Théâtre Italien before 1791 the clarinet was heard only sporadically in operatic repertoire, including four works by André-Ernest-Modeste Grétry. However, Grétry subsequently used the clarinet in at least twenty-five operas until 1803, helping to establish the instrument in the comic opera genre. The "Pas de deux" in act 2, scene 9 of *Anacréon chez Polycrate* (1797) opens with a clarinet solo and closes with a duet. This use of the instrument in a pastoral context reflects its versatility (see ex. 4.1). Among Dalayrac's comic operas, both *La soirée*

---

6   This work was premiered on December 14, 1779. During the 1760s and 1770s musicians employed as clarinetists by the French crown for the Musique du Roi at Versailles also played other instruments, including violin, viola, bassoon, and trumpet: Michael Greenberg, "Le personnel et les effectifs de la Musique du Roi (1732–1792)," *Musique, images, instruments* 12 (2010): 27, 29. This confirms that the clarinet was yet to become a specialist instrument.

7   "Sa voix est celle de l'héroïque amour": Hector Berlioz, *Grand traité d'instrumentation et d'orchestration modernes* op.10 (Paris: Schonenberger, 1844), 138.

Example 4.1. André-Ernest-Modeste Grétry, *Anacréon chez Polycrate* (1797), act 2, scene 9, "Pas de deux," clarinets.

orageuse (1790) for the Comédie-Italienne and *La jeune prude* (1804) for the Opéra-Comique open with a clarinet solo. Indeed, from the 1790s there was something of an explosion in the number of comic operas utilizing the clarinet, taking advantage of the instrument's availability in a greater number of theaters. Composers, some of whose careers continued well into the nineteenth century, included Henri-Montan Berton, François-Adrien Boieldieu, Antonio Bruni, Pierre-Antoine-Dominique Della Maria, François Devienne, Pierre Gaveaux, Antoine-Frédéric Gresnick, Louis-Emmanuel Jadin, Rodolphe Kreutzer, C. François Lescot, Jean-Pierre Solié, and Daniel Steibelt.

Luigi Cherubini is a significant figure because of his innovative works in both the comic and the tragic genres. During the early
Napoleonic years, Cherubini and Étienne-Nicolas Méhul skillfully
integrated the clarinet within an expanding range of orchestral timbres, among which were Méhul's *Mélidore et Phrosine* (1794), *Uthal*
(1806), and *Joseph* (1807), and Cherubini's *Les deux journées* (1800).
Praised for its originality, what survives of the music of their contemporary Jeanne-Hippolyte Devismes's *Praxitèle* (1800) features some
prominent clarinet writing.[8]

We can now be confident that Isouard included clarinet in at
least twenty-five operas, of which twenty-three were premiered in
Paris between June 1801 and February 1822. He treats the clarinet
as a distinct timbre, although using it less frequently than the other
woodwinds. Isouard's works for the Opéra Comique Feydeau exploit
the instrument to the full, and among them solo passages in *La ruse
inutile* (1805), *Cendrillon* (1810), and *Joconde* (1814) encapsulate early
nineteenth-century clarinet technique, comparing favorably with contemporary treatment of the instrument in Jean Xavier Lefèvre's op.
2 sonatas. Isouard's contemporaries included Charles-Simon Catel,
André-Frédéric Eler, Valentino Fioravanti, Sophie Gail, Ferdinando
Paer, Louis-Luc Loiseau de Persuis, and Charles-Henri Plantade. Gail's
two operas, *Les deux jaloux* (1813) and *La sérénade* (1818), make idiomatic use of the clarinet; see example 4.2.

Among Gaetano Spontini's early operas, *La vestale* (1807), *Olimpie*
(1819 and 1826), and *Fernand Cortez* (1809 and 1817) synthesize elements of Gluck's lyric tragedies with a bel canto melodic style. Michele
Carafa, also active throughout Europe, embraced both comic and fairy
genres in his operas for Paris beginning in 1822. In contrast, during
the 1820s François Henri Joseph Castil-Blaze introduced Parisian audiences to German and Italian operas, through his own adaptations of
pre-existing music by Beethoven, Domenico Cimarosa, Mozart, Paer,
and Rossini, among others. Remembered today for his ballet music,
Adolphe Adam composed music for one-act plays and vaudevilles in
the 1820s and, following *Pierre et Catherine* (1829), comic operas at least
until 1840. In the music of these composers we witness something of
the fluency and versatility enabled by a contemporary instrument with
thirteen keys.

---

8   Jacqueline Letzter and Robert Adelson, *Women Writing Opera: Creativity
    and Controversy in the Age of the French Revolution* (Berkeley: University
    of California Press, 2001), 36–37.

Example 4.2. Sophie Gail, *Les deux jaloux* (1813), "Il faut qu'entre eux je me plante," opening clarinet solo.

Rossini's appointment as director of the Théâtre Italien in 1824 marked a decisive moment for Parisian opera. In 1825 the seventy-four members of the orchestra at the Paris Opéra included three clarinets,[9] the ensemble for which Rossini deftly revised three earlier works. Enjoying considerable success in their new Parisian guises were *Le siège de Corinthe*, after *Maometto II* (1826); *Moïse et Pharaon*, after *Mosè in Egitto* (1827); and *Le comte d'Ory* (1828), based on the earlier but less successful *Il viaggio a Reims*. Further fueling the Parisian appetite for his music, these operas by Rossini exerted a profound influence on music by Daniel-François-Esprit Auber and Ferdinand Hérold. Recognized as the "first grand opera," Auber's *La muette de Portici* (1828) synthesizes elements of comic opera with the Italian style of Rossini.[10] Despite the success of Auber and Hérold in the genre, neither one exploited the clarinet's versatility to the extent of Rossini, making fewer demands on players especially in terms of articulatory nuances. In the years that followed, grand opera, in particular, enabled the clarinet to reach its full potential in the Parisian opera orchestra, a topic examined further in chapter 5 of this volume.

---

9   Hervé Lacome, "The 'Machine' and the State," in *The Cambridge Companion to Grand Opera*, ed. David Charlton (Cambridge: Cambridge University Press, 2003), 34.

10 Sarah Hibberd, "La Muette and Her Context," in Charlton, *The Cambridge Companion to Grand Opera*, 149 and 164.

London

Mid eighteenth-century-London was a thriving, affluent, and multi-cultural metropolis. During the seventy years spanning the reigns of King George III (r. 1760–1810) and his more flamboyant son George (r. 1811–20 as regent Prince of Wales and 1820–30 as King George IV), England enjoyed military success in Europe despite the loss of colonies in North America. Relative political stability fostered an economy in which an emerging middle class joined the aristocracy in availing itself of London's artistic offerings. Theatrical entertainment was paramount in the city's buoyant musical life, where a hierarchical system encompassed both local and foreign works. Unlike in Paris, Naples, and Vienna, there was no court-based system of operatic patronage, and all theaters were run as commercial enterprises.[11] The King's Theatre held sway until the mid-nineteenth century as the leading house for the performance of works in Italian. Managed by an impresario, this venue derived revenue from performances of pasticcios and revivals of opera seria and buffa. Its imported repertoire was adapted by in-house composers, who included J. C. Bach, P. A. Guglielmi, and others. The two patent theaters of Covent Garden and Drury Lane staged works mixing song and speech in English, often adaptations of Continental works. Like the King's Theatre, Covent Garden and Drury Lane employed in-house composers, including Charles Dibdin, William Shield, Thomas Linley, Stephen Storace, Henry Bishop, and Thomas Cooke. A host of smaller theaters such as the Lyceum, the Pantheon, and the Theatre Royal in the Haymarket variously mounted works in Italian or English.

Arrangements and adaptations of pre-existing material characterized much of what was heard on stage in London during the eighteenth and early nineteenth centuries. London's cosmopolitan environment nurtured pasticcio, which thrived during the second half of the eighteenth century. A truly collaborative art form, embracing singers, in-house composers, directors of music, and theater managers, pasticcios were underpinned by a set of values with less emphasis on originality and the authority of a single creator. Although London at this time was a major European center of engraving, the majority of stage works published were vocal-score anthologies, including some but not all

---

11 Michael Burden, "Opera in Eighteenth-Century England: English Opera, Masques, Ballad Operas," in *The Cambridge Companion to Eighteenth-Century Opera*, ed. Anthony R. DelDonna and Pierpaolo Polzonetti (Cambridge: Cambridge University Press, 2009), 202.

of the musical numbers performed on stage. In comparison to works premiered in Naples, Vienna, and Paris, very little London repertoire has surviving manuscript full scores and sets of orchestral parts. We are therefore heavily reliant on cues in vocal scores to understand the extent to which the clarinet appeared in this music. Although these publications were issued well into the nineteenth century, their prevalence and the loss of countless manuscripts work against our understanding of the clarinet's use in such repertoire.

An account of opera in London must also include music performed at pleasure gardens, mostly consisting of songs taken from works staged in the various theaters. Small-scale operas also featured regularly as the second of an evening's two acts of entertainment. Synthesizing features of Italian opera and English ballad opera, some were even staged in dramatic representations. Among this music, works by J. C. Bach and James Hook demonstrate a cross-fertilization of genres. Two of Bach's Vauxhall songs including clarinet warrant mention here because they demonstrate a further interaction between stage music and concert repertoire. Both composed for the soprano (Mrs.) Frederika Weichsell, "By my sighs you may discover" (1766) later appeared as "Thirst of Wealth" in the pasticcio *Tom Jones* (1769), and "See the kind indulgent gales" (1777) is one of three adaptations of "Se spiego le prime vele" from Bach's *Zanaida* (1763). The works of Hook, in particular, while often not original in today's sense of the word, embody the ebb and flow between homegrown and imported music in London. We note the presence of clarinet in two of his Vauxhall songs: "The Flower Song" (1799), which contains an alternative flute part to substitute for the obbligato clarinet, and "Ye bold sons of Nimrod" (ca. 1800), which uses the clarinet-horn combination so popular in pleasure gardens.[12]

In 1726 the first documented clarinetists in London, August Freudenfeld and Francis Rosenberg, were players of Germanic origin, confirming the presence of musicians from continental Europe in the English capital since the early eighteenth century.[13] We are less sure, however, of the date of the clarinet's arrival in the opera orchestra before Arne's *Thomas and Sally* of 1760, discussed in chapter 2.

---

12 Michael Winesanker, "Musico-Dramatic Criticism of English Comic Opera, 1750–1800," *Journal of the American Musicological Society* 2, no. 2 (1949): 94–95.

13 Their benefit concert was advertised in *The Daily Courant* on March 24, 1726: Albert Rice, "The Clarinet in Public Concerts," *Early Music* 16, no. 3 (1988): 389.

Even though a third version of an aria from Handel's 1724 *Tamerlano* includes a pair of clarinets in its scoring, we cannot be certain whether it dates from circa 1744 or the 1770s.[14]

Over the next seventy or so years, London audiences heard the clarinet in stage works by both foreign and native composers. Together with Arne and J. C. Bach, the first generation of composers to include the instrument were François-Hippolyte Barthélemon, Dibdin, P. A. Guglielmi, Venancio Rauzzini, Sacchini, and Mattia Vento, in newly composed works as well as pasticcios. We note Arne's inclusion of clarinet in his masque *The Fairy Prince* (1771). Given that he was composing at least until 1777, it is likely that Arne's clarinet writing is more substantial than surviving scores suggest. As well as his three stand-alone works, Vento includes clarinet in his contribution to the pasticcios *Ezio* (1764) in the aria "Belle luci," and *Solimano* (1765) in "Vuoi che lasci" (ex. 4.3). In each of the published "Favourite Songs" from these works, separate parts for wind instruments affirm an ensemble of flutes, clarinets, horns, and strings. Oboes are also used in both works, but never at the same time as clarinets. The conservative nature of the clarinet writing in example 4.3 is due to the fact that the part largely doubles the violins. In corroborating evidence from documentary sources, these two factors confirm that specialist clarinetists were yet to emerge.

As noted by Rice in chapter 2, the clarinet-horn combination was celebrated in Arne's *Thomas and Sally*; it continued to be used by Dibdin in *The Jubilee* (1769), and in Jackson's *The Lord of the Manor* (1780) and *The Metamorphosis* (1783). This feature was explicitly commended

---

14 The aria "Par che mi nasca in seno" is sung by the character Irene in act 2, as found in the British Library, London, Egerton MS 2920, vol. XI (ff. i + I 10). "Tamerlane." This copy of the opera was made for Handel's friend Bernard Granville by John Christopher Smith. The date of ca. 1744 appears in Jens Peter Larsen *Handel's Messiah: Origins, Compositions, Sources* (London: Adam & Charles Black, 1957), 211. Until further documentary evidence emerges connecting this manuscript to a performance of *Tamerlano*, we must acknowledge that it may have been copied during the 1770s. See the discussion in Colin Lawson, *The Early Clarinet: A Practical Guide* (Cambridge: Cambridge University Press, 2000), 114–15. Furthermore, we cannot be certain whose wishes are represented by the inclusion of clarinet, Handel's, Smith's, or Granville's.

Example 4.3. Mattia Vento, *Solimano* (1765), "Vuoi che lasci," clarinets.

in Linley's air "O ponder well" for *The Beggar's Opera* (1777)[15] and Giordani's *Il bacio* (1782).[16]

From the mid-eighteenth century London theater orchestras numbered between twenty and thirty players, but in reading these figures we must take account of the fact that many musicians were known to be proficient on more than one instrument.[17] Even by the late 1780s

---

15 William Shield, *Introduction to Harmony* (London: the author, 1800), 100. Despite the lack of surviving music, we know of Linley's use of clarinet in *The Heiress* (Drury Lane, January 14, 1786) because of a review published two days later remarking on how "the clarinets heightened the effect of her [Mrs Crouch's] voice." *Morning Herald and Daily Advertiser,* January 16, 1786.

16 While this music has not survived, a contemporary account reports on the "very exhilarating" effect of the clarinet-horn combination in the French air "De tous mes veuës" sung by Giuseppe Viganoni; quoted in Frederick C. Petty, *Italian Opera in London* (Ann Arbor, MI: UMI Research Press, 1980), 190.

17 Vanessa L. Rogers, "English Caricature and the Playhouse Orchestra at London's Drury Lane Theatre," *Musique, images, instruments* 12 (2010): 48. Clarinets are most likely excluded from the list of instruments for Drury Lane's 1778–79 season simply because the instrument was among those played by the violinists George Smart, Sr., John Gilham, and Thomas Shaw, Jr.; see Peter Holman, "Worth 100 Words: Edward Francis Burney at Drury Lane in 1779," *Early Music* 45, no. 4

the clarinet was a frequent but not established fixture in these ensembles; during the 1788–89 season a performance by the castrato Luigi Marchesi was hampered "only for want of a clarinet to accompany his voice."[18] A contemporary account from 1794 confirms that London-based clarinet players undertook a variety of engagements, in the theaters and pleasure gardens, at Westminster Abbey, for musical societies, and in military bands. Thirty-one individuals, just over 2 percent of the musicians listed in Doane's 1794 *Directory*, included proficiency on the clarinet among a portfolio of skills.[19]

In the hands of Arnold, Hook, Martín y Soler, Paisiello, Shield, and Storace, the clarinet was exploited as a more individual orchestral timbre, emancipated from its kinship with the oboe, a relationship which no doubt arose from the necessity to have one player for both instruments. By the late eighteenth century, three major composers all held positions in rival establishments: Storace at Drury Lane, Shield at Covent Garden, and Arnold at the Little Theatre in the Haymarket. Surviving music confirms how the skill of these musicians lay in their judicious selection and incorporation of borrowed music, from works premiered in Europe as well as folk material, and its integration with their original contributions.

Despite the overlap between Hook's pleasure gardens music and stage works, his treatment of the clarinet is not genre-specific. In works premiered between 1782 and 1808, Hook and his contemporaries Shield and Arnold make frequent and effective use of the instrument as an obbligato, either solo or as a pair. Arnold's collaboration with Dorothea Plowden, *Virginia* (1800), is among a very small number of extant works with music by a woman, and includes a clarinet cue for

(2017): 649. The situation was unchanged by the early 1790s. James Oliver, Richard Oliver, and Samuel Tattnal, Drury Lane musicians for the 1791–92 season, are listed as performers on clarinet and other instruments including the violin; see Jane Girdham, *English Opera in Late Eighteenth-Century London: Stephen Storace at Drury Lane* (Oxford: Clarendon Press, 1997), 74.

18 Antoine Le Texier, *Ideas on the Opera …* (London: J. Bell, 1790), 5.

19 Joseph Doane, *A Musical Directory for the Year 1794* (London: R. H. Westley, 1794). Concerning theater musicians, Girdham reports that "despite their competence, the orchestral members were considered the lowliest of the musical performers in the London theatres"; Girdham, *English Opera*, 77.

the air "To bid adieu to her I love."[20] John Mahon, among the first English clarinet virtuosi, composed an obbligato for his sister Sarah's 1796 Covent Garden debut in Shield's *The Woodman*. Although not overtly virtuosic, "Hope thou cheerful ray of light" is an adroit combination of instrument and voice. In contrast, music composed for London stages by Martín y Soler, Paisiello, and Storace displays their more systematic training and subsequent experience writing for different Continental companies. Storace's works combine his own music and material recycled from his *Gli equivoci* (Vienna, 1786), typical of the self-borrowing prevalent at this time, with dexterous incorporations of numbers from Continental operas. The quartet "Ah perche," scored for pairs of flutes, oboes, clarinets, bassoons, and horns, is used again in *La cameriera astuta* (1788) and, as the sextet "Hope a distant joy," finally in *No Song, No Supper* (1790). Storace's treatment of the clarinet as an equal and distinct part of the wind choir appears in *The Siege of Belgrade* (1791), where three numbers altogether demonstrate the clarinet's standing: the act 1 air "The Rose and the Lily," co-written with Martín y Soler, as well as Storace's airs "My plaint in no one pity moves" and "Love and honour now conspire." Two late works by Martín y Soler, *La scuola dei maritati* (1795) and *L'isola del piacere* (1795), make frequent use of clarinet, although not as an obbligato or solo timbre.

By the late 1790s, London's vibrant opera scene included new venues such as the Lyceum, adding to musicians' employment opportunities. Conditions still militated against loyalty to a particular theater, and most clarinetists continued to be vocationally mobile. Composers often worked alone, but the collaborative process brought forth a myriad of newly composed stage works from the likes of Attwood, Braham, Cooke, Davy, Horn, Kelly, King, Lee, Mazzinghi, Moorehead, Reeve, Sinclair, Smith, Ware, and Whitaker, many of whom were also active as performers. Works such as Davy's *The Blind Boy* (1808), King's *Oh, This Love* (1810), Whitaker's *Who's to Have Her?* (1813), and Ware's *Harlequin Asmodeus* (ca. 1815) confirm that the clarinet was recognized as a distinctive woodwind timbre and a soloist, both within the orchestral texture and in obbligatos. These features are also found in the music of Henry Bishop, whose career embraced positions in-house at both Covent Garden and Drury Lane.

---

20 It has been suggested that Plowden's tunes were harmonized by Arnold; Barbara Garvey Jackson, *Say Can You Deny Me: A Guide to Surviving Music by Women from the 16th through the 18th Centuries* (Fayetteville: University of Arkansas Press, 1994), 313–14.

Bishop synthesized elements of bel canto with popular taste, enabling his music to permeate the many sub-genres of English stage entertainment. By 1830 his output included over thirty-six works with clarinet: stand-alone original works, collaborations, and adaptations of Continental operas. The score of *The Knight of Snowdoun* (1811) is remarkable for its naming of a clarinetist, "Mr. Hopkins." The violinist and clarinetist Edward Samuel George Hopkins played the latter instrument at Covent Garden at least until 1818, and then at Drury Lane in the 1821–22 season. He was also active as a military musician, in the band of the Guards Third Regiment and then as bandmaster of the Scots Guards.[21] Bishop's writing for clarinet in this early work utilizes the instrument's distinctive tone qualities and its suitability for subtle melodic nuances, as well as the long-standing success of its combination with horns and other *Harmonie* instruments. Bishop's mature handling of the clarinet is apparent in *The Two Gentlemen of Verona* (1821) and *Clari* (1823), no doubt as a result of his familiarity with the works of Continental composers of earlier generations. He uses the instrument as an obbligato color, to introduce a number's melodic material, and to interject as a comment on the sung text, as well as in various accompanying roles. The concertante parts for flute, oboe, and clarinet in the overture to *Brother and Sister* (1815; see ex. 4.4) were favorably received at the work's premiere.[22]

Another distinguishing feature of early nineteenth-century opera in London was the adaptation of Continental operas, manifesting each theater's particular approach. The King's Theatre staged the first professional London productions of Mozart's *La clemenza di Tito* (1806), *Die Zauberflöte* (as *Il flauto magico*) and *Così fan tutte* (both 1811), *Le nozze di Figaro* (1812), and *Don Giovanni* (1817), the latter production securing the composer's place in the London operatic canon.[23] Fre-

---

21 Doane, *A Musical Directory*, and also Philip H. Highfill, Kalman A. Burnim, and Edward A. Langhans, *A Biographical Dictionary of Actors, Actresses, Musicians, Dancers* ... (Carbondale: Southern Illinois University Press, 1982), 7:406. Hopkins is also named by Ware in *Harlequin Asmodeus*, mentioned above.

22 William T. Parke, *Musical Memoirs* ... (London: Henry Colburn and Richard Bentley, 1830), 2:111.

23 Rachel Cowgill, "'Wise Men from the East': Mozart's Operas and their Advocates in Early Nineteenth-Century London," in *Music and British Culture, 1785–1914: Essays in Honor of Cyril Ehrlich*, ed. Christina Bashford and Leanne Langley (New York: Oxford University Press, 2000), 61.

Example 4.4. Henry Bishop, *Brother and Sister* (1815), overture, clarinet solo.

quent alterations to a work's orchestration suggest that this feature was not viewed as integral to the work's identity, as it was by Castil-Blaze in contemporary Paris.[24] For example, in 1814 Boieldieu's *Jean de Paris* received different treatment, at the hands of Bishop at Covent Garden and Horn at Drury Lane. We have only vocal score evidence for Bishop's Covent Garden reinventions of Mozart's *Don Giovanni* as *Don Juan or the Libertine* (1817) and *Le nozze di Figaro* as *Marriage of Figaro* (1819). Bishop substituted a clarinet for Mozart's oboe and bassoon in the duet for Susanna and the Countess, "How gently, when the sun's descending," and in his own aria for Susanna, "The youth in his blooming array." In this case, however, the substitution suggests an understanding of the instrument's use in amorous contexts.[25]

The performance in Italian of at least twelve of Rossini's operas in London between 1818 and 1824 added to the public's continuing appetite for foreign opera, although surviving materials tell us little about Bishop's use of clarinet in his 1830 Drury Lane adaptation of *Guillaume Tell* as *Hofer, the Tell of the Tyrol*. While opera sung in German was banned, in 1824 four different composers, William Hawes, Montague Philip Corri, Barham Livius, and Henry Bishop, capitalized on the popularity of Weber's *Der Freischütz* by staging their own English-language versions, all in the space of four months.[26] Livius's clarinet writing is likely to be more widespread than the scant number of

---

24 Christina Fuhrmann, *Foreign Opera at London Playhouses: Mozart to Bellini* (Cambridge: Cambridge University Press, 2015), 14.

25 Mozart's duet "Che soave zefiretto" appears in act 3. The use of clarinet as a signifier in such contexts is discussed below in relation to opera in Vienna.

26 Appendix 1 in Fuhrmann, *Foreign Opera at London Playhouses*, 196.

surviving scores suggests, given his reworking of operas by Auber, Onslow and Weigl. Similarly, while the clarinet appears in Hawes's adaptation of Ries's *Die Raüberbraut* as *The Robber's Bride* (1829) his use of the instrument is likely to be more prolific. The success of *Der Freischütz* saw Weber commissioned to write an English-language work for Covent Garden; *Oberon* (1826) was soon imitated by Bishop's *Aladdin* (1826). Weber's treatment of the clarinet in this London context, at the end of his life, reflects his expectations that local clarinetists were the equal of those he had encountered in his native Germany. In *Oberon*, he uses the instrument as a soloist within the orchestra and as a distinctive voice in the wind section, which requires fluency throughout the whole compass as well as dexterity of articulation.

Naples

Eighteenth-century Naples was easily the largest city on the Italian peninsula and a true "European cultural epicenter."[27] In 1737, three years after his ascent to the thrones of Naples and Sicily, the Spanish-born monarch Charles commissioned the building of the Teatro San Carlo. This venue, bearing his name, remains the oldest public opera house in the world. Lasting from 1759 until 1825, the reign of Charles's successor, Ferdinand, endured both a republican uprising and the aspirations of Napoleon Bonaparte. It is important to acknowledge that during the last thirty years of the eighteenth century the San Carlo orchestra was "among the finest in contemporary Europe."[28] Comic opera also thrived in theaters such as the Teatro dei'Fiorentini, Teatro Nuovo, and the Teatro del Real Fondo di Separazione. The Spanish line continued with Francis, whose short reign lasted from 1825 until 1830, during which time Naples remained a vibrant operatic center. Neapolitan traditions combining local dialects with spoken dialogue eventually gave way to a style clearly influenced by French art and politics, as well as by the works of Rossini.

Naples's conservatories played a crucial role in stimulating opera. Three of the initial four conservatories existed between 1743 and

---

27 Anthony R. DelDonna, "Opera in Naples," in *The Cambridge Companion to Eighteenth Century Opera*, ed. Anthony R. DelDonna and Pierpaolo Polzonetti (Cambridge: Cambridge University Press, 2009), 214.

28 Anthony R. DelDonna, "A Documentary History of the Clarinet in the Teatro San Carlo Opera Orchestra in the Late-18th Century," *Studi musicali* 37 (2008): 410.

1797: Santa Maria di Loreto, Sant'Onofrio a Porta Capuana, and Santa Maria della Pietà dei Turchini.[29] The clarinet had almost certainly been taught at one of the conservatories by the time of its first documented use at the opera in 1765.[30] Between 1797 and 1807, despite the political upheavals of the Napoleonic wars, the Santa Maria di Loreto and Sant'Onofrio were still flourishing. In 1807 they merged to form the Real Collegio di Musica, housed initially at the San Sebastiano monastery and from 1826 in its current location at San Pietro a Majella.[31] It is highly significant that over half of the musicians identified for this chapter who wrote opera for Naples before 1830 studied at one of these institutions. The completion of a stage work as a condition of graduation eased young composers into the profession, while further confirming the city's international reputation.[32] These composers cut their operatic teeth with comic operas and insertion numbers before trying their hand at opera seria.

The first appearance of the clarinet in Neapolitan opera is in Sacchini's *Il Creso* (1765), where the clarinet is never heard alongside the oboe, confirming the practice of woodwind doubling. A pair of clarinets appear in the act 2, scene 9 aria "Perche, oh Dio! fra tanti affanni" in at least one manuscript.[33] The instrument's next appearance seems to be some six years later, in Paisiello's *I scherzi di amore e di fortuna*, premiered at the Teatro Nuovo. Although by the early 1770s Paisiello already enjoyed a reputation on the Italian peninsula as a composer of opera, he used the clarinet conservatively, treating it as simply a contrasting wind timbre in relation to the more prevalent oboe, and once again it seems that the oboe and clarinet parts were most likely performed by the same players because the instruments are never heard together. A similar manner of clarinet writing and, in the majority of cases its demarcation from the oboe, was also a feature of contemporary stage works by Pasquale Anfossi, Pasquale Cafaro, P. A. Guglielmi, and Josef Mysliveček, premiered between 1772 and 1776 at San Carlo. In example 4.5, we see how Anfossi's Naples revision (1772) of his *La clemenza di Tito* (1769), originally for Rome, utilizes the availability of

---

29 Antonio Rostagno, "18th Century," §I.5 of the article "Italy," *Grove Music Online.*

30 DelDonna, "A Documentary History," 414–15.

31 Rostagno, "18th Century."

32 DelDonna, "Opera in Naples," 216.

33 Biblioteca del Conservatorio di Musica S. Pietro a Majella, Naples, 31.4.22–24. The opera was revived for performance at San Carlo in 1776; DelDonna, "A Documentary History," 439.

Example 4.5. Pasquale Anfossi, *La clemenza di Tito* (1772 revision), act 2, "Pensa, pensa, in qual pena amara," mm. 1–6.

the clarinet. Included in only one number, the act 2 aria "Pensa, pensa, in qual pena amara," the clarinet is used in a similar vein to Vento (see ex. 4.3 above). Such conservative writing again is indicative that the instrument was almost certainly played by musicians who, for the rest of the opera, were oboists.

Documentary evidence attests to the presence of Raffaele Battimelli and Raffaele Cuomo as clarinetists at San Carlo at least from 1775, albeit in a supernumerary capacity, but it is likely that these musicians also performed on other instruments.[34] It is possible that Battimelli and Cuomo appeared in Cimarosa's *Le stravaganze d'amore* (1778) if the presence of the instrument in one manuscript reflects the work's premiere.[35] The 1779–80 San Carlo season marked the appointment of Guglielmo (Wilhelm) Hattenbauer and Leopold Vinitzki as permanent clarinet players, joining an orchestra numbering some fifty-nine

34 DelDonna, "A Documentary History," 410–11 and 413.
35 Bibliothèque Nationale de France, Paris, Département de la Musique, D.2148-9.

musicians.[36] This arrival of specialist clarinetists soon heralded a change in the way the instrument functioned within the opera orchestra. In stage works composed by Francesco Bianchi, Cimarosa, Giuseppe Gazzaniga, Giacomo Insanguine, Martín y Soler, Rosetti, Joseph Schuster, Johann Sterkel, and Zingarelli, the clarinet assumed a more individual role including obbligato and solo passages, particularly alongside the oboe. Bianchi was a prolific composer of operas, completing almost eighty works between 1772 and 1807. His use of muted clarinets, among an ensemble of muted horns and strings, in Arbace's act 1, scene 7 cavatina "Mentre un soave oblio" in the opera seria *Arbace* (1781) now appears to be the earliest documented use of this technique.[37] This is but one example of how the orchestration in Bianchi's Neapolitan works made effective use of the available wind instruments.

Similarly productive was Cimarosa, whose output includes over seventy operas composed between 1772 and 1801. From the late 1770s until the end of the century the clarinet established itself as a permanent member of the opera orchestra in Naples. Two clarinets appear in the list of the San Carlo orchestra following Paisiello's re-organization circa 1796.[38]

Although heard most often at San Carlo, clarinetists also supplemented the smaller orchestras of the Fiorentini, Fondo, and Nuovo, and others took part in performances of stage works in venues associated with the nobility. The majority of works from this time are opera seria; however, the clarinet's coming of age in Naples coincided with a flourishing of comic opera. Among the most active and innovative composers writing for the stage at this time were Cimarosa, P. A. Guglielmi, Paisiello, and Giacomo Tritto.[39] They worked across comic and serious genres with considerable flair, their music enjoying more

36 DelDonna, "A Documentary History," 414. The 1780 evidence comes from Pasquale Cafaro, *maestro di cappella*; Michael F. Robinson, *Naples and Neapolitan Opera* (New York: Da Capo Press, 1985), 160.

37 The score indicates "clarinetti con sordine"; Biblioteca del Conservatorio di Musica S. Pietro a Majella, Naples, 24.3.15–17.

38 Ulisse Prota-Giurleo, *La grande orchestra del R. Teatro San Carlo nel Settecento: da documenti inediti* (Naples: the author, 1927), 53, cited in Robinson, *Naples and Neapolitan Opera*, 161.

39 Guglielmi's works with clarinet span 1776–1802, Paisiello's 1771–1808, Cimarosa's 1778–98, and Tritto's 1783–1815. While his works are currently out of fashion, during his career Guglielmi senior composed almost 100 operas, confirming his pre-eminence as a composer for the stage. See the worklist in "Pietro Alessandro Guglielmi," in James

performances in the late eighteenth century than Mozart's Da Ponte works. Other composers, many of them now overlooked, also wrote for the clarinet with an awareness of the instrument's versatility particularly in terms of characterization. For example, Francesco Antonio de Blasis, whose opera buffa *Il geloso ravveduto* (1784) utilizes the clarinet as a soloist within the orchestra. That so much of this music is not available to us today serves to remind us of the pitfalls of a system of dissemination reliant on manuscripts rather than printed music.[40]

Two operas that demonstrate how the clarinet was used in the late 1780s and 1790s are Paisiello's *Fedra* (1788) and *Elvira* (1794). *Fedra* employs four clarinets with pairs of bassoon and horns in act 1, scene 3, and the "Serenata" prologue to *Elvira* combines obbligato clarinet and guitar with oboes, bassoons, and horns. From the late 1770s, operas staged at San Carlo often made use of an on-stage band or *banda sul palco*, an additional ensemble which enhanced the orchestral palette.[41] This practice was well utilized by composers of serious opera and sacred dramas, continuing well into the nineteenth century, as Rossini's *Ricciardo e Zoraide* (1818) testifies. Additionally, from the late 1780s until the early nineteenth century, *azione sacre* or staged oratorios were performed at San Carlo during Lent.[42] Enjoying considerable success beyond Naples, the most celebrated of these was P. A. Guglielmi's *Debora e Sisara*, which makes idiomatic use of the clarinet as a solo instrument as well as in the on-stage band.[43] Other Lenten dramas with clarinet are Guglielmi's *Gionata Maccabeo* (1789); Piccinni's *Gionata* (1792), including pairs of muted oboes and clarinets in the chorus in part 1, scene 13; and Andreozzi's *Sofronia e Olindo* (1793).[44]

L. Jackman, Kay Lipton, and Mary Hunter, "Guglielmi Family," *Grove Music Online*.

40   *Il geloso ravveduto*, overture and Margherita's cavatina "Ragazza poveretta"; Conservatorio di Musica Luigi Cherubini, Florence, Biblioteca, B.46, B.I.60.

41   For an account of the use of this feature see Rey Morgan Longyear, "The Banda sul Palco: Wind Bands in Nineteenth-Century Opera," *Journal of Band Research* 13, no. 2 (Spring 1978): 25–40.

42   Anthony R. DelDonna, *Opera, Theatrical Culture and Society in Late Eighteenth-Century Naples (London: Routledge, 2016)*, 147–49.

43   Biblioteca del Conservatorio di Musica S. Pietro a Majella, Naples, 27.4.36–37.

44   For a list of performances of these works see DelDonna, *Opera, Theatrical Culture*, 158.

Rossini drew on this tradition for *Mosè in Egitto* (1818), as did Donizetti in *Il diluvio universale* (1830).

By the turn of the nineteenth century, the clarinet was in regular use in at least four Neapolitan theaters, with performers often moving between venues to optimize conditions of work and pay.[45] Ferdinando Sedelmajer and his successor Michele Rupp, holders of the position *maestro di clarinetto* at Santa Maria della Pietà dei Turchini between 1801 and 1807, performed at the opera. Sedelmajer joined the orchestra of the Fiorentini for the first time in the 1801–02 season.[46] Rupp is known to have performed in the orchestras at San Carlo and the Fondo.[47] In the last fifteen years of Napoleonic rule, an array of composers took advantage of the instrument's availability; apart from Simon Mayr, however, most remain relatively unknown today. Among their works, the cavatina no. 13 in Valentino Fioravanti's *Il bello piace* (1806) and the opening of the act 2 finale of Stefano Pavesi's *Aristodemo* (1807; see ex. 4.6) demonstrate the melodic fluency of the clarinet register.

Rossini's first opera for Naples was *Elisabetta, regina d'Inghilterra* (1815), and over the next seven years he premiered another nine operas in the city. Although not as often performed today as *Il barbiere di Siviglia* (Rome 1816), *Guillaume Tell* (Paris, 1829), *La Cenerentola* (Rome, 1817), and *La gazza ladra* (Milan, 1817), the eight works for San Carlo took full advantage of the theater's orchestral and vocal prowess, exerting a profound influence on later Italian operatic composition.

Among other operas premiered in Naples in the years up to 1830, we note the continual presence of works by composers trained locally, including Saverio Mercadante. Mercadante's Neapolitan works embraced serious and comic genres, but his opposition to contemporary operatic practices has overshadowed the achievements of his output. San Carlo retained its status well into the nineteenth century, although the majority of works were staged at comic theaters, confirming the distinctive nature of Neapolitan comic opera.

---

45 Anthony DelDonna, "Eighteenth-Century Politics and Patronage: Music and the Republican Revolution of Naples," *Eighteenth-Century Music* 4, no. 2 (2007): 232–35.

46 Ibid., 234.

47 Adriano Amore, *La scuola clarinettistica italiana: virtuosi e didatti* (Benevento: Frasso Telesino, 2006), 67.

Example 4.6. Stefano Pavesi, *Aristodemo* (1807), act 2 finale, opening clarinet solo.

Vienna

As the largest German-speaking city between the mid-eighteenth century and the first decade of the nineteenth, Vienna was the capital of an empire encompassing Austria, Bohemia, Moravia, Hungary, Transylvania, Croatia, Lombardy, and Belgium. Under Maria Theresa's successors, Joseph II (r. 1765–90) and Leopold II (r. 1790–92), the court continued to dominate Viennese operatic life, controlling the principal theaters and, with wealthy aristocrats, providing a source of employment for musicians. During the reign of Francis II (r. 1792–1835) the leasing of venues to impresarios enabled a broader base for the patronage of opera, although aristocratic support remained vital. In addition, Vienna's status as a major European center of music engraving and publishing continued well into the nineteenth century.[48] As Wolfgang Amadeus Mozart wrote to his father Leopold in April 1781, Vienna was "the best place in the world" for his profession.[49]

Joseph II made two fundamental gestures in support of opera which proved highly advantageous for the clarinet. His 1776 decree converted the Habsburg Court Theater into the National Theater. Housed at the Burgtheater, this company began to employ the clarinet initially in a supplementary capacity, not unlike contemporary Naples and Paris some thirty years before. During the next nine years a prominent feature of the orchestra's gradual expansion was the transition of wind players to salaried positions. The Stadler brothers,

---

48 Donald W. Krummel, "The Age of Engraving, 1700–1860," §II.3 of the article "Printing and Publishing of Music," *Grove Music Online*.

49 Letter of April 4, 1781, in *Letters of Wolfgang Amadeus Mozart*, ed. Hans Mersmann, trans. M. Bozman (New York: Dover Publications, 1972), 161.

Anton and Johann, first contracted in the latter half of the 1779–80 season, became regular players two years later.[50] Archival evidence supports the claim that the Stadlers were the two "Clarinetti" in the Burgtheater orchestra during the 1786–87 season.[51] Similarly, Joseph's establishment, in 1778, of the National Singspiel enabled the creation of German-language comic operas, among the earliest works staged in Vienna with clarinet. Mozart's *Die Entführung aus dem Serail* K. 384 (1782), seems surprisingly late in the century, given the establishment of the clarinet in other major European cities.[52] In the nine years from 1783 until 1792, at least sixty new operas were staged at the Burgtheater under the patronage of Joseph II and his successor Leopold II.

Rice notes in chapter 2 above that the chalumeau featured in operas written by composers working at the Habsburg court in the early part of the eighteenth century. As I have shown elsewhere, this instrument was often used to portray delicate, sentimental, and intimate contexts.[53] It is no accident, then, that later in the century the clarinet appeared in similar contexts, in works such as Mozart's *Così*, premiered at the Burgtheater in January 1790, and we can be fairly

---

50 Dexter Edge, "Mozart's Viennese Orchestras." *Early Music* 20, no. 1 (1992): 71.

51 The Court Theater account list is reproduced in Stephen Storace, *Gli equivoci*, ed. Richard Platt (London: Stainer & Bell, 2007), xliv.

52 Although clarinet parts have been attributed to a 1723 revival of Caldara's *Ifigenia*, we cannot be certain of the date or provenance of these (Conservatoire Royal de Bruxelles, Bibliothèque/Koninklijk Conservatorium Brussel, Bibliotheek, MS 2048). Fricke has drawn attention to the use of the clarinet by Matthias (Michael) Baumgartner (Baumgärtner, Paumgärtner) in his only extant opera, *Alcidoro* of 1773, but this remains to be confirmed; Heike Fricke, *Die Klarinette im 18. Jahrhundert: Tendenzen und Entwicklungen am Beispiel der Sir Nicholas Shackleton Collection* (Falkensee: Finkenkruger Musikverlag, 2013), 234–37. The earliest documentary evidence of the Stadler brothers as musicians dates from March 21, 1773; Pamela L. Poulin, "The Basset Clarinet of Anton Stadler and Its Music" (master's thesis, University of Rochester, 1976), 1:3–4. Therefore, it is possible that the Stadlers may have performed in Baumgartner's opera.

53 Ingrid Pearson, "Delicacy, Sentimentality and Intimacy: The Chalumeau as 'Signifier,'" International Clarinet Association, November 27, 2018, http://clarinet.org/wp-content/uploads/2016/03/Pearson-Chalumeau.pdf.

certain that Viennese opera audiences would have understood such extramusical messages being conveyed on stage.[54]

An important Viennese musical partnership with substantial ramifications for the clarinet was that of (Johann) Theodor Lotz, instrument maker to the imperial royal court and chamber, and his fellow Freemason Anton Stadler. They collaborated in the 1780s to create what we now term the "basset clarinet."[55] Although the earliest trace of basset clarinet writing in an opera is not until *Così*, Stadler probably used this type of clarinet almost exclusively from 1788. The second clarinet part of "Ah lo veggio, quell'anima mia," Ferrando's aria in act 2, scene 2 of *Così*, includes two instances of the written note D^3. Although this use of basset notes is far more conservative than that in "Parto, parto" in *La clemenza*, it may be that the instrument's timbre was just as appealing as its range.

Following the premiere of *Die Entführung*, the Stadlers probably played in the first performances of the operas at the Burgtheater by Paisiello, Salieri, Gazzaniga, Martín y Soler, and Carl Ditters von Dittersdorf, and both versions of Mozart's *Figaro* (1786 and 1789) as well as the Vienna version of *Don Giovanni* (1788).

In addition to *Die Entführung*, *Figaro*, *Don Giovanni*, and *Così*, we should take into account Mozart's inclusion of clarinet in other stage works for Vienna, particularly if we are to appreciate his innate understanding of the instrument's capabilities: *Der Schauspieldirektor* K. 486 (1786), the second version of *Idomeneo* K. 366 (1786), and *Die Zauberflöte* K. 620 (1791),[56] stand-alone dramatic pieces, and individual operatic numbers for his own operas as well as works headlined by other composers.[57]

The friendship between Anton Stadler and Mozart is well documented, but we also observe the influence of this fruitful acquaintance in operas by Storace, Franz Süssmayr, and Georg Joseph Vogler. Storace's two comic operas, *Gli sposi malcontenti* (1785) and *Gli equivoci* (1786), were written for the Italian opera buffa troupe in residence during the suspension of the National Singspiel in the mid-1780s. His

---

54 Rushton discusses this in relation to the use of different dance forms to portray the social standing of characters in Mozart's *Don Giovanni*; Julian Rushton, *W. A. Mozart: Don Giovanni* (Cambridge: Cambridge University Press, 1981), 16.

55 Melanie Piddocke, "Lotz, Johann Theodor," *Grove Music Online*.

56 This work also utilizes the basset horn.

57 Mozart also includes clarinet in an oratorio and a sacred cantata: *Davidde penitente* K. 496 (1785) and *Die Maurerfreude* K. 471 (1785).

use of both clarinet and basset horns is clearly influenced by the scoring of *Die Entführung*. Storace writes quite cautiously, using the basset horn for its timbre rather than its range, perhaps because of his relative inexperience as a composer for the stage. Süssmayr's tenure in Vienna was similarly productive for the clarinet, assisted by positions at Burgtheater and the Kärntnertortheater. While at least eight of his surviving operas for Vienna include clarinet, from *L'incanto superato* (1793) to *Phasma* (1801), two works use the basset horn as well, namely *Der Wildfang* (1797) and *Phasma*, a further testimony to the nature of his association with Mozart and the Stadlers. The Stadlers' legacy continued with Vogler's use of both clarinet and basset horn in *Samori* (1804). While Anton Stadler had left the orchestra in 1799 and Johann died in 1804,[58] it seems likely that further operas with both clarinet and basset horn were composed and may well come to light in the future.

Like Mozart before them, Beethoven, Cherubini, and others sought the opportunities that Vienna offered, while the city's theaters also staged operas premiered elsewhere. Beethoven's only opera was first performed as *Leonore* at the Theater an der Wien (1805) before being staged as *Fidelio* (1814). His incidental music for Goethe's *Egmont*, op. 84 (1810), includes clarinet, as do the finales for two Singspiel pasticcios: "Germania" (1814) for *Die gute Nachricht* (which includes other music by Adalbert Gyrowetz, Johann Nepomuk Hummel, Mozart, and Joseph Weigl), and "Es ist vollbracht" (1815) for *Die Ehrenpforten* (with other music by Handel and Weber). The clarinet is a prominent wind color in *Faniska* (1806), Cherubini's only opera for Vienna, particularly in the Andantino instrumental interlude toward the end of act 1 and the trio no. 11 toward the end of act 2.

Schubert's operatic aspirations were fraught with obstacles largely because of his dissatisfaction with the librettos he encountered.[59] Of the eighteen works he began between 1811 and his death in 1828, he completed nine, of which only the Singspiel *Die Zwillingsbrüder* (1820) and the melodrama *Die Zauberharfe* (1820) were staged in Vienna in his lifetime.[60] Schubert used clarinets in the incidental music to *Rosamunde* (1823); the clarinet's association with matters pastoral in no. 6, "Hirtenmelodien," and no. 7, "Hirtenchor," possibly foretells the

---

58 Poulin, "The Basset Clarinet of Anton Stadler and Its Music," 55.

59 Maurice J. E. Brown, Eric Sams, and Robert Winter, "Dramatic Music," §2(iv) of "Schubert, Franz," *Grove Music Online*.

60 Seven complete and six incomplete works were premiered between 1854 and 1971; see the worklist in Brown, Sams, and Winter, "Schubert, Franz."

instrument's obbligato role in *Der Hirt auf dem Felsen* of 1828. *Die Zauberharfe* continues the tradition of *Zauberspiel* exemplified in Mozart's *Die Zauberflöte* and Süssmayr's *Der Spiegel von Arkadien*. Clarinet writing in these works, as well as in *Der vierjährige Posten* (1815), embraces the instrument's pastoral and military characters, utilizing *Harmonie* textures and obbligato solos. The three completed works from the early 1820s, *Alfonso und Estrella* (1821–22), *Die Verschworenen* (1822–23), and *Fierrabras* (1823), make more soloistic use of the clarinet. The obbligato "Ich schleiche bang" from *Die Verschworenen* should surely be as well known to clarinetists as the Octet, composed the following year. It is a testimony to certain favorable circumstances, the interaction of particular key individuals, and current taste that certain Viennese operatic repertoire of this time has become so central to our appreciation of both the clarinet and the genre.

Conclusion

In surveying the clarinet in opera before 1830 we begin to realize the extent to which our understanding of this music is colored by the availability of a relatively limited amount of evidence. Despite our easy access to a range of sources, such as individual clarinet parts, miniature scores, vocal scores, full scores, and manuscripts, as well as audio and video recordings, these represent a disproportionately small amount of eighteenth- and nineteenth-century operatic repertoire. While the digital age may well help redress this imbalance, we will probably only ever have a completely unrepresentative understanding of the clarinet's role in opera at a time that was vital and exciting for both instrument and genre.

This repertoire also invites us to question the notion of artistic originality, when we bear in mind that many composers of the past were often also compilers and/or arrangers of the music of others. This feature stands in stark contrast to our current expectations of an artist who completes a work which is then consumed in perpetuity, usually in only one version. Perhaps the production of so-called scholarly editions has tricked us into an understanding of opera based almost entirely on standardized snapshots of what are, in fact, fluctuating artistic entities.

Among our four centers, Paris accommodated a large number of composers, and the city's printing technology ensured the survival of this music in appropriately representative detail. Opera in London was facilitated by a considerable number of collaborations, including the judicious tailoring of foreign products for local audiences. While music composed for Naples was mainly distributed in manuscript form, those who studied at one of the conservatories left a lasting effect on opera, at home and abroad. That Viennese repertoire is among the most celebrated today is no doubt a result of the special affiliations between certain individuals.

During the eighteenth and early nineteenth centuries technological innovations and the emergence of specialist players enabled the clarinet to begin to assume a distinctive and vital role in the opera orchestra. Social and cultural changes, at local, regional, national, and international levels, spanning the Enlightenment and the Industrial Revolution, exerted a profound influence on its music. It is indeed this operatic repertoire which enables us to recognize the clarinet's coming of age.

5

THE CLARINET IN
NINETEENTH-CENTURY OPERA

Julian Rushton

Whereas in earlier orchestral music (symphonies, concertos, operas) the clarinet was an occasional participant in the orchestra, by the early nineteenth century it was fully integrated. Throughout the century its popularity as a solo instrument exceeded that of other woodwinds. But, as Colin Lawson reminds us, for performing musicians "before the enthusiasm for virtuosity as an end in itself during the nineteenth century ... the communication of emotion was an absolute priority."[1] Alongside the instrument's other capabilities, clarinetists playing in nineteenth-century opera can often enjoy rapid passagework, especially ascending arpeggios, like those that occur profusely in concertos, but they do not have obbligatos in the fashion of Floquet (*Hellé*) or Mozart (*La clemenza di Tito*). Sometimes such figuration can be interpreted from a simple musical standpoint, as textural enrichment, but at other times it may be intended to contribute to the collaborative dramatic whole that, ideally, is an opera. The opera composer responds to action, establishes atmosphere, and enhances characterization, by orchestral means; and the communication of dramatic emotion and insight is of paramount importance.[2] The palette

---

1   Colin Lawson, *The Early Clarinet: A Practical Guide* (Cambridge: Cambridge University Press, 2000), 2.
2   This formulation is indebted to Joseph Kerman, *Opera as Drama*, 2nd rev. ed. (London and Boston: Faber & Faber, 1988), 215.

of woodwind colors was greatly enriched by the regular inclusion of clarinets and, later, the bass clarinet.

What follows cannot be comprehensive; the repertoire is too large to cover every important opera composer in equal detail, never mind every opera. I hope that by studying certain sections, and even operas, in sharper focus, I shall at least indicate how much composers from Weber and Berlioz to Tchaikovsky and Puccini valued the instrument, and how they made effective use of its particular qualities. To those whose favorite clarinet passages are not mentioned, I can only apologize.

The form of this essay is first, and primarily, to consider the clarinet as a kind of voice, in which the "clarion" or "cantabile" register, above the break, is most used; then to review its use as part of an ensemble, and as a frequent contributor to dark, even tragic, coloring, where the middle and especially the lowest "chalumeau" register are likely to be employed. The latter discussion leads naturally to the operatic use of the bass clarinet.

The Clarinet as "Voice"

The clarinet was integral to the sound-world of composers such as Spontini, Spohr (notably in *Faust*), and Weber. These, with Mendelssohn and Berlioz, fueled Romantic interest in color as expression, which was not confined to opera. The clarinet became a wordless voice. For a non-operatic example, consider the recapitulation of the lyrical theme in Mendelssohn's *Die Hebriden*, where the second clarinet joins the first, soaring into a high register, sunshine over the northern sea. Within an operatic overture, human emotion is more directly invoked. Berlioz, enraptured by the clarinet solo in Weber's *Der Freischütz* overture, asks (rhetorically): "Isn't this the lonely virgin, the fair bride of the huntsman who, raising her eyes to heaven, mingles her tender plea with the uproar of trees shaken by a storm? ... O Weber!!!"[3] As early as 1830, Berlioz quoted with no less enthusiasm a passage from Spontini's *La vestale*, divided between clarinet and oboe; "this superhuman melody" ("ce chant surhumain") is

---

3   "N'est-ce pas la vierge isolée, la blonde fiancée du chasseur qui, les yeux au ciel, mêle sa tendre plainte au bruit des bois profonds agités par l'orage? ... O Weber !!!" Translated from Hector Berlioz, *Grand traité d'instrumentation et d'orchestration modernes*, ed. Peter Bloom, *New Berlioz Edition*, 24 (Kassel: Bärenreiter, 2003), 204. Translations in this chapter are mine, unless otherwise noted.

associated with the troubled Julie, the title role.[4] A substantial catalogue could be made of occasions in nineteenth-century opera that introduce a female character by a musical gesture, or a more extended melody, on the clarinet. In *Der Freischütz* flute and clarinet in octaves, later a favorite doubling for Berlioz, are prominent in Max's aria "Durch die Wälder" as he reflects on his love for Agathe; in act 2 her *scena* begins with expressive gestures from the A clarinet, and within her aria ("Leise, leise") she sings the melody introduced by the (B-flat) clarinet in the overture. The lesson was not lost on later composers.

These solos exploit the clarinet's "cantabile" (or "clarion") register, above the break. Although its contribution to operatic expression is by no means confined to that register, it is, at least until the invention of the saxophone, of all instruments closest to the singing voice. A similar claim has sometimes been made for the violin, but the voice is a wind instrument, and of that family the most intimate member and hence most "vocal" was perceived throughout the nineteenth century to be the clarinet. Carl Baermann (*Vollständige Clarinett-Schule*, 1864–75) refers to the cantabile register as able to match "a superlatively fine and full soprano." In this, Baermann followed the lead of Franz Joseph Fröhlich's more general music tutor, *Vollständige theoretisch-praktische Musikschule* (Bonn, 1810–11): "Among all wind instruments, none approaches the tone of the full, female soprano voice as much as does the clarinet." Late in the century, François-Auguste Gevaert in his instrumentation treatise followed Berlioz's lead, and Robert Vollstedt (*Clarinetten Schule zum Selbstunterricht*, 1892) states as a fact that the sound of the clarinet "is closest to the human voice."[5]

Authors of clarinet tutors are perhaps not entirely unbiased in claiming this special status for their instrument, but the practice of composers tends to bear them out. Berlioz orchestrated the low–high dialogue in Weber's piano work *Aufforderung zum Tanz* for cello (as baritone) and clarinet (as soprano); this (as *L'invitation à la valse*) was for inclusion in the Paris Opéra staging of *Der Freischütz* in 1841. A few years earlier on the same stage, Meyerbeer's *Les Huguenots* (Paris Opéra, 1836) matched the brilliant soprano passagework of Queen Marguerite (act 2: "O beau pays de la Touraine") with the flute (although this is no mad scene à la *Lucia*). Some of her shorter

---

4   Hector Berlioz, *Correspondance générale*, ed. Pierre Citron, vol. 1, *1803–1832* (Paris: Flammarion, 1972), 386.

5   Baermann, Fröhlich, and Vollstedt are quoted in Lawson, *The Early Clarinet*, 19 and 63. See also François-Auguste Gevaert, *Nouveau traité d'instrumentation* (Paris: Lemoine, 1885), 165 and 174.

phrases, however, are reflected by the clarinet, like an orchestral mirror, with the composer's instruction "Imitez la voix" (pp. 250, 253); a little later on, the clarinet actually anticipates a vocal phrase.[6]

Disappointingly, however, there is only a little support for this clarinet–feminine association in an earlier, and epoch-marking, grand opéra, Auber's *La muette de Portici* (1828). Fenella, the mute title role, cannot sing. While she conveys her meaning by dumb-show the clarinet does not take much part in Auber's gestural orchestral music (admired by Wagner). At her first entrance, pursued by police, she explains the disaster that has befallen her (rape) to the sympathetic Elvire. She "answers" Elvire's question "What could have been your crime?" with gestures that convey that "she swears by heaven that she is not guilty." This "speech" Auber marks with a quartet of clarinets and bassoons, perhaps evoking the sound of an organ (the instrument of the church); then the first clarinet (in C) briefly flowers into melody. Fenella's more agitated "speeches" are underlined by a larger orchestra, with little privileging of woodwind. The following year, however, the clarinet is prominent at the first appearance of Matilda in Rossini's *Guillaume Tell*, its triplets being the most mobile orchestral "voice" in the introduction and her recitative ("Ils s'éloignent enfin"). The following Romance ("Sombre forêt") is colored by flutes and clarinets, sometimes doubled in octaves, in dialogue with the voice, but without oboes.[7]

In many of Gluck's operas, still in repertoire at the Paris Opéra in the 1820s and greatly admired by Berlioz, the favored solo woodwind was the oboe, sometimes in scenes evoking female distress or agitation (Iphigenia, Armida). When Orpheus meditates on the beauty of the Elysian Fields, the oboe represents his longed-for Eurydice. Gluck's oboe–female connotation remained part of Berlioz's aesthetic, and some examples from Gluck appear in his *Traité*. In his overture *Le roi Lear* (1831), separate oboe solos in the slow introduction and the Allegro are usually associated with Cordelia, and in his dramatic symphony *Roméo et Juliette* (1839) the solo oboe (second movement) seems to represent Romeo's image of the so far unattainable Juliet. Chronologically between these instances, Meyerbeer features a solo oboe in act 5 of *Les Huguenots* (p. 829) as the Protestant women sing of their distress.

---

6   Page references for *Les Huguenots* are to the first published score (Paris, 1836; repr. New York: Garland, 1980).

7   *Guillaume Tell* (Paris, 1829), 339. Full score: *Edizione critica delle opere di Gioachino Rossini*, vol. 2, ed. M. Elizabeth C. Bartlet (Pesaro: Fondazione Rossini, 1992), 564–73.

The feminine association lingered: a solo oboe (*piano, Ausdrucksvoll*) accompanies Eva's first words in act 3 of Wagner's *Die Meistersinger*.

However, nineteenth-century composers also used the clarinet in this way, strongly associated with female characters and sometimes also with males. In *Les Huguenots* a florid clarinet marks the first entry of the tenor, Raoul ("Sous ce beau ciel"), as he is politely received by a group of nobility now that Protestants and Catholics are (temporarily) at peace; an instrument in the tenor register (bassoon, horn) would not perhaps match so closely his appreciation of the favor he is receiving (ex. 5.1). But the feminine association is more apt as to register, and thus, perhaps, more persuasive when, in act 3, the clarinet introduces the unhappy Valentine (ex. 5.2)—a more florid solo than Weber or Berlioz would have written, covering a wide range, with trills two octaves apart. In act 4 as Raoul prepares to leave Valentine—before their mutual declaration of love—the clarinet perhaps represents her (p. 727). An interesting detail here is that during their rapturous duet, the first clarinet is pitched in B-flat, but despite the six flats (the key is G-flat) the second clarinet is pitched in A, enabling Meyerbeer to use it for a low dominant pitch (its written E sounds Db).

Berlioz's response to *Der Freischütz*, quoted above, suggests his equal willingness to make eloquent use of the clarinet, and not only the oboe, as an instrumental identifier or metaphor for a female character. In his early Rome Prize cantata *La mort d'Orphée* (1827), the clarinet offers a wistful memory after Orpheus (tenor) has died with the name "Euridice" on his lips. Much later, in act 1 of *Les Troyens* (composed 1856–59), the clarinet is associated with two unhappy Trojan women. Act 1, scene 2 is a monologue for the prophetess Cassandra, daughter of King Priam. In the recitative, like Meyerbeer and for the same reason, Berlioz changes the second clarinet to A, although the key signature is three flats (p. 35).[8] In her aria "Malheureux roi," a figure for the two clarinets in thirds (both now in B-flat) marks the point where her thoughts turn to her lover Chorœbus (p. 41). Then at her regretful farewell to dreams of love ("Plus de doux rêves de tendresse") the clarinets introduce a new melodic shape (p. 43, echoed by flutes, see ex. 5.3a); and they contribute to the expressive accompaniment in the following measures, with a delicate arpeggio to color the reprise (p. 44, see ex. 5.3b; the reprise is

---

8   *Les Troyens* was premiered as two operas, acts 3–5 in 1863 as *Les Troyens à Carthage*, acts 1–2 in 1879 as *La prise de Troie*. Berlioz's original intention (published as a vocal score, Paris: Choudens, 1863) is restored as a single five-act opera in *New Berlioz Edition*, vol. 2a–c, ed. Hugh Macdonald, through-paginated (Kassel: Bärenreiter, 1970), reprinted as a miniature score in one volume (Edition Eulenburg, no. 925 [1973]).

Example 5.1. Giacomo Meyerbeer, *Les Huguenots* Paris, Opéra, 1836), act 1. Full score (see n. 6), p. 41.

Example 5.2. Meyerbeer, *Les Huguenots*, act 2. Full score, p. 477.

Example 5.3. Hector Berlioz, *Les Troyens* (Paris, Théâtre Lyrique, 1863), act 1, no. 2 (in concert form, Paris, Cirque d'Hiver and Théâtre du Châtelet, 1879; see n. 8). Full score, *New Berlioz Edition*, vol. 2a: (a) p. 43, (b) p. 44.

(a)

(b)

in E-flat major, whereas the aria opened in the parallel minor). Clarinets and flutes in octaves reprise the motive of example 5.3a to begin the coda, where Cassandra's thoughts return to her lover, who immediately enters (p. 46).

One of the most remarkable of all operatic clarinet solos occupies a whole movement within the second tableau of *Les Troyens* (act 1, no. 6, "Pantomime," pp. 115–22). The solo clarinet in A plays in eighty-two of this movement's ninety-three measures, always as the principal voice, a veritable instrumental aria, representing Hector's lamenting widow Andromache, who is mute. The clarinet rests only for a short but imposing passage when the king and queen bless her child. In the central major-key section, the clarinet rises to E^6 above an enriched orchestral texture, the accompaniment having previously been by strings. The movement ends in a lower key than its opening (F-sharp minor rather than A minor). Perhaps for that reason, in the recapitulation (from m. 53), violins double the melody of the solo clarinet, which is lightly decorated. This doubling continues until the arching clarinet phrase rises alone, then falls over two octaves. In the coda the instrumental "voice" is almost unsupported; by exploiting its low register, playing a sighing semitone, this coda reflects the truth of Cassandra's grim prophecy, heard during the scene: "Alas! Keep back your tears, Hector's widow; you will need bitter ones for future sorrows."[9]

Like Meyerbeer, Berlioz also used the clarinet in connection with male voices. In act 5 of *Les Troyens*, two B-flat clarinets in parallel thirds take over the melody of the "Chanson d'Hylas" as the homesick Trojan sailor falls asleep (p. 600); clarinets in a more folksy vein open the comic duet for two Trojan sentries that follows (p. 615). But the female connection remained strong. Soon after Berlioz's *Troyens* was performed, in 1863, Ambroise Thomas opened the overture to his opéra-comique *Mignon* (1866) with a clarinet solo, which perhaps represents the (female) title role, and in his *Hamlet* (1868) he associated the clarinet with Ophelia.

---

9   "Hélas! Garde tes pleurs, veuve d'Hector ... A de prochains malheurs Tu dois bien des larmes amères."

Verdi and Wagner

One of the longest and most eloquent operatic clarinet solos of the nineteenth century appears in a crucial scene in Verdi's *La forza del destino* (1862; revised 1869). Verdi's orchestral writing in general, and his use of wind instruments in particular, developed to a remarkable degree during his long career (along with increasing harmonic subtlety). In *La forza del destino* there is again evidence to connect the clarinet with the principal female role. Discussing the well-known overture, Julian Budden points out that "unexpectedly a new theme is announced ... associated with Leonora."[10] It is on clarinet, in E major, and Leonora duly sings this melody in act 2, near the end of her duet with the Father Superior. Earlier in act 2 her *scena* brings back ideas from the overture, including another lyrical theme; after the aria, as she waits nervously for the Father Superior, calling on the protection of the Virgin Mary, this theme reappears on the clarinet over a string tremolo.

Act 3, in accordance with a convention used elsewhere by Verdi, begins with a short chorus followed by what Budden calls a "concertino" for clarinet, an Andante in ⅜ of over fifty measures, shorter than Berlioz's clarinet solo in *Les Troyens* but considerably more virtuosic.[11] This is not, however, a scene in mime; it stands alone as an instrumental interlude. But as the "concertino" ends, Alvaro (tenor) enters; in his recitative ("La vita è inferno all'infelice"), he thinks of his ruined life and of his beloved Leonora, whose father he has accidentally killed. Her name is framed by versions of the principal motive of the concertino, still on the clarinet.[12] The concertino itself ends with a lavish cadenza; it seems that the principal clarinetist in St. Petersburg, the opera house that commissioned *La forza del destino*, was a friend of Verdi (see also chapter 6 in this volume).

Like Berlioz and Verdi, Wagner used clarinet solos in association with female characters. There, perhaps, the resemblance ends, as his musical language is less dependent on extended melodies. In the overture to *Tannhäuser* (in which he used both A and C clarinets), the A clarinet contributes to the main motives of the "Venusberg" music, first with arpeggios (diminished sevenths, doubled by violas) rising to a phrase doubled by oboes, then on its own (ex. 5.4), a sinuous melody that

---

10 Julian Budden, *The Operas of Verdi*, vol. 2, *From "Il trovatore" to "La forza del destino"* (London: Cassell, 1978), 473.

11 Ibid., 477.

12 In the published vocal score (Milan: Ricordi, 1863), the "concertino" appears on pp. 176–77 and the recitative on p. 178.

Example 5.4. Richard Wagner, *Tannhäuser* (Dresden, Königliches Sächsisches Hoftheater, 1845), overture, mm. 195–204, within the second group of themes that prefigure the first scene (Venusberg) of act 1.

recurs within the first scene, sung by Venus herself ("Geliebte, komm! Sieh' dort die Grotte"); it is what Ernest Newman calls her "cajoling invocation" to Tannhäuser, in an attempt to keep him with her.[13]

The energetic opening of the prelude to act 3 of *Lohengrin* represents the wedding festivities of the Grail knight Lohengrin and Elsa of Brabant. But the wedding is ill-omened (a fact probably unknown to most of those who choose the famous march that follows for their nuptials). In an episode within the prelude, while the orchestra continues its bounding rhythms, albeit at a lower dynamic level, the A clarinet soars above, with chromatic inflections and extreme dynamic indications (ex. 5.5). Perhaps this anticipates the forthcoming agony of the unhappy Elsa, who cannot bear to lie with a man whose name she does not know.

Throughout his later operas, Wagner uses clarinet and bass clarinet resourcefully, in a variety of contexts. In act 1 of *Die Walküre* the burgeoning love of Siegmund and Sieglinde is evoked by new thematic material, the most tender music of the entire *Ring* cycle. It is introduced mainly by strings, but as Sieglinde hands her brother (as yet unrecognized) a draught of mead, a pair of A clarinets adopts the curving motive emblematic of their love. Then, following an intervention of horns, the first clarinet (*Sehr langsam*) gives forth a double version of their love motive (p. 33).[14] Later, when invited to explain himself to Hunding, Siegmund falls into a reverie; above the falling "Wälsung" motive two B-flat clarinets ascend sequentially on the curving motive, while the cycle's principal love motive passes to the oboe (p. 51).

---

13 Ernest Newman, *Wagner Nights* (London: Putnam, 1949), 69.

14 Page references for Wagner's later operas—the *Ring* cycle, *Tristan und Isolde, Die Meistersinger*, and *Parsifal*—are taken from the Eulenburg miniature scores.

Example 5.5. Wagner, *Lohengrin* (Weimar, Grossherzogliches Hoftheater, 1850), act 3, Vorspiel, mm. 75–79.

Wagner's affection for the clarinet was not necessarily greater than his feeling for other high woodwinds, but such eloquent instances may be found throughout his mature works. The clarinet among others imitates birdsong in act 2 of *Siegfried* (e.g., p. 573), in anticipation of the soprano voice of the suddenly articulate "Vogelstimme" (voice of the Forest Bird), which Siegfried understands thanks to his taste of dragon's blood. In 1876 the first audiences at Bayreuth would surely have recognized, as act 3 of *Götterdämmerung* began, that the music for three clarinets reintroduces the three Rhinemaidens, even though the theme at this point is new, not a direct reminiscence of their music in *Das Rheingold*. And in *Parsifal*, Kundry's seductive *Langsam* ("Gelobter Held!") contains ravishing solos, intertwined, for A clarinet and solo violin (pp. 247–53).

Russian Composers

Russian composers of the late nineteenth century are fully a match for their French and German contemporaries in the richness of their orchestral polyphony, and clarinetists in opera orchestras are among the beneficiaries of their imaginative and colorful scoring. The feminine association seems to remain: Nikolai Rimsky-Korsakov's orchestration treatise includes an example from his opera *The Snow Maiden* (*Snegurochka*; his example 8), in which the clarinet is associated with the maiden Kupava (ex. 5.6). As she is led across the stage as part of a wedding ritual, the first clarinet soars above the second clarinet, two bassoons, strings (upper strings pizzicato), and harp, with tenor-register cellos in nearly canonic imitation; as the clarinet descends, the other instruments stop abruptly, leaving the clarinet isolated.[15] Two other Russian operas make good case studies of very diverse characters,

---

15 Nikolai Rimsky-Korsakov, *Principles of Orchestration with Musical Examples Drawn from His Own Works*, ed. Maximilian Steinberg, trans.

Example 5.6. Rimsky-Korsakov, *The Snow Maiden* (St. Petersburg, Mariinsky Theater, 1882). Rimsky-Korsakov, *Principles of Orchestration*, vol. 2, ex. 8.

in which composers have used the clarinet in a variety of ways, often, though not exclusively, in association with female characters.

Alexander Borodin, Prince Igor (Knyaz' Igor')

The orchestral score of *Prince Igor* is complicated by the fact that Borodin died before fully completing it.[16] The overture was not notated by him, but written down after his death by Alexander Glazunov, from his memory of Borodin's piano playing. It is possible, even likely, however, that Borodin gave indications of his orchestral intentions including, perhaps, introducing a new theme on the A clarinet (at rehearsal letter C, from m. 87); this solo of fifteen measures is recalled more briefly at letter S. At letter Q, the cellos recapitulate another theme, first heard on the horn, to the accompaniment of rippling arpeggios from the first clarinet.

For the most part, the resourceful and imaginative clarinet writing in *Prince Igor* exploits the upper range of the instrument, and can be associated with the composer's preoccupation with Russian folk music and the depiction of the Polovtsian Khan; the exoticism of some of this material anticipates Richard Strauss's use of the instrument in *Salome*. In practice, all higher woodwind instruments are likely to be involved in the evocation of the Orient; for example, in the dances

---

Edward Agate, 2 vols. (Berlin, Moscow, and Leipzig: Éditions Russe de Musique, [1922]); the music examples form the second volume.

16　Page references are to the published score in two volumes, separately paginated (Leipzig: Belaieff, 1889). Attributions of orchestration are taken from this score. Richard Taruskin notes that Rimsky-Korsakov was already assisting Borodin from 1879, himself assisted initially by Anatoly Liadov, then by Glazunov; see Taruskin, "Prince Igor," *The New Grove Dictionary of Opera*, ed. Stanley Sadie (London: Macmillan, 1992), 3:1098–1102.

from Saint-Saëns's *Samson et Dalila* (1877) flutes and double reeds are especially prominent. The clarinet writing in the Borodin opera could have been affected by the folk instruments of central Asia.[17] This is especially so in act 2, which is set in the Polovtsian camp. The high solo in no. 8 ("Dance of the Polovtsian Maidens") comes in a section orchestrated by Rimsky-Korsakov, as do the rhapsodic solos in later numbers. The familiar sequence of Polovtsian dances, however, was orchestrated by Borodin himself. He chose the clarinet for the prominent solo at the start of the sequence, soon passed to the oboe. The sequence includes other solos, the dance in $\frac{6}{8}$ having the clarinet in dialogue with the oboe. Nevertheless, there are still reasons to infer an association of the instrument with the female voice. The solo in no. 9 is folkloric, even (vol. 2, p. 31; ex. 5.7); the singer is the Polovtsian maiden Konchacovna, who anticipates meeting her lover Vladimir. The following love duet (no. 12) includes a brilliant clarinet cadenza (vol. 2, p. 83). These are both Rimsky-Korsakov orchestrations; he was later to compose still more virtuosic clarinet music in his own *The Golden Cockerel* (performed 1909; the clarinet already takes the characteristic chromatic motive in the introduction to act 1). In the final act of *Prince Igor*, no. 25, in Borodin's own orchestration, the clarinet plays in dialogue with the voice as Igor's wife Yaroslavna laments his supposed death in war (ex. 5.8); this aria includes the vocal version of the lyrical theme presented in the overture by horn and cellos.

Tchaikovsky, The Queen of Spades (Pikovaya dama)

For Tchaikovsky, the association of clarinet and female lead singer remains, but is not automatic. An early example is in the act 1 soprano aria in *Vakula the Smith* (*Kuznets Vakula*, 1874). A good many striking uses of the instrument mentioned below are associated with the central figure in *The Queen of Spades*, Hermann. He is, admittedly, often thinking of his beloved Lisa; but equally often he is obsessed with the possibility of winning a fortune by gambling on the Countess's "three cards." One might have expected more from the clarinet in Tatiana's "letter scene" in act 1 of *Eugene Onegin* (1878); rather than playing a solo love theme (as in his fantasy-overture *Francesca da Rimini*, of the same year), it merely echoes the voice for six notes, and is otherwise

---

17   Janet Page refers to "the *balaban* of the Uzbek and Tadjik peoples." See Janet K. Page et al., "Clarinet," *The New Grove Dictionary of Music and Musicians*, 2nd ed., ed. Stanley Sadie and John Tyrrell (London: Macmillan, 2001), 5:895.

Example 5.7. Borodin, *Prince Igor* (St. Petersburg, Mariinsky Theater, 1890), act 2, no. 9 (orchestrated by Rimsky-Korsakov). Full score (see n. 16), vol. 2:31.

Example 5.8. Borodin, *Prince Igor* (1890), act 4, no. 25. Full score, vol. 2:365–68.

less prominent than the oboe, or is heard in the familiar doubling, an octave below the flute. *The Queen of Spades,* however, provides an object-lesson in resourceful use of the clarinet, which may be roughly divided into categories:

1 Independent counterpoint, often against the strings, the other woodwinds not active.
2 Participation in the woodwind choir.
3 As a soloist, including passages that might have been used in a concertante work.
4 Unusual expressive use of the "weak" middle register around the break.

Category 1, independent counterpoint, occurs in the orchestral introduction. The first measures of act 1 (scene 1, p. 13)[18] are a falling figure in the violins, one of the many such descending patterns associated by David Brown with "fate."[19] Beneath this, two A clarinets in unison play a counterpoint over a string bass pedal. Although not an

---

18 Page references for *The Queen of Spades* are to the full score (Moscow: Musyka, 1983).
19 David Brown, *Tchaikovsky: A Biographical and Critical Study,* vol. 4, *The Final Years* (London: Gollancz, 1991), 259–62.

obviously tragic gesture, this curious texture strikes an ominous note. A similar texture appears in the third scene. The clarinets change to B-flat and offer a flowing sixteenth-note counterpoint in their lowest register (p. 19). Later in this scene, a solo clarinet sustains below string filigree and repeated eighth-note chords in the horns (p. 77). Near the end of this scene, a variant of the opening violin figure twice recurs, but on the clarinet, descending from B^5, then from C^6. Similar independence of the clarinets within a texture is represented by expressive accompaniment figures such as the one when Lisa enters, agitated, in act 2, scene 3 (p. 328), when the clarinet part is strikingly like a passage in Rimsky-Korsakov's *Scheherazade*. As the Countess thinks of past times (scene 4), prior to singing a melody (by Grétry) ostensibly remembered from her youth, the clarinet has a strange figure (a half note followed by a rapid "tuplet" of nine sixteenth notes, in a low register); this comes eleven times, like an obsession (pp. 381–82).

In Tchaikovsky's orchestral palette, the clarinet often performs the serviceable function of providing the middle of the harmonically controlled texture (category 2). There are some unison melodies and octave doublings; indeed, the orchestral introduction to act 1 begins with clarinet and bassoon in octaves (p. 1). In act 1, scene 2 (p. 192) there is an actual unison of clarinet and bassoon, which is then reiterated, this time in double octaves, flute, clarinet, and bassoon. Tchaikovsky's charming evocation of an early eighteenth-century pastoral does not imitate the eighteenth-century sound of that courtly genre; instead, clarinets lead the dance of shepherds and shepherdesses, evoking an ancestral folk instrument (act 2, scene 3; p. 281). A strange sonority is created in scene 4 (p. 361), with A clarinets in thirds, doubled an octave *below* by oboes, and partnered with bassoons, also in thirds but in contrary motion. In the penultimate scene (act 3, scene 6), Lisa's arioso is introduced by a woodwind quartet (two each of clarinets and bassoons, from p. 465).

Category 3, concertante work, appears in a rippling clarinet accompaniment to Hermann's first solo (but with a feminine association; he is thinking of his unknown beloved); it rises, concerto-like, into the high register (pp. 51–53). If one were to assume that the characters in an opera can hear the orchestra, this ebullience might explain his friend Tomsky's cynical response to Hermann's uncharacteristic behavior. In act 1, scene 2, with Laura and her friends in the garden, the female singers are orchestrally colored by flutes rather than clarinets or oboes (shades, perhaps, of the first finale of *Così fan tutte*), but the passage is punctuated by a lovely B-flat clarinet phrase (ex. 5.9). In the

Example 5.9. Tchaikovsky, *The Queen of Spades* (St. Petersburg, Mariinsky Theater, 1890), act 1, scene 2. Full score (see n. 18), pp. 141, 143.

same scene, Pauline's Romanza involves clarinet, but Lisa's more intro-spective solo is colored by English horn, then oboe. When the Count-ess enters, in angry mood, the clarinet has a swooping descent over two octaves; and when Hermann appears, the B-flat clarinet reflects his agitation with sextuplets grouped in fours, going across the beat (ex. 5.10). The Countess calls, and two clarinets in parallel thirds sweep up over two octaves, with crescendo. The motivic shapes in this passage are a diminution of the characteristic figure associated with her "three cards" (pp. 200–201). When Lisa is alone, in act 3, scene 5, sixteen concertante-like measures of clarinet scales and arpeggios may reflect the cause of her suffering: Hermann has not come to meet her, despite being forgiven (by letter) for causing the death of the Countess (pp. 476–79, repeated on pp. 496–08).

The fourth category, unusual use of the "weak" middle register below the break, reveals Tchaikovsky's complete understanding of its expressive potential; taking over from the more robust English horn, the clarinet (here in A) moves around the break in a manner that a pedantic orchestration teacher might suggest should be avoided, but which in this context sounds an appropriate note of pathos; Her-mann's death, as he recalls his love for Lisa, coincides with the end of this passage (ex. 5.11).

Puccini

Associating the clarinet with the heroine's problems is apparent in the operas of Giacomo Puccini; my examples are mostly from *Tosca* (1900). In act 1 the painter Cavaradossi sings of the unknown lady, some of whose features he has incorporated into a painting ("A te, bella ignota"). But his thoughts are of his lover, the singer Floria Tosca, who has also contributed to his composite "portrait" of the Madonna. He sings in unison with the cellos, doubled by clarinet an octave

Example 5.10. Tchaikovsky, *The Queen of Spades*, act 1, scene 2. Full score, p. 185.

Example 5.11. Tchaikovsky, *The Queen of Spades*, act 3, scene 7. Full score, pp. 603–5.

higher (after fig. 18, p. 26).[20] When Tosca herself appears, the clarinet is again in an octave partnership, this time with bassoon, and in unison with Tosca herself; the passage is marked *dolce* (p. 37). Near the end of the act, the villainous Scarpia is also thinking of her ("Tosca è un buon falco"), and the A clarinet has a short solo, again marked *dolce* (p. 192).

The final act opens with a song for a shepherd, for which Puccini used the traditionally pastoral flutes. Cavaradossi is led in by guards who leave him alone prior to his execution. Low clarinets turn the pastoral atmosphere into something more ominous; the principal melody of his aria is anticipated by the strings, and may suggest where his thoughts are turning, for he expects never to see his beloved Tosca again. At the opening of the aria itself ("E lucevan le stelle"), he delivers the words on a monotone; all the musical eloquence of the aria's principal melody is heard from a solo clarinet. It is this phrase that notoriously recurs at the very end of the opera – notoriously because Joseph Kerman says of this reprise that "the orchestra screams the first

---

20 References to Puccini operas are to the full scores (*Tosca*, 1899, *Madama Butterfly*, 1906, also in smaller format: Milan: Ricordi).

thing that comes into its head."[21] The melody is irrelevant, Kerman suggests, because the aria about self-pity rather than love. But a person about to be shot, especially one whose "crime" is his love of liberty, may be permitted a degree of self-pity; moreover, this arises from memories of his love for Tosca. Kerman adds that Tosca never heard this melody. Again, that question is too wide to address here: do operatic characters hear the orchestra? If they do not, Kerman's point seems meaningless; and in any case the earlier appearance of the melody of "E lucevan le stelle" on the instrumental timbre nearest to the soprano voice identifies it with Tosca. The orchestra addresses the audience; as she jumps to her death, the brutal reprise of a tender clarinet melody reflects the tragic failure of her attempt to save her lover. Puccini's association of the clarinet with a woman continued in *Madama Butterfly*. In act 2, when Sharpless, whom she has not yet seen, addresses her as "Madam Butterfly" she corrects him ("Madam Pinkerton"), to a lyrical moment on the clarinet which, as she turns and realizes that this distinguished visitor may have news of her husband, reflects a moment of embarrassment by mutating into fluttering arpeggios (p. 242).

I conclude that standard (A and B-flat) clarinets played a major role in supporting the presentation of rounded female characterizations throughout the nineteenth century. The instrument's cantabile register matches the tessitura of the soprano and mezzo-soprano, so it can be used as a substitute for the voice of a silent character (Andromache in *Les Troyens*) or a character not present on stage (Lisa, Tosca) when the singer is a male. It also serves to introduce voices in the same range (for this the Rhinemaidens of *Götterdämmerung* provide a particularly ravishing example), and as a partner in dialogue with a soprano or mezzo-soprano voice.

Clarinets in Ensemble

In his orchestration treatise, illustrated entirely with his own music, Rimsky-Korsakov concentrates on ensemble writing; he implies that as woodwind solos are heard all the time, they are not an orchestration problem.[22] Instead, he turns his attention to combinations of instruments, with examples where the clarinet plays in unison with violas or an oboe, or in octaves with a flute. Some instances of the

---

21 Kerman, *Opera as Drama*, 15.
22 Rimsky-Korsakov, *Principles of Orchestration*, 1:5 and passim.

latter combination have been mentioned already; to them may be added the introduction to act 4 of Georges Bizet's *Carmen*, where the frenetic atmosphere prior to the scene by the bullring is colored not only by percussion but by a doubling of piccolo and clarinet, *two* octaves apart (pp. 478–80).[23]

The use of clarinets in ensembles has inevitably been touched upon in the more detailed studies above. Particularly telling is the use of the clarinet as the highest instrument in a generally low-pitched ensemble. In nineteenth-century orchestration, woodwind combinations are ubiquitous; but sometimes the ensemble has a special coloring achieved by omitting the higher instruments (flute, oboe), leaving the clarinet on top of the texture (one such example has been mentioned already, in act 2, scene 4 of *The Queen of Spades*). Félicien David in *Herculanum* (1859), an opera that has recently received its first recording, uses the clarinet resourcefully in many ways. In Hélios's aria "Je veux aimer toujours" (I want to be in love forever) it is employed as a soft accompaniment, and it participates with flute and English horn in dialogue with the voice (p. 136).[24] Wagner, throughout the *Ring* cycle, with three clarinets and bass clarinet, was able to embed clarinet tone in such rich textures as the introduction to Siegmund's "Spring Song" (*Die Walküre*, p. 150, "Winterstürme wichen dem Wonnemond").

Woodwind groupings are prominent in certain distinct characterizations, for which a light staccato attack is often required. Stravinsky tells us that "at the beginning of my career the clarinet was considered incapable of long fast-tongue passages." This seems surprising, although founded on his memory of a clarinetist who objected to such a passage in his orchestration of *Les sylphides* ("Monsieur, ce n'est pas une musique pour la clarinette.").[25] At least from Weber's *Oberon* (1826), fast, light clarinet staccato in varied woodwind combinations had been a resource for composers in music intended to suggest fairies or other fantastical beings. Following Berlioz ("Queen Mab" in *Roméo et Juliette*) and Mendelssohn (Scherzo from the incidental music to *A Midsummer Night's Dream*), this articulation features for the false fairies in Otto Nicolai's *Die lustigen Weiber von Windsor*

---

23 Page references for *Carmen* are to the full score (Leipzig: Peters, n.d.; repr. New York: Dover, 1989).

24 Page references to *Herculanum* are from the published score (Paris: Michel Lévy Frères, 1859). I am indebted to Ralph Locke for access to this edition.

25 Igor Stravinsky and Robert Craft, *Conversations with Igor Stravinsky* (London: Faber & Faber, 1959), 30.

(1849; overture and final act, the tormenting of Falstaff). In act 4 of *Les Troyens* the symphonic interlude ("Chasse royale et Orage") requires fast staccato from all woodwinds for the hunting music (p. 449) and the approaching storm (p. 453). Exquisite use of oboe and clarinet solos in David's *Lalla Roukh* (1862) evokes what Ralph Locke describes as "an imaginary world not far from fairy tale."[26] Without any supernatural connotation, the clarinet staccato was also employed by Puccini in *Tosca* (pp. 153–54).

It seems that composers find clarinet tone, often in close collaboration with other instruments, to be particularly useful in introductory material; some of the gloomier examples are mentioned in the next section. A good instance, admittedly evoking the atmosphere of a dark and mysterious forest in which the characters are lost, opens Debussy's *Pelléas et Mélisande*; from measure 5, a motive associated with Golaud is presented by a reed ensemble: two oboes, English horn, and two clarinets. These are also important in the coloring of Golaud's entry (pp. 5–6).[27]

The Clarinet as Somber Color: The Low Register

Berlioz's instrumentation treatise points to the value of the clarinet's lowest register for dark colors. Again, the paradigmatic examples are from *Der Freischütz*: in the overture, with string tremolo from measure 30; in Max's aria "Durch die Wälder" when he thinks heaven has abandoned him; and elsewhere in connection with the demon Samiel. In David's *Herculanum*, as Hélios kneels before Olympia, she, like Mephistopheles in Berlioz's *Faust*, sings "Il m'appartient, il est à nous"; the low clarinet above two bassoons, sustained, forms a somber background (p. 135).

The low clarinet does not always evoke evil, however. In the prelude to *Les Huguenots* it is used (as, perhaps, in *La muette de Portici*: see above) as a substitute for the organ. In a relatively low register, it takes the melody in a woodwind group for the exposition of the archetypical Protestant chorale *Ein feste Burg* that recurs throughout the opera. In act 5, as tragedy looms, low clarinets are more ominous, this time, strikingly, an octave below the first bassoon (p. 809). Both these instances

---

26 From a pre-performance talk at Lincoln Center, communicated to me by Professor Locke, to whom, again, my thanks.

27 Page references are to the orchestral score (Paris: Durand, 1905); repr. as miniature score (New York: International Music Company, 1962).

seem to foretell the final slaughter of the Protestants. Weber's sinister use of the lowest clarinet register is taken up by Wagner in the fourth scene of *Das Rheingold*. A throbbing rhythmic motive on three clarinets accompanies Alberich as, freed from his bonds, he prepares to curse the ring (p. 363). This motive recurs, like the "curse" motive itself, throughout the remainder of the *Ring* cycle. In *Carmen*, the clarinet is heard in the orchestral prelude, with bassoons, coloring the first hearing of the sinister motive, with its augmented intervals, that foretells the tragedy to come (pp. 14–16). The motive recurs, with varied instrumentation, throughout the opera; when Carmen throws her flower to José, a moment that seals their fate, the clarinet is the only woodwind doubling violas and cellos (p. 98). The lowest note of the B-flat clarinet (sounding D), for Winton Dean, "points Carmen's amazed anger when José says he must answer the recall to barracks."[28] In discussing the same passage, Susan McClary notes that *Der Freischütz* was "one of Bizet's favorite works."[29] Throughout *Carmen*, Bizet deploys the clarinet with a skill and imagination not inferior to Tchaikovsky's; the confrontation of lovesick José and Carmen in act 2 makes much use of soft arpeggios (responding to the harp in the "Flower Song"). The clarinet's military associations mark the entr'acte before act 2, when it takes over the lively tune first heard on bassoon; in the next entr'acte clarinet and flute join in a duet. Bizet has a fondness for doubling clarinets and cellos, and makes further telling use of the low register when Michaela tells José that his mother is dying (p. 471). In *Tosca*, the hollow middle- and low-register clarinets color the entry of the terrified Angelotti (p. 3), in chords with viola and bassoon, and with scalar flickers that could have been chromatic scales but that they might accidentally have seemed to quote the "Dies irae" of Verdi's Requiem.

Other Clarinets High and Low

Early uses of the bass clarinet in French operas mark points of crisis, and this is the case with much other nineteenth-century usage. The bass clarinet was improved in reliability and flexibility through the ingenuity of Adolphe Sax (1814–94). However, for the famous bass clarinet solo in act 5 of *Les Huguenots* Meyerbeer must have used an older model, as

---

28 Winton Dean, *Georges Bizet: His Life and Work* (London: J. M. Dent, 1965), 235.

29 Susan McClary, *Georges Bizet: Carmen* (Cambridge: Cambridge University Press, 1992), 66.

Sax patented his improvements only in 1838, before moving to Paris. The instrument was so unusual that the full score contains an explanation of the notation (p. 847); Meyerbeer used the treble clef convention, which offers identical fingering to the clarinetist but, as the footnote explains, sounds an octave lower. In the final act, while the severe Huguenot elder Marcel interrogates the young lovers on their faith before presiding over their marriage (all three die in the ensuing massacre), the orchestra is silenced and the only instrumental voice for forty-six measures is the bass clarinet. Berlioz praised this scene in his 1836 review: "the low sounds of the bass clarinet, filled with sadness, are the sole accompaniment for the voice of Marcel; this very orchestral silence also contributes, giving the musical character of the scene something of an air of unexpected grandeur and solemnity."[30] A few years later Berlioz quoted the scene in his orchestration treatise (1844). The 1836 full score (ex. 5.12) differs in several particulars from the version in Berlioz's treatise, which alters certain rhythmic values and excludes the highest notes, despite the fact that by this time the Paris Opéra had acquired one of Sax's instruments.[31] A few measures later, in a direction absent from the 1836 score, the version Berlioz used invites the bass clarinet, like the clarinet earlier in the opera, to "imitate the voice" (that of Marcel, a bass). The bass clarinet also plays a role in the Huguenot martyrs' vision of heaven, evoked by contrary-motion arpeggios of clarinet and bass clarinet (p. 857).

Berlioz himself used the bass clarinet only in dramatic works, selectively and to telling effect. In *Benvenuto Cellini* (1838) it adds gravitas to the music for the Pope, first in the overture at measure 67 (p. 73), then when the Pope finally appears (p. 853).[32] In his operas Berlioz used only two clarinet players, one of them doubling on bass. However, in

---

30 "les sons graves et pleins de tristesse de la clarinette basse, seul accompagnement du chant de Marcel; ce silence même de l'orchestre, tout contribue à donner à l'ensemble musical de cette scène quelque chose de grandiose et d'imprévu dans sa solennité." Hector Berlioz, *Critique musicale 1823–1863*, vols. 1–6, ed. H. Robert Cohen, Yves Gérard, et al. (Paris: Buchet/Chastel, 1996–2008), 2:437.

31 Berlioz, *Grand traité d'instrumentation et d'orchestration modernes*, ed. Bloom, 216–18. Different editions of the treatise (including English translations) contain differences of note values, phrasing, and dynamics, perhaps because Berlioz consulted a vocal score or notated the passage from memory.

32 Page references for *Benvenuto Cellini* are to *New Berlioz Edition*, vol. 1a–c, ed. Hugh Macdonald, through-paginated (Kassel: Bärenreiter, 1994–96).

Example 5.12. Meyerbeer, *Les Huguenots*, act 5, scene 2. Full score, p. 847.

La damnation de Faust (1846)—a "dramatic legend" intended for concert performance rather than strictly an opera, but frequently staged—he has three players, the third taking only the relatively short bass clarinet part. The instrument first appears in part 3, to add weight to the near-atonal wind unison that opens Mephistopheles's "Évocation des follets" (p. 273).[33] In the refrain of the sinister "Menuet des follets" (Minuet of will-o'-the-wisps) that follows, it contributes to the devilish sonority by playing, alone, an octave below the second bassoons and fourth horn. It reappears in part 4 to develop a significant motive during the grotesque "Course à l'abîme" ("Ride to the abyss," pp. 413–14), and it is used in the "Pandaemonium"—but not in the final scene in heaven, for which Berlioz at one point proposed using two saxophones (the idea was abandoned, and the staves visible in the autograph are blank).

Berlioz's most eloquent use of bass clarinet is in *Les Troyens*, again at points of crisis. The instrument is withheld until the final act. When ghosts order Aeneas's departure from Carthage (p. 639), the bass clarinet is the root, without bassoons, of a woodwind chord in which most of the instruments employ their lower registers. The bass clarinet's contribution, its lowest G (sounding F), lies a full tenth below the next pitch (English horn, sounding A♭; the other instruments are clarinet, oboe, and two flutes). After Aeneas leaves, Dido realizes that her rage is futile, and she must die (p. 701). As she summons the priests of Pluto, god of the underworld, the bass clarinet signals a change of atmosphere (although when these priests appear, in the final tableau, the bass clarinet is not used). Again, there are no bassoons in

---

33 Page references for *La damnation de Faust* are to *New Berlioz Edition*, vol. 8a, ed. Julian Rushton (Kassel: Bärenreiter, 1979).

these ominous harmonies, the hollow sound of the bass clarinet prov-
ing more evocative in that register. When Dido sings "I am going to
die" ("Je vais mourir") the bass clarinet is given its own motive (p. 706)
which is then developed, to emerge from the texture in an arpeggio of
over two octaves, recalling the solo in *Les Huguenots* (ex. 5.13). It continues as the lowest wind instrument almost throughout the moving
Gluck-like serenity of the Carthaginian queen's acceptance of death,
her aria "Adieu, fière cité" ("Farewell, proud city").

Verdi also used the bass clarinet to add ominous coloring to the
orchestra in the final act of *La forza del destino*, as Leonora, murdered
by her dying brother Carlo, is dying in her turn. But this is not a solo
like example 5.13, or the solo that appears in another great work of the
1850s, Wagner's *Tristan und Isolde*. Like Berlioz with the English horn,
Wagner, in later works other than *Die Meistersinger*, adopts the bass clarinet as a standard part of his orchestral lineup, rather than withhold-
ing it for special effect. His bass clarinet parts are therefore designed
for a specialist, rather than being given to one of the regular clarinetists. In the *Ring* cycle, the bass is the first member of the clarinet family
to play (prelude to *Das Rheingold*, p. 4), though only as an additional
sustaining instrument, and it is often used in that capacity. But if the
clarinet suggests a female character, the bass clarinet logically suggests
a male. Fully aware as he was of Meyerbeer's *Les Huguenots*, Wagner
gives the bass clarinet one of the longest solos in its entire repertoire
in act 2 of *Tristan und Isolde*, accompanying the opera's lowest voice-
type: bass (King Mark). Wagner specified bass clarinet in A, an instrument that hardly any players or opera houses nowadays possess. The
prevailing tonality in this scene, however, is D minor, and although the
music modulates widely the solo is perhaps hardly more awkward to
play on the B-flat instrument; and, whereas with clarinets in C, B-flat,
and A the timbral differences, while less marked with the latter pair,
are often perceptible and affect a player's approach, this distinction is
unlikely to be noticeable with the B-flat bass clarinet which, moreover,
routinely extends the standard range by at least a semitone to (written) low E♭ or lower to C, reaching the lowest note of the bassoon.

The bass clarinet solo in *Tristan* comes in the long sequel to the
great love scene, its bass-baritone register matching Mark's tender
reproaches. It introduces the gravely descending opening motive
that precedes his first words (p. 673), which are in a Wagnerian kind
of recitative. A new, more passionate motive (p. 678) introduces
what amounts to the betrayed king's aria. As Mark's speech reaches
its climax, Wagner follows Meyerbeer by introducing sixteenth-note

Example 5.13. Berlioz, *Les Troyens*, act 5, no. 47. Full score, *New Berlioz Edition*, 2b:707.

ascending arpeggios (pp. 687–88), although these are not solos emerging from the texture, but fill it out, in unison with the cellos.

Meyerbeer's fluid writing for the bass clarinet perhaps also impressed Rimsky-Korsakov, who made use of its agile capabilities in *The Snow Maiden* at figure 243.[34] Like Berlioz in *Les Troyens*, Tchaikovsky in *The Queen of Spades* reserved the bass clarinet for scenes where the drama darkens, though its first appearance (requiring a third player) accompanies the Countess's grumbling in scene 4 (p. 377). The bass clarinet is prominent in the fatal third act. Following a convention in opera that letters are spoken rather than sung, it plays alone, to accompany Hermann reading Lisa's letter of forgiveness, a solo less extended than Meyerbeer's equally isolated solo, but no less poignant (ex. 5.14). In act 3, scene 6, Hermann, believing himself reconciled to Lisa, announces that he must go to the gaming tables, a decision that leads to her despair and suicide. At this point, the bass clarinet adopts the kind of role previously taken by clarinets (see above), an independent counterpoint of accented triplets, over ten measures with scanty support from the bassoons, one of the darkest colors in this opera. Darker still is Puccini's *verismo* one-act *Il tabarro*; the bass clarinet contributes to the somber atmosphere of the opening. But the instrument's depth also has the simple function of extending clarinet tone downward, as in the parallel chords of the orchestral introduction to Ravel's *L'heure espagnole* (1911), where the bass clarinet joins as an equal in swooping arpeggios, a fantastic sonority with flutes, clarinets, strings, and harp glissando (p. 73).[35]

Among other members of the clarinet family, Berlioz's celebrated use of the E-flat clarinet in his "Dream of a Witches' Sabbath" (*Symphonie fantastique*, final movement: "Songe d'une nuit de Sabbat") forms an

---

34 Example 47 in Rimsky-Korsakov, *Principles of Orchestration*, 2:47.
35 Page references for Ravel's *L'heure espagnole* are to the (miniature) orchestral score (Paris: Durand, 1932).

Example 5.14. Tchaikovsky, *The Queen of Spades*, act 3, scene 5.

element in his bold transfer of scenic elements into the concert hall. The second clarinet, in C, is the first to play the cruelly distorted form of the "idée fixe"; then the E-flat clarinet gives it in full. Just so might an opera composer represent the imminent presence, and then the entry, of a principal character, in this case the artist's beloved, transformed into a witch. But this instrument was otherwise little used in the nineteenth century (Mahler's use of it in his first two symphonies is generally attributed to Berlioz's example rather than to Mahler's experience as an opera conductor); and in the twentieth century, despite a possible temptation to use the E-flat instrument, Ravel introduces his cat duet (*L'enfant et les sortilèges*, p. 125) with arpeggios from B-flat clarinets.

The C clarinet was a standard part of the nineteenth-century clarinetist's equipment; the modern practice of transposing, to play its part on a B-flat clarinet, undoubtedly loses some of the variety of color presumably intended by composers such as Smetana, whose pastoral comedy *The Bartered Bride* (*Prodana nevěsta*, 1866) is scored for C clarinet in several movements, including the well-known overture. Dealing with three instruments is not easy, and composers were not always as considerate as they might have been. David, in *Herculanum*, requires the first clarinet, who has recently been playing on the instrument in C, and then on the B-flat, to change again to A for an exposed and florid passage in a new tempo and meter (ex. 5.15); however, there is time to change earlier and use the A clarinet, transposing up a semitone the simple held notes that precede the Air.

In *Salome* (1905), Richard Strauss continued the tradition of associating clarinet themes with a principal female character, in this case the title role and (as in *Tannhäuser*) a *femme fatale*. Strauss then revived a member of the family beloved of Mozart, intermediate between

Example 5.15. Félicien David, *Herculanum* (Paris, Opéra, 1859). Full score (see n. 24), p. 78.

clarinet and bass clarinet: the basset horn, which he deployed within an enlarged clarinet ensemble in *Elektra* (1909) and *Der Rosenkavalier* (1911). In this same period (closing the "long" nineteenth century) Arnold Schoenberg's one-act operas *Erwartung* (1909) and *Die glückliche Hand* (1913) each require five clarinetists: three regular clarinets, "little" clarinet (in D), and bass clarinet. Shortly after this, Schoenberg began to implement his radical suggestion that orchestras might include a "section" of clarinets, as do wind orchestras (the first of his songs op. 22, composed 1913–16, requires six clarinets playing in unison as well as in harmony; the third song requires three bass clarinets and contrabass clarinet). In practice, economic conditions meant that such visions of a reformed orchestra, in effect combining the standard wind band with the traditional string-based orchestral ensemble, could not be realized. Nevertheless, the clarinet alongside its increasingly prominent cousin the saxophone continued to play major roles in dramatic coloring in operas by composers who matured before World War I, for instance the later Strauss operas, the operas of Franz Schreker, Schoenberg's *Von heute auf morgen*, and Alban Berg's *Lulu*.

6

INNOVATION AND CONVENTION IN THE GOLDEN AGE OF THE CLARINET CONCERTO, CA. 1800–1830

David E. Schneider

In 1869 the renowned Viennese critic Eduard Hanslick recognized that the funeral knell for concertos for woodwinds had long since begun to toll: "At the present time, the piano and violin almost exclusively occupy the field of solo virtuosity. Other than these, only the violoncello makes an occasional appearance. Concertos for wind instruments, which used to be so popular, have been on the verge of extinction for the past 20 years."[1] Indeed, the mid- to late nineteenth century, which saw the production of many of the most beloved concertos in the piano and violin repertoires by the likes of Mendelssohn, Schumann, Brahms, Saint-Saëns, Tchaikovsky, and Dvořák, was virtually barren of the production of concertos for woodwinds. Between 1830 and 1900 no major composer wrote a clarinet concerto, and the few concertos written for the instrument in this time period have not found a secure place in the repertoire.[2] As Hanslick indicates, this long dry stretch followed

---

1   Eduard Hanslick, *Geschichte des Concertwesens in Wien* (Vienna: Wilhelm Braumüller, 1869), 418–19. Translations in this chapter are mine unless otherwise noted.

2   Nikolai Rimsky-Korsakov's short Concerto for Clarinet and Military Band (1878) is the only clarinet concerto written by a well-known composer in the period 1830–1900. This short work, which lacks substantial ritornelli and places only modest technical demands on the solo clarinet, is more properly a concertino than a concerto.

a period rich in wind concertos. In the first three decades of the nine-teenth century the clarinet concerto in particular occupied an impor-tant position in the output of some of the leading composers of the day. The years from 1800 to 1830 saw the composition of a generous handful of clarinet concertos by major composers and several dozen more by less renowned composers—many of which are artistically satisfying, and all of which are useful for understanding the conventions of the genre.

The present chapter grows out of an examination of some thirty-two clarinet concertos beginning with Mozart's Concerto in A Major, K. 622 (1791) and ending with the Concerto in G Minor, op. 29 (1854), by Julius Rietz. The two leading composers of clarinet concertos after Mozart in this period, Carl Maria von Weber (1786–1826) and Louis Spohr (1784–1859), wrote their concertos for the two most promi-nent clarinet virtuosi of the day: Heinrich Baermann (1784–1847) and Johann Simon Hermstedt (1778–1846), respectively. The third most important composer of clarinet concertos in this period, Bernhard Henrik Crusell (1775–1838), a Swede of Finnish origin, was the most sophisticated composer among the clarinet virtuosi who also composed for their instrument. Other important clarinet virtuosi-*cum*-composers included Baermann's, Crusell's, and Hermstedt's teacher Franz Tausch (1762–1817) in Berlin, whose career had begun as a clarinetist in the Mannheim orchestra of Mozart's day; Baermann himself; the German J. G. H. Backofen (1768–1839); and the Estonian-born German Iwan Müller (1786–1854), active in Russia, Germany, and France, who was responsible for important innovations in the clarinet's construction.

A general craze for virtuoso wind players was evident already in the last decade or two of the eighteenth century, when their number exceeded that of solo violinists and pianists in Vienna for several decades.[3] The clarinet, the woodwind considered best able to imitate the human voice, seems to have been particularly favored, surpassing the oboe in popularity both as a solo instrument and as the primary instrument in military bands.[4] Indeed, the large number of clarinetists required by the military provided a robust pool of talent, from whose ranks extraordinary

---

3   Oskar Kroll, *The Clarinet*, rev. Diethard Riehm, trans. Hilda Morris, ed. Anthony Baines (New York: Taplinger Publishing Co., 1968), 68.

4   Documentary evidence of the clarinet overtaking the oboe's reputa-tion as the instrument best able to imitate the human voice in the years around 1800 is given in Kurt Birsak, *The Clarinet: A Cultural History*, trans. Gail Schamberger (Buchloe: Obermayer, 1994), 9–16. For the clarinet becoming more popular than the oboe around 1800 see J. Page and M. Vigneau, "Oboe," *Grove Music Online*.

players rose to occupy principal positions in orchestras and to perform as soloists (Baermann, Crusell, and Hermstedt all got their first training and began their careers in military bands). Because the clarinet became a regular member of some European orchestras only as late as the second half of the 1790s, excitement about the instrument was particularly high in the years around 1800.[5] This excitement was paired with composers making increasing demands on the clarinet, which in turn inspired changes to the instrument's construction that resulted in facilitating the ease with which it could play in a wide range of keys, execute extended chromatic passages, and produce a uniform tone throughout its extraordinarily large range (E^3–C^7).[6] At the same time clarinetists began abandoning the earlier dominant technique of playing with the mouthpiece turned reed-side up in favor of the new method of playing with the reed resting on the lower lip, which facilitated greater speed and clarity of articulation and improved clarinetists' ability to control tone.[7]

Of the numerous works written for clarinet and orchestra in this golden age of clarinet virtuosity, only a minority were concertos. Sets of variations, potpourris, divertissements, and similar light, one-movement pieces abound, but so do many more substantial works appearing under such titles as Concert Piece (*Konzertstück*), Concertino, and, less frequently, Sonata for Clarinet and Orchestra, some of which consist of multiple movements and compete with works designated as concertos in terms of length and gravitas.[8] Although composers in the nineteenth century continued the standard three-movement form (fast–slow–fast, generally Allegro–Adagio–Allegretto)

---

5   A rarity in orchestras before 1780, clarinets became indispensable in the 1790s. For example, clarinetists were first regularly employed in the Dresden court orchestra in 1794, although they had already been included in the orchestra on an ad hoc basis for some time. See Charles Arthur Coltman III, "Carl Gottlieb Reissiger (1798–1859): Forgotten Composer for the Clarinet" (DMA diss., University of North Texas, 2002), 13.

6   For a summary of the developments in the construction of the clarinet in this time period, see Johan van Kalker, *Die Geschichte der Klarinetten: Eine Dokumentation* (Oberems: Verlag Textilwerkstatt, 1997), 89–90.

7   Birsak, *The Clarinet*, 41–45.

8   The worklist of Heinrich Baermann (1784–1847) is a case in point. His compositions for solo clarinet and orchestra include four sets of variations, three concertinos, three divertissements, two sonatas (!), a fantasy, and a concerto. See Gudula Schütz, "Heinrich Joseph Baermann," in *MGG*, 2nd ed. (Kassel: Bärenreiter, 1994–2008), *Personenteil*, 1:1616.

established as the norm for concertos in the eighteenth century, the number of movements seems to have been a less important feature of the genre than the structure of the first movement, typically sonata form with ritornelli. Saverio Mercadante's two-movement Concerto in B-flat Major, op. 101 (1819?) (Allegro maestoso—Andante theme and variations), and Karol Kurpinski's one-movement Clarinet Concerto in B-flat (1823) suggest that even in concerted works lacking three movements, the presence of a proper first movement sufficed to qualify the work as a concerto.[9] Heinrich Baermann's two sonatas for clarinet and orchestra further help to define the genre. Both are highly virtuosic works with first movements in sonata form, but they lack the requisite ritornelli to qualify as concertos.[10]

In what follows I consider only concertos proper. Specifically, I focus on aspects of early nineteenth-century concertos that differ in important ways from concertos of an earlier generation: the solo entrance, formal innovations, and the role of virtuosity in first movements; Romantic tendencies in slow movements; and, briefly, the joy of acrobatics in the codas of third movements.

For Starters

Looking back from the early twentieth century, Ferruccio Busoni confirmed the importance of first movements of concertos, which, he

---

9   Dieter Klöcker's recording of Mercadante's Concerto in B-flat inserts a short slow movement before the theme and variations movement, but there is no support for this addition in the manuscript.

10 Baermann's worklist in *MGG* lists these two sonatas, one for clarinet and orchestra in F major, op. 33 (Mus Mss 1807, Bayerische Staatsbibliothek, Munich), and one in F minor, op. 31, for clarinet and strings with *ad libitum* parts for two horns, two bassoons, and contrabass, suggesting the possibility of orchestral performance. Dieter Klöcker mentions a third "Sonata for Clarinet concertante and Orchestra" in the notes to his recording *Heinrich Joseph Baermann: Klarinettenkonzerte* (Orfeo C 065 011 A, 2002, compact disc). Baermann's C-Minor Concertino op. 29 (1818—not to be confused with the *Andante avec variations*, given as op. 29 in the *MGG* worklist) adheres to the three-movement form of a concerto, but its first movement lacks a recapitulation. Although it is listed as a concertino in *MGG*, the score to this work has been erroneously published as a concerto: *Concerto in C minor for Clarinet and Orchestra* (Massa, Italy: Nico Bertelli Edizioni Musicali, 2015).

wrote, "were given the outward shape of a symphony" in order to provide respectability for a genre that was, in essence, little more than a
display of virtuosity, a "*bravura* piece" or a "*morceau d'occasion*." With
its symphonic shape the concerto's first movement "put on the mask
of a certain dignity, but in the following movements the mask was
gradually dropped, until the finale brazenly displayed the grimace of
an acrobat."[11] Although describing concertos in the late nineteenth
century, Busoni's observation also holds true for clarinet concertos in
the early nineteenth century, some of which exhibit something of a
Beethovenian tension between adherence to classical forms and the
Romantic tendency to break free of those forms. We see this particularly in a few first movements, the genre-defining form of which lent
concertos their symphonic weight, and whose conventions at the same
time carried challenges to the more continuous, goal-oriented dramaturgy gaining prevalence in the nineteenth century.

The sometimes-contradictory dual aspirations for rhetorical weight
and flamboyant virtuosity typical of the first movements of concertos
often makes itself clear in the solo entrance. In the eighteenth-century
tradition, exemplified by Mozart's and Franz Krommer's clarinet concertos, both in wide circulation in the early nineteenth century, the soloist
enters in the solo exposition with a straightforward repetition of the first
theme of the opening ritornello.[12] Such openings in eighteenth-century
clarinet concertos generally duplicate the first violins' initial statement
of the first theme at pitch when it is in the clarinet's clarion register or, as
is the case in Franz Tausch's and J. G. H. Backofen's Concertos in E-flat
major, transpose it up an octave if rendering the violin line at pitch would
bring the clarinet into a lower range. Although this opening strategy of

---

11   Ferruccio Busoni, program note for a performance of his Piano
     Concerto, February 21, 1934, trans. Edward J. Dent, repr. in Larry
     Sitsky, *Busoni and the Piano* (New York and Westport, CT, and London:
     Greenwood Press, 1986), 92.

12   For discussion of whether the clarinetist should play during the open-
     ing ritornelli of late eighteenth-century clarinet concertos, see Carey
     Campbell, "Should the Soloist Play during the Tuttis of Mozart's
     Clarinet Concerto?" *Early Music* 38, no. 3 (2010): 423–36. What the
     author fails to point out, however, is that solo parts often included
     notation of the first violin part as a means of allowing the soloist to
     lead the orchestra in rehearsal. What is notated in the solo parts
     should not, therefore, necessarily be taken as an indication of perfor-
     mance practice. I am grateful to Robert Mealy, director of historical
     performance at the Julliard School, for this observation.

straightforward repetition of the main ritornello theme remained an option in the clarinet concertos of the next generation, later composers tended to be more concerned with establishing the clarinet's voice as distinct from the orchestra from the outset. One straightforward and effective technique of achieving this goal was to compose a solo part in which the clarinet, as if improvising, rendered the first theme, perhaps preceded by an *Eingang*, in an elaborately embellished version. Crusell takes this approach in his opp. 1 and 11, as does Pierre Cremont (1784–1846) in his E-flat Major Concerto (ex. 6.1a–c). In these solo entrances, the embellishments extend the theme beyond the range in which it had been presented by the violins and, without exception, deep into the clarinet's chalumeau register.

A desire to begin with a flashy presentation of the clarinet's full range also appears to motivate another common opening strategy, in which the clarinet begins with something akin to a fanfare in advance of playing the first theme. In the Concerto no. 1 in D Minor by Iwan Müller, the clarinet covers a range of over three octaves (G^6 to E^3) in its opening gesture. Crusell introduces his solo instrument in a similar way in his opus 5; and Weber's famous three-octave leap from F^6 to F^3 (and then down another step to E^3) in his Concerto no. 2 presents the traversal of the extremes of the clarinet's registers in a dramatically distilled and compact form (ex. 6.2a–c).

Formal Innovations, Programmatic Gestures

Gentle solo openings for the clarinet in this period occur in two important clarinet concertos, both of which present novel approaches to form. The first, Spohr's Clarinet Concerto no. 1 in C Minor (1808–09), begins the solo entrance with a literal rendition of the lyrical main theme in the clarinet, but what precedes the solo entrance is exceptional (ex. 6.3).[13] The movement lacks a proper opening ritornello in the sense that the slow introduction and the first eight measures of the Allegro that occur before the clarinet enters present only the beginning of a first theme, omitting the bridge, second theme, and

---

13 Simon Hermstedt famously needed to have six keys added to his instrument to be able to perform Spohr's Clarinet Concerto no. 1. See Spohr's preface to the first edition of the Concerto, reprinted in facsimile and translation in Louis Spohr, *Klarinettenkonzert Nr. 1 c-moll, Opus 26, Klavierauszug*, ed. Ullrich Scheideler (Wiesbaden: Breitkopf & Härtel, and Munich: G. Henle, 2015), viii–ix.

Example 6.1 a) Crusell, Clarinet Concerto in E-flat Major, op. 1 (published
1811), mvt. 1, comparison of the opening ritornello, violin 1, mm. 1–3, with
the solo entrance, mm. 64–66; b) Crusell, Clarinet Concerto in B-flat Major,
op. 11 (published 1829), mvt. 1, comparison of the opening ritornello,
violin 1, mm. 1–2, with the solo entrance, mm. 52–53; c) Cremont, Clarinet
Concerto no. 1 in E-flat Major (ca. 1810), mvt. 1, comparison of the opening
ritornello, violin 1, mm. 1–4, with the solo entrance, mm. 87–90.

closing material of a traditional orchestral exposition. Following a
half cadence, but no halt to the orchestra's forward momentum, the
clarinet's repetition of the theme already underway in the orchestra initially feels almost like another woodwind solo from within the
orchestra—the oboe and flute having already had prominent solo or

Example 6.2. a) Müller, Clarinet Concerto no. 1 in D Minor (1810), mvt. 1, mm. 81–83, solo entrance; b) Crusell, Clarinet Concerto in F Minor, op. 5 (published 1818), mvt. 1, mm. 61–62, solo entrance; c) Weber, Clarinet Concerto no. 2 in E-flat Major (1811), mvt. 1, mm. 50–51, solo entrance.

soli turns.[14] The clarinet becomes a true soloist only when it departs from the primary theme six measures into its solo.

The effect of the abbreviated ritornello and early initiation of the solo exposition creates a more continuous flow to the movement than was common for the time, somewhat akin to that of Mendelssohn's Violin Concerto in E Minor (1844), famous for postponing the first orchestral ritornello until after the solo presentation of the first theme.[15] Indeed, in Spohr's First Concerto, the tutti following the solo

---

14 Clarinets in the orchestral accompaniments to eighteenth-century and early nineteenth-century clarinet concertos are rare. Crusell and Weber do not use clarinets in the orchestras of their clarinet concertos, and Spohr uses clarinets in the orchestras of only his Third (1821) and Fourth (1828) Concertos. Likely the earliest, and possibly the only example of orchestral clarinets in a clarinet concerto prior to Spohr's Third is Joseph Eybler's Clarinet Concerto in B flat (1798), which calls for pairs of flutes, clarinets, and bassoons, the clarinets playing a role similar to that more commonly given to oboes.

15 Mendelssohn already takes this approach in his Piano Concerto in G Minor (1831).

Example 6.3. Spohr, Clarinet Concerto no. 1 in C Minor (1808–09), mvt. 1, mm. 1–28, head motive of primary theme in the opening tutti of the slow introduction and Allegro through the entrance of the solo clarinet.

rendition of the primary theme features the head motive of the primary theme (mm. 40–43) in a manner that initially could be taken as a Mendelssohnian reversal of the order of the solo and opening ritornello. Spohr's tutti is ultimately too short to serve such a function, and the orchestral passage in the Allegro before the solo entrance is longer and more thematic than Mendelssohn's short tonic burbling before the entrance of the solo violin. Still, Spohr, some thirty-six years before Mendelssohn, achieves a continuity and unity in this movement greater than what was commonly found in "double-exposition" form, in part by avoiding the stop and start that comes from the introduction of the soloist only after the closing material of the opening ritornello.

Other aspects of Spohr's approach in this movement that create greater continuity than is generally found in concerto first movements of the period include the omission of a cadenza and a soft ending, in which the clarinet fades away in its lowest range—an effect that, like Mendelssohn's famous held note in the bassoon at the end of the first movement of his Violin Concerto, appears designed to forestall applause between movements. Spohr also provides continuity between movements by referring to the first theme of the first movement in the coda to the third movement (ex. 6.4). This thematic recall between movements and Spohr's quiet ending of the coda in the third movement are rarities that make this work notable in the history not only of the clarinet concerto,

Example 6.4. Spohr, Clarinet Concerto no. 1 in C Minor, mvt. 3, m. 315–end, solo clarinet, head motive of primary theme from mvt. 1 recalled in closing measures of coda.

but also of the concerto writ large. It would be well over a century before Carl Nielsen would again end the finale of a clarinet concerto quietly.

Like Spohr, who may have inspired him, Weber continued the tradition of formal innovation in the first movement of his Clarinet Concerto no. 1 in F Minor (1811).[16] Weber's first movement also shares with Spohr's its minor mode, quiet ending (again, avoiding applause between movements seems a likely goal), lack of cadenza, and lyrical entrance theme for the clarinet.[17] Yet, despite its similarity to Spohr's, the first movement of Weber's concerto is exceptional for at least two reasons: it is the only first movement among the works examined for this chapter to be written in triple meter as opposed to common time; and, more important, Weber's modifications to sonata form dramatize the relationship between the orchestra and soloist in a manner unique among clarinet concertos of the day.

In the opening ritornello (see ex. 6.5), Weber eschews convention by omitting the customary presentation of two themes, focusing instead on the orchestra's primary theme, initially presented in a goblinesque *pianissimo* in the cellos and basses, then exploding with a violent *fortissimo* blast (m. 11). The imbalance of this material sets the tone of violence and unpredictability that will recur at several junctures throughout the movement. The primary theme begins regularly with two bars of i followed by two bars of V^7, the second highlighted

---

16 Although we have no documentary proof of a connection between their two first clarinet concertos, Spohr likely influenced Weber, whom he first met in early 1808. The two composers remained friends and rivals. See Louis Spohr, *The Musical Journeys of Louis Spohr*, trans. and ed. Henry Pleasants (Norman: University of Oklahoma Press, 1961), 68–69.

17 Heinrich Baermann's insertion of a cadenza into the first movement will be discussed below.

by a sighing ♭6–5 appoggiatura (m. 4). Instead of providing a four-measure consequent phrase ending on i to round off the first theme, however, Weber uses the motive from measure 3 to push forward without a break to the sudden *fortissimo* half cadence in measure 11. The stormy bridge that follows continues to use motives from the first theme, ending, conventionally enough for a non-modulating bridge of an orchestral exposition, on V^7 (m. 46). Instead of the expected second theme in the orchestra, however, the solo clarinet enters. Playing *con duolo* (plaintively), the clarinet articulates its own, doleful voice with a balanced, four-plus-four, antecedent-consequent phrase that, by definition as the solo entrance, functions as the primary theme of the solo exposition. Still, there is some degree of formal ambiguity in this theme given that its straightforward structure and lyricism (not to mention its rendition by a solo woodwind) carry the associations of a secondary theme, the place of which it initially appears to have taken.[18]

At least as striking as the ambiguous structural function of the solo clarinet's theme is the fact that the clarinet and the orchestra never play each other's primary themes and thus, from the outset, occupy two separate expressive spheres: one violent, aggressive, the other quiet, withdrawn, lamenting. In the dynamic field of the concerto it is possible to hear the solo clarinet's laments as a mournful reaction to the violence of the orchestral introduction, an attempt to sooth with calm, rational sympathy what has been a seemingly irrational process of unequal phrase lengths and sudden dynamic shifts.

This quasi-programmatic dialogue between the soloist and orchestra becomes more prominent in the retransition, recapitulation, and coda (ex. 6.6). In measure 223, the orchestra settles on a dominant pedal that signals the beginning of the retransition. The clarinet attempts to initiate the recapitulation by returning to its primary (*con duolo*) theme in the tonic (m. 231). The orchestra, however, thwarts the clarinet's attempt at recapitulation by continuing to build tension typical of retransitions. Although the orchestra resolves to F minor, it denies the clarinet the stability of root-position tonic support, using instead a i$^6_4$ chord that extends the dominant pedal in the bass by some eighteen measures (mm. 231–48). This odd disjunction of melodic recapitulation over the harmonic continuation of the retransition

---

18   Another factor that makes the solo clarinet's entrance theme similar to a second theme is the tradition of featuring solo winds in second themes in symphonies, overtures, and concertos of the period: Rossini's famous woodwind solos in the second themes of his overtures are perhaps the most emblematic examples of this tradition.

Example 6.5. Weber, Clarinet Concerto no. 1 in F Minor (1811), mvt. 1, mm. 1–13, primary theme of opening ritornello, and mm. 30–55, portion of bridge to solo entrance, primary theme.

—(*continued*)

Example 6.5—*concluded*

precipitates something of a crisis, its tension reflected in the strings' *pianissimo* tremolo (mm. 231–41) and in the clarinet's increasingly forceful and agitated (*sempre più crescendo ed agitato*) gestures culminating with a *fortissimo* C^6, the seventh of a V7 chord (m. 247), the line of the solo clarinet ending before it is allowed to achieve harmonic resolution. Having denied the clarinet the satisfaction of a cadence, Weber finally brings the orchestra to a forceful resolution on a root-position tonic chord that initiates the true recapitulation with the reiteration of the orchestra's primary theme only after the clarinet has been silent for a full measure (m. 249). Undermining the clarinet's attempt at recapitulation and thus undercutting its heroic role in the concerto, the orchestra thrusts its own primary theme into the more commanding position. In the narrative of this concerto, violent disruption triumphs, as it were, over doleful rationality.

Example 6.6. Weber, Clarinet Concerto no. 1 in F Minor, mvt. 1, mm. 223–50, retransition through recapitulation.

[Retransition]

dolce

Hn.

p

[False Recapitulation]

pp

cresc.

—(*continued*)

Weber continues the contest between the clarinet and the orchestra in the coda (ex. 6.7), which commences immediately after a radically shortened recapitulation.[19] The coda begins with a series of explosive rising gestures for the clarinet: first scales, starting on tonic

19 In my reading of the movement, the recapitulation begins at measure 149 and lasts only nine measures until the beginning of the coda (m. 158). The recapitulation omits repetition of the secondary theme as well as transitional and closing material.

Example 6.6—*concluded*

G^3 in the depths of the clarinet's chalumeau, then a series of trills that finally arrive at a hard-won resolution on a glorious altissimo G^6, the highest note for the clarinet in the movement, strategically saved for this climax. The victory is, however, pyrrhic, being undermined yet again by the orchestra, which violently takes over with its F-minor primary theme and a jagged descending scale (mm. 273ff.). The clarinet's response is mimetic of death. As if almost literally torn apart, it is

Example 6.7. Weber, Clarinet Concerto no. 1 in F Minor, mvt. 1, mm. 258–87, coda.

—(*continued*)

able only to utter two fragments of its doleful theme in response, the second of which returns, with resignation, to rest on the chalumeau G^3 from which it began its ascent in the coda. Weber's performance indication, *morendo* (dying away), both shows off the clarinet's unusual ability to fade out seamlessly on a long, sustained note in its lowest range and embodies the tragic topic of the movement.

Example 6.7—*continued*

—(*continued*)

While all concertos tailor their content to the solo instrument to some extent, adhering as they must to the solo instrument's range and other limitations, Weber's concluding *morendo* as a logical outcome of the clarinet's opening *con duolo* is unusual in the sense that the dramatic shape of the movement is built so clearly around the careful deployment of three of the clarinet's intrinsic abilities: to sing (in the primary theme, to lament) in the clarion register, to arrive triumphantly in the altissimo, and to fade to nothing in the chalumeau.

Example 6.7—*concluded*

Retrenchment

However dramatically effective the first movement of Weber's Clarinet Concerto no. 1, it inspired a critique from Heinrich Baermann, the clarinetist for whom it was written. The criticism took the form of a sixteen-measure-long passage of brilliant sixteenth-note runs and a cadenza, which Baermann composed to be inserted in place of the last two measures of the solo exposition. The insertion brings an abrupt change in affect that provides a level of technically brilliant display for the soloist that is otherwise missing from the movement. Implicit in Baermann's insertion is that he found the movement lacking in just the type of flamboyance that Busoni would deride in concertos as circus-like acrobatics. The fact that an overwhelming number of clarinetists who perform the work play Baermann's insertion suggests that this is just the sort of high-wire antics that performers and audiences want in concertos. Baermann's critique thus exposes precisely the conflict between the demands of dramatic continuity, rhetorical weight, and acrobatic display, a conflict that Busoni identified as a central problem for concertos in the nineteenth century.

Weber's decision to write a significantly more virtuosic first movement for his Second Clarinet Concerto suggests that he learned a
lesson from his experience with Baermann. Tellingly, the first movement of his Second Concerto includes extended sixteenth-note passagework in the closing material of the solo exposition, providing the
same type of acrobatic technical display in exactly the same formal
position as Baermann's addition to the First Concerto.[20] Furthermore,
while in the first movement of his First Clarinet Concerto Weber has
the clarinet enter with a lyrical theme that takes its time in exposing
the extremes of the instrument's range, in the first movement of his
Second Clarinet Concerto he makes the entrance of the soloist brilliant and declamatory by having the clarinet forcefully proclaim the
extremes of its range already in its first entrance (cf. ex. 6.2c).

Weber's conformity to the expectations of his soloist, and presumably to his public, did, however, come at a price. He exchanged the
dramaturgy of expression intimately tied to formal novelty for the tried
and true formulas of virtuosity. No wonder that the form of the first
movement of the Second Concerto is conservative: its dramatic tra-
jectory is no more original than what was found in the vast majority
of concertos of its day. In conformity with the norms of the time, the
Second Concerto's first movement has a full-blown opening ritornello
complete with a march-like first theme and cantabile second theme.
The orchestra and solo clarinet share the materials introduced in the
opening ritornello in the solo exposition, and the orchestra ends the
movement with a brief ritornello that caps off the clarinet's final display with seven measures of heroic E-flat-major tonic, sure to inspire
applause. Unlike the first movement of his First Concerto, the first
movement of the Second Concerto has no formal ambiguity, no tanta-
lizing departure from convention to suggest a programmatic narrative,
no invitation to hold one's breath or wipe one's eye before the beginning of the second movement.

Like Weber, Spohr also turns away from formal innovation in
the first movements of his clarinet concertos after his first. In the
first movement of his Second Clarinet Concerto (1810), he briefly
steps outside convention by giving the clarinet a short solo turn in
the course of the opening ritornello (mm. 5–8), but the clarinet
is otherwise silent until its entrance at the beginning of the solo
exposition in measure 71. There is little else remarkable about the

---

20 The passage in the first movement of Weber's Second Concerto that
    corresponds to Baermann's addition in the first movement of Weber's
    First Concerto is measures 118–36.

movement in terms of form. The first movements of Spohr's Third (1821) and Fourth (1828) Clarinet Concertos are even less original formally, although in the former Spohr finds an elegant solution to smoothing over the disjunction between the end of the opening ritornello and the solo entrance by bringing the clarinet in on a *pianissimo* D^5, which is held for two measures before emerging as the first note of the first theme. (A similar effect, but with the dynamics reversed—*forte* decreasing to *piano*—connects the retransition to the recapitulation in mm. 217–19). Spohr's Fourth Concerto holds the more dubious distinction of likely being the first clarinet concerto in which the solo entrance is in the clarinet's weakest "throat" register, although the theme, marked *piano dolce*, does not require great power, and Spohr's reduction of the orchestral to a few sparse pizzicato chords shows sensitivity to the weakness of the register of the clarinet. Like Spohr in the first movement of his Second Concerto, Crusell writes a novel obbligato line for the solo clarinet near the beginning of the opening ritornello of his Concerto in B-flat, op. 11 (published 1829; mm. 7–13). The form of the movement is otherwise unremarkable.

&♦ &♦ &♦

Joseph Haydn's student Joseph Eybler (1765–1846) begins his Clarinet Concerto in B-flat Major (1798) for the clarinetist Anton Stadler with what must be considered a reference to the Clarinet Concerto of his and Stadler's good friend Wolfgang Mozart.[21] The first two measures of the first theme of Eybler's Concerto begin with the same rhythm as does Mozart's, and the shape of Eybler's theme is virtually an exact inversion of what must have been his model (ex. 6.8). Once we leave Mozart's immediate circle in Vienna and step into the nineteenth century, however, aside from the generic tendency to adhere to "double exposition" form and a lack of cadenzas[22]—qualities

---

21 Eybler was close enough to the Mozart family and familiar enough with the composer's works that Mozart's widow Constanze first chose him to complete Mozart's Requiem K. 626. See E. Badura-Skoda and H. Herrmann-Schneider, "Eybler, Joseph Leopold, Edler von," *Grove Music Online.*

22 Perhaps inspired by Mozart, whose Clarinet Concerto omits the traditional first-movement cadenza, cadenzas in the first movements of clarinet concertos in the early nineteenth century are more the exception than the rule. While Eybler includes a cadenza in the traditional

Example 6.8. Comparison of head motives of first themes of Mozart, Clarinet Concerto (1791), movt. 1, mm. 1–2, and Eybler, Clarinet Concerto (1798), mvt. 1, mm. 1–2.

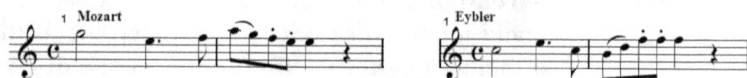

hardly unique to the first movement of Mozart's Clarinet Concerto— the first movements of post-1800 golden age clarinet concertos show little specific debt to Mozart's Concerto, their greatest predecessor. The achingly beautiful second movement of Mozart's Concerto, however, cast a longer shadow.

Slow Movements, Romantic Gestures

Crusell, who had Mozart's Clarinet Concerto in his repertoire, seems to have been channeling his predecessor especially strongly in the second movement of his Clarinet Concerto in B-flat Major, op. 11.[23] In addition to its overall Mozartian quality, at least three sections of Crusell's slow movement recall specific gestures of the earlier work:

position in the first movement of his Clarinet Concerto (m. 298), none of Spohr's clarinet concertos contains a cadenza in any of the movements. Like Mozart, Crusell, Spohr, and Weber generally confined cadenzas in their clarinet concertos to slow movements. Of this group only Crusell's F-Major Concerto, op. 5, has a fermata point (mvt. 1, m. 317) suitable for cadenza-like embellishment outside the second movement. In Riotte's Concerto in B-flat Major, op. 24 (1809), an orchestral accompaniment during the cadenza in the first movement helps ameliorate the discontinuity between the cadenza and the rest of the movement. See Philipp Jakob Riotte, *Konzert B-dur für Klarinette und Orchester*, ed. Jost Michaels (Hamburg: Hans Sikorski, 1960), 2. The nineteenth-century trend away from cadenzas was not limited to clarinet concertos. None of Spohr's fifteen violin concertos has a cadenza.

23 Crusell performed Mozart's Clarinet Concerto at least twice, in 1802 and 1804. See John Payne Spicknall, "The Solo Clarinet Works of Bernhard Henrik Crusell (1775–1838)" (DMA diss., University of Maryland, 1974), 55.

the arpeggiation of an F-major chord at the beginning of the main theme with the violins' groups of descending eighth notes in thirds used to connect phrases (ex. 6.9a, m. 6;)[24] the arpeggiation in the clarinet and the rhythmic intensity of the orchestra in the build-up to a fermata indicating a cadenza from B♭[5] (the seventh of a V7 chord) that leads back to the return of the opening theme (ex. 6.9b); and the quick summary of the clarinet's range in preparation for the end of the movement: first high, then low, before a fourfold iteration of the concluding tonic pitch (ex. 6.9c). Although Crusell's B-flat-Major Concerto was published only in 1829, the Mozartian echoes in its slow movement are one of several factors that suggest a much earlier date of composition for its second and third movements.[25]

The term "echo," however, holds more than a metaphorical meaning in the relationship between Crusell's and Mozart's writing for the clarinet in the slow movements of their concertos. Although we have no documentary evidence to support the practice of playing repeated phrases as echoes in the slow movement of Mozart's Concerto, clarinetists have long relied on this expressive effect, which is possible on the clarinet to a much greater degree than on other woodwinds.[26] In the slow movement of his Concerto in F Minor, op. 5, Crusell marks each of the clarinet's last four entrances *Echo, pianississimo*, thus making explicit what was likely a matter of individual interpretation in Mozart.

In the slow movement of Crusell's opus 5 there are two types of echoes at play: the clarinet either repeats its own previous phrase (mm. 46–49), or, as in the last three echoes, it repeats lines played more expressively by the first violins (mm. 50–64) (ex. 6.10). The last three echoes recall exchanges (echoes, although not labeled as such) between the clarinet and the first violins in the movement's B section (mm. 26–30, ex. 6.11). In this intense passage marked *con espressione* in the emotionally fraught key of A-flat minor, the violins seem to express empathy for the clarinet as they reiterate its sighs.

---

24 Although the second movement of Mozart's Clarinet Concerto is in D major and that of Crusell's is in E-flat major, because Mozart's Concerto is for clarinet in A and Crusell's is for clarinet in B-flat, the clarinet parts are both written in F major.

25 Bernhard Henrik Crusell, *Klarinettenkonzert B-dur Opus 11, Klavierauszug*, ed. Nicolai Pfeffer (Munich: G. Henle, 2015), iii–iv.

26 In the slow movement of Mozart's Concerto, clarinetists regularly play measure 85 as an echo of measure 84, and the beginning of the return to the A section (mm. 60ff.) as a long-range echo of the opening phrase.

Example 6.9. a) Crusell, Clarinet Concerto in B-flat Major, op. 11, mvt. 2, mm. 3–6; b) Crusell, Clarinet Concerto in B-flat Major, op. 11, mvt. 2, mm. 34–37; c) Crusell, Clarinet Concerto in B-flat Major, op. 11, mvt. 2, mm. 61–67.

Example 6.10. Crusell, Clarinet Concerto in F Minor, op. 5, mvt. 2, mm. 53–67, echoes between clarinet and first violins.

Example 6.11. Crusell, Clarinet Concerto in F Minor, op. 5, mvt. 2, mm. 26–30, dialogue between first violins and solo clarinet.

In contrast, the literal echoes at the end of the movement are emotionally cool. Crusell instructs the violins to play with expressive gestures—crescendos, decrescendos, a *sforzando*, and a *smorzando*—while the clarinet repeats the violins' lines without inflection. Its responses are not empathetic. Like an echo in nature, the clarinet impassively reflects the violin's lines in a muted, disembodied tone that creates a sense of loneliness and distance. Crusell's move into the realm of nature at the end of the movement corresponds both to the space in which echoes are heard and the pastoral mood implied by his tempo designation, "Andante pastorale."

Given the general lack of detail in the reviews from Stockholm reported in the "Communications" section of the *Allgemeine musikalische Zeitung*, it is surprising that a reviewer singled out Crusell's echo effects for praise at the earliest known performance of his Clarinet Concerto op. 5 in March 1815.[27] Like the end of the first movement of Weber's First Concerto, these echoes are particularly effective because they show off a technique especially suited to the clarinet. They also embody something of the musical aesthetics of the generation following Mozart. The slow movement of Mozart's Clarinet Concerto embodies a graceful purity similar to Ferrando's expression of pure love in the aria "Un'aura amorosa" from *Così fan tutte*. Crusell's slow movement with echo reflects something less idyllic if no less poignant than Mozart's, conveying an image of nature as an impassive backdrop to human alienation—a quintessential Romantic conceit.

The slow movements of Weber's clarinet concertos come even closer to program music than Crusell's Andante pastorale, especially in the extended passages that connect Weber's contrasting B sections to the varied A sections that round off the movements. In the second movement of Weber's Second Concerto this connecting passage, marked "Recitative," carries the implication of a text unusually clearly (mm. 63–73).[28] Already the movement's title, "Romanza," suggests an opera aria, supported not only by the recitative section, but also by the movement's song-like A section (mm. 1–46) and its bel canto–like B section (mm. 47–62). The impetus for the clarinet to "speak" appears as part of a dramatic process that bears exploration.

---

27 *Allgemeine musikalische Zeitung*, July 1815, 451. "A concerto from Mr. Crusell. He played a concerto for clarinet that he himself composed. Quite beautiful—especially the Adagio [*sic*] with echo."

28 Weber in fact writes "Recit." twice in this passage: once at the beginning, and once at measure 70 following several tempo changes.

The A section of the movement consists of four phrases: two multi-sectional statements for the clarinet, each answered by an identical orchestral interlude. These gentle, optimistic orchestral passages in G major contrast with the more somber and fraught clarinet solos in G minor (mm. 3–20) and C minor (mm. 29–38) in a manner that appears operatic—the clarinet's lines expressing what is being sung, presumably pertaining to the singer's present condition, the orchestral interludes suggesting a vision of something emotionally lighter, perhaps a pleasant memory, thoughts of a brighter future, or a cheerful scene enacted elsewhere on stage.

The B section of the "aria" brings contrast as expected. The key switches to ♭VI (E-flat), a common tonal shift for excursions to alternative realities in Romantic music. The clarinet sheds its former introspection, replacing it with brilliant *fioritura* and proud declamations culminating in a truly heroic leap of more than three octaves (E^3–G^6, m. 56). The B section ends, again traditionally for this aria type, with a cadenza-like passage over a dominant chord resolving to the local tonic. The straightforward path of harmonic return to the thematic material of A and the G-minor tonic of the movement would be easily achieved by an augmented-sixth chord on E♭.[29] Instead, Weber veers in an entirely new and unexpected direction, introducing the recitative with a sudden shift to Allegro and a forceful gesture in the orchestra that marks the shift in discourse (mm. 62–63). As if awakened from a dream expressed in the bravura exploits in the B section, the clarinet at first reacts slowly and softly and then with increasing passion, volume, and speed, only to retreat back to a series of sweeter (*dolce*) phrases. The passage ends with a seven-note gesture in the clarinet typical of the last phrase of a recitative, and the orchestra supplies the D7 chord that leads back to G minor for the last statement of A.[30] Notable in this process is the turmoil of the recitative section: the whirlwind of emotions the orchestra and clarinet express in accomplishing the transition from the world of the B section back to the world of the A section. The effort to bridge the distance between these two worlds becomes so highly charged as to require breaking the normal bounds of instrumental expression for the gestures of operatic declamation.

---

29 Weber uses this formula to return to G minor after harmonic wandering in the A section (mm. 18–19).

30 Traditionally recitative is composed of randomly alternating lines of seven and eleven syllables. The clarinet's final seven-note phrase recalls this practice.

Weber was not the inventor of heightened contrast for the B section in clarinet concertos. A year before his First Clarinet Concerto, Spohr had written a highly contrasting B section in the slow movement of his Second Clarinet Concerto, notable for likely being the first slow movement of a clarinet concerto to begin with a theme in the chalumeau range, an effect that reflects the increasing strength of the clarinet's low register due to improvements in its construction. In contrast to the song-like, chalumeau-based A-flat-major material of the A section, marked *piano dolce* and featuring eighth- and sixteenth-note subdivisions, the B section of Spohr's movement is in the tenser key of C minor, featuring more agitated sextuplet-sixteenth-note subdivisions, jarring *forte–piano* effects, and dramatic arpeggios reaching into the clarinet's altissimo range. Despite the high degree of contrast, Spohr, unlike Weber, does not dramatize the return from the B back to the A section. Instead, he smooths over the return with a diminuendo and gradual slowing of motion. Spohr further finesses the return by initially giving the main theme of A to the obbligato flute as the clarinet plays a countermelody below (mm. 35–38; ex. 6.12). Equally important for the sense of flow is that this thematic return does not coincide with a return of the tonic but occurs over a dominant pedal that resolves only with the clarinet taking up the main theme after seven bars (m. 42).

Weber's use of contrast for the B section in the slow movement of his First Concerto is similar to Spohr's and suggests that Weber may have been keeping an eye on his friend's writing for the clarinet. He also shifts mode (C major in the A section turns to C minor in the B section), introduces a more animated tempo (*poco più animato*), and writes a clarinet line featuring wide-ranging arpeggios in contrast to the aria-like material of A.[31] As he would with the recitative section in his Second Concerto, Weber does not slide back directly to A from B, but inserts an extended section (mm. 41–65) before the return. This passage is much more than a transition: it is harmonically stable and self-contained enough to constitute a discrete section, C. In it, Weber introduces a complete change of scene with three solo horns acting as the sole accompaniment to the clarinet.[32] Throughout the section the

31 Heinrich Baermann clearly models the contrasting section of the slow movement of his Concertino in C Minor (1818) on this section of Weber's First Concerto.

32 Weber calls for a third horn only in chorale-like sections of the second movement of the First Concerto. The first and third movements use the customary two horns.

Example 6.12. Spohr, Clarinet Concerto no. 2 in E-flat Major (1810), mvt. 2, mm. 35–38, return of main melody in flute over countermelody in solo clarinet (over dominant pedal).

horns play in a homophonic texture reminiscent of a hymn, beginning and ending in stereotypical fashion with the basic chord progression I–IV–V7–I, while the clarinet weaves a line of descant. In addition to the religious implications of Lutheran hymnody, the horn-passage implies a particularly Germanic setting, the woods so prominent in German folklore—*Waldhorn* (literally "forest horn") tellingly being the German word for the instrument.

Given the symbolic power of hymns and woods for German national identity, it is perhaps no surprise that the C section of the slow movement of Weber's First Clarinet Concerto was singled out to memorialize Weber in a concert dedicated to his memory in 1831. On this occasion, Weber's friend and favorite clarinetist Heinrich Baermann made explicit the vocal connotations of the horn hymn by arranging the horn parts for three male voices, setting them with the following text by the German poet and politician Eduard von Schenk:

Er ist dahin, der Schöpfer dieser Klänge!
Der Hohe Meister, der von hinnen schied,
Er lehrt den Engelchören nun Gesänge;
Doch ewig lebt auf Erden auch sein Lied!

[He is gone, the creator of these strains!
The sublime master, who is departed,
Now teaches hymns to the angelic choirs;
But here on earth his song lives on forever!][33]

---

33 John Warrack, *Carl Maria von Weber*, 2nd ed. (Cambridge: Cambridge University Press, 1976), 128. I am grateful to Christian Rogowski for help with this translation.

Third-Movement Acrobatics

I have almost entirely eschewed discussion of the third movements of clarinet concertos because of their largely formulaic construction. They are charming, technically spectacular rondos (often rhythmically charged polonaises) that serve to round off these works brilliantly; the dramatic arc of their form is exciting, effective, and reassuringly predictable. They tend to follow a tried-and-true formula for "bringing down the house," often with the switch to blisteringly fast sextuplet sixteenth notes in the coda as part of the final display of fireworks. That composers took little opportunity for exploring exceptions to this norm speaks both to the effectiveness of the formula and to the enduring tradition of the *lieto fine* (light, happy ending) in concertos long after composers had begun to shift the weight of symphonies toward their last movements.

The third movement of Weber's First Concerto is, however, like so much in that concerto, exceptional. Likely out of deference to the $\frac{3}{4}$ time of the first movement, the rondo finale of this concerto is not the customary $\frac{3}{4}$ polonaise, but a spritely contredanse in $\frac{2}{4}$. Perhaps because Weber was overly cautious about making excessive technical demands on his soloist, the movement's coda features the straight sixteenth notes already found throughout the movement rather than introducing the effect of sixteenth-note sextuplets regularly used in codas. Weber's creative solution to this absence of virtuosic display is a novel and spectacular series of quarter-note trills (mm. 347–50). As was the case with the first movement, the finale of Weber's Second Clarinet Concerto is more conventional than that of the First. When Weber does arrive at the expected sixteenth-note triplets in the coda of this polonaise, however, the fireworks are more brilliant and catchier than in any other concerto examined for this study. In Weber's hands, what Busoni disparaged as "the grimace of an acrobat" becomes tumults of pure joy.

The Twilight of the Clarinet's Golden Age

By 1831, the year of Baermann's memorial concert for Weber, Weber had been dead for five years, and two decades had passed since he had composed his clarinet concertos. The *Grand duo concertant*, Weber's last virtuosic work for the clarinet, was completed in 1816. Spohr would live until 1859, but his last clarinet concerto dates from 1828. Backofen died in 1839. Crusell would live for another seven years, but his last concerto to be published, likely begun in 1807, appeared in 1829. Baermann hung on a bit longer, giving his last solo appearance in 1839. Hermstedt died in 1846. In short, the golden age of clarinet virtuosi was drawing to a close, and with the passing of these soloists, some of whom were also composers, the composition of clarinet concertos would remain largely moribund until the twentieth century.[34] Baermann's homage to Weber, therefore, can also be seen as a eulogy for the era in which the clarinet was not only a novel medium for virtuosic display, but also an instrument weighty enough to elicit substantial, three-movement concertos for it from the likes of Weber and Spohr, among the most important and progressive composers of their day.

Although the reasons for changes in fashion are notoriously hard to pin down, the decline in the popularity of the clarinet as a solo instrument in concertos appears to be tied to its burgeoning success as a member of the orchestra. The unusually wide expressive range of the clarinet had quickly made it not only an indispensable member of the orchestra, but a favorite obbligato instrument in symphonic music and opera. There was no shortage of work, some of it highly virtuosic, for orchestral clarinetists. When Giuseppe Verdi was commissioned to write an opera for the Imperial Theater in St. Petersburg, he was aware that his countryman Ernesto Cavallini (1807–74), who had performed Verdi's works under the direction of the composer when he had been principal clarinetist at La Scala, was playing in the Russian orchestra. Verdi responded by giving the clarinet an unusually prominent role in *La forza del destino* (1862), including a solo lasting more than three minutes near the beginning of the opera's third act, a gesture that fitted into the trend of incorporating much of the best solo writing for the clarinet into large-scale works other than clarinet concertos.[35] Cavallini, himself a composer of virtuosic works for his instrument, had written two

---

34 Fantasies, concertinos, and sets of variations for clarinet and orchestra, while not plentiful, were more common in the period 1830–1900 than clarinet concertos.

35 See David Lawton, "Verdi, Cavallini, and the Clarinet Solo in *La forza del destino*," *Verdi: bollettino dell'Instituto di Studi Verdiana* 2, no. 5 (1966): 1726–45. Lawton acknowledges that proof is lacking for Verdi having intended the clarinet solos in *Forza* for Cavallini, but provides substantial circumstantial evidence supporting the claim. There is no doubt that Verdi was familiar with Cavallini's playing at La Scala, and he would have also been aware of Cavallini's appointment in St. Petersburg, which was reported in the Italian press.

clarinet concertos at the tail end of the golden age in the late 1820s.[36] A remark by Eduard Hanslick, writing in his infamously cantankerous tone in 1864, supports the notion that by the middle of the nineteenth century the best clarinetists had generally abandoned a position standing in front of orchestras as a concerto soloist for the first chair in an orchestra's clarinet section: "Go and join an orchestra! That is the proper place for us to appreciate clarinet, flute, oboe, and bassoon players; the time is past when these artists arrived in hordes and discharged concertos on their tedious single pipes."[37] Hanslick's caustic tone also suggests that the end of the golden age of clarinet concertos came not only because of their occupation in orchestras, but also because the aesthetics of the concerto had changed since the early nineteenth century. His dismissive pronouncement did not, however, predict the future for the long run. When the dominant aesthetic in serious instrumental composition shifted away from maximalist German trends in the twentieth century, concertos for clarinet (and other woodwinds) would once again occupy some of the century's leading composers.

New Directions

The only possible exception to the moribund state of clarinet concertos in the mid- to late-nineteenth century is the Concerto for Clarinet and Orchestra in G minor, op. 29 (1854), by the Leipzig composer Julius Rietz (1812–77).[38] This concerto, which came to light only with Thea King's recording of it in 1981 and was published in a modern edition

---

36 Cavallini's Clarinet Concerto no. 1 in E-flat Major (1827) and his Clarinet Concerto no. 2 in C Minor (1830) are not available in modern editions, but have been recorded by Giuseppe Porgo, clarinet, and the Norddeutsche Philharmonie Rostock (CPO 777 948-2, 2015). The First Concerto, more properly a concertino, has four movements, the first of which is not in sonata form.

37 Quoted in Birsak, *The Clarinet*, 64.

38 Interestingly, Rietz seems to have been familiar with all of Weber's works for clarinet and orchestra. According to the IMSLP website, https://imslp.org/wiki/Clarinet_Concerto_No.1_in_F_minor%2C_Op.73_(Weber%2C_Carl_Maria_von (accessed August 13, 2019), Rietz was the copyist of *12 Instrumental Pieces*, a collection of works by Weber including his Concertino for Clarinet and both of his clarinet concertos. A facsimile of the manuscript is available through the Sächsische Landesbibliothek, Dresden, accessed August 13, 2019, https://digital.slub-dresden.de/en/workview/dlf/185297/1/.

only in 2008, is notable for realizing some tendencies detected in the First Clarinet Concertos of both Spohr and Weber: a reduced opening ritornello—in this case drastically reduced to a few measures—and a section at the end of the first movement that connects it to the second movement without pause. These features, in addition to the musical language of the work, show a strong debt to Schumann's Cello Concerto and the Violin Concerto of Rietz's friend and close musical associate Felix Mendelssohn. In a clear reference to the sustained note in the bassoon at the end of Mendelssohn's first movement, Rietz initiates a thirty-two-measure transition at the end of the first movement of his Clarinet Concerto with a long *pianissimo* A^5 in the solo clarinet. Despite the clear debt to Mendelssohn, this detail can also be seen as prophetic. In it, I hear an early example of what would become an important feature of some of the most important works for clarinet and orchestra in the twentieth century. Exploiting the clarinet's ability to "float" or "whisper" notes at low dynamic levels would become a crucial effect in works for clarinet and orchestra beginning with Claude Debussy's *Première rhapsodie* (1910) and continuing throughout the century with the clarinet concertos of Carl Nielsen (1928), Aaron Copland (1948), John Corigliano (1977), and John Adams (1996). What is notable about these great twentieth-century works in terms of the history of the concerto as a genre is that they all achieve what Busoni considered so important for the healthy development of the genre: they break free of the formal structure of concertos that had remained largely unchanged throughout the nineteenth century. The longevity of the form makes Spohr's and Weber's experiments with it in the early nineteenth-century all the more prescient.

7

JOINING THE CONVERSATION

The Clarinet Quintet in Classical and Romantic Chamber Music

Marie Sumner Lott

Different notions of "dialogue" or conversation lie at the heart of the chamber music experience. Composers collaborate with performers to highlight an instrument's or its players' strengths and avoid weaknesses; players engage in verbal and non-verbal communication throughout the rehearsal and performance of a work; and the works themselves enter into an ongoing dialogue with earlier and contemporaneous pieces. The personal relationships that developed between renowned virtuoso clarinetists and influential composers in the first hundred years of the instrument's history led to the creation of innovative pieces that experiment with new textures and timbres while exploring the clarinet's evolving capabilities, and reflect the unique situations and relationships that brought them into being. This chapter will explore three seminal works for clarinet and string quartet that exemplify the multiple dialogues at play in the creation, performance, and enjoyment of chamber music. An examination of quintets by Mozart (K. 581, 1789), Weber (op. 34, 1811–15), and Brahms (op. 115, 1891) shows how the social settings and broader culture of musical life influenced compositional choices that had a lasting impact on the history of the genre and the instrument. These three works demonstrate the technical development of the clarinet from its early acceptance in the concert hall nearly to its modern state of design, as well as the evolution of chamber music's role in the social life of fashionable Europe during the long nineteenth century, circa 1789–1914. But the main reason why these three works continue to be performed, recorded, and heard throughout the world is that they exemplify the breadth and depth of musical expression that continues to make chamber music so alluring for performers and listeners in a wide variety of settings and circumstances.

Mozart and Stadler Create a Genre

Perhaps the most famous collaboration between a clarinetist and composer was that which resulted in the first generally accepted masterworks for the instrument. Wolfgang Amadeus Mozart (1756–91) composed several pieces featuring the clarinet and/or the basset horn for virtuoso clarinetists Anton Stadler (1753–1812) and his brother Johann.[1] Mozart seems to have met Stadler in 1781 shortly after his arrival in Vienna. He composed a seven-movement serenade for thirteen instruments, known today as the *Gran Partita* (K. 361/370a), that contains virtuosic writing for two clarinets and two basset horns. This work was almost certainly intended for performance by the Stadler brothers, though that performance appears to have been delayed by several years; the first documented interaction between the two men occurred in 1784, when Stadler was making arrangements for a Vienna concert that would include the serenade. Mozart and Stadler developed a close friendship around this time and played together on a number of occasions, both professionally and recreationally, leading to several magnificent works composed at the apex of Mozart's fame and artistic potency. In addition to the serenade and the Piano Quintet in E-flat Major (K. 452, 1784), these include the light-hearted "Kegelstatt" Trio in E-flat Major for Clarinet, Viola, and Piano (K. 498, 1786), the Quintet in A Major for Clarinet and String Quartet (K. 581, 1789), and the Clarinet Concerto (K. 622, 1791).[2] Mozart's works for clari-

---

1   The Stadler brothers held positions in the wind ensemble (the *Harmonie*) at the Habsburg imperial court in Vienna from 1779 and later in the court orchestra as well as other aristocratic musical establishments. Pamela L. Poulin, "Stadler, Anton," *Grove Music Online*.

2   Stadler was also the intended performer of the obbligato basset clarinet and basset horn parts in Mozart's last operas *La clemenza di Tito* and *Die Zauberflöte*, both of which premiered in September 1791. Mozart

net encapsulate many aspects of his mature style, which is synonymous with the peak of Viennese Classicism. They employ elegant sonata-cycle structures with clear, cleanly articulated forms that take full advantage of the harmonic language of the late eighteenth century. They emphasize complementary thematic materials, often using symmetrical melodic patterns with antecedent and consequent phrases, in contrasting keys audibly established with logical modulations and elaborate cadential procedures. Typical of Mozart's style, they are filled with inventive themes and clever harmonic gestures on the musical surface that enliven the listening or playing experience and provide welcome surprises, but never obscure the overriding narrative of a goal-oriented form intended to bring contrasting or conflicting ideas into a pleasing reconciliation. More than any of his contemporaries, Mozart excelled at manipulating expectations built on a finely tuned system of dances and topical styles familiar to audiences who played and heard dance music, sonatas, songs, and church music every day.[3] Such pleasant manipulations abound in the clarinet works he completed for and with Anton Stadler.

One of Stadler's aims in commissioning works for this relatively new instrument was to establish a reputation and a repertoire that would show off its unique advantages in comparison to other woodwind instruments of the day, and to demonstrate that the clarinet was more than capable of performing subtle, nuanced music alongside

---

also composed several pieces for basset horn in a variety of apparently ad hoc ensemble types to suit particular performance needs, such as the *Masonic Funeral Music (Mauerische Trauermusik* K. 477) he composed in 1785 and several choral settings of Metastasio texts accompanied by clarinets and basset horns composed in 1786–88. On the basset horn's association with Masonic gatherings, see Colin Lawson, *Mozart: Clarinet Concerto,* Cambridge Music Handbooks (Cambridge: Cambridge University Press, 1996), 19–22.

3   On topical styles and their analytical uses, see Leonard Ratner, *Classic Music: Expression, Form, and Style* (New York: Schirmer, 1980). Later scholars have extended Ratner's list of topics and styles significantly; see, for example, Wye J. Allanbrook, *Rhythmic Gesture in Mozart: "Le nozze di Figaro" and "Don Giovanni"* (Chicago: University of Chicago Press, 1984); Kofi Agawu, *Playing with Signs: A Semiotic Interpretation of Classic Music* (Princeton, NJ: Princeton University Press, 1991); Janice Dickensheets, "Nineteenth-Century Topical Analysis: A Lexicon of Romantic Topoi," *Pendragon Review: A Journal of Musical Romanticism* 2, no. 1 (2003): 5–19; and Raymond Monelle, *The Musical Topic: Hunt, Military, and Pastoral* (Bloomington: Indiana University Press, 2006).

instruments with a more refined pedigree (such as the violin family).[4] Stadler was one of a small number of players who championed the clarinet before 1800. Although Carl Stamitz (1745–1801) and a few others had used the clarinet in chamber works and composed concertos for it—Stamitz was inspired by the playing of Joseph Beer in Paris—the repertoire was still somewhat restricted. Mozart's works, particularly the Clarinet Quintet, serve the dual purpose of displaying the instrument's (and its player's) technical capabilities while also providing a demonstration that the clarinet, perhaps unlike the other woodwind instruments, was capable of the same learned and ennobling dialogue that music connoisseurs had come to associate with chamber genres epitomized by the string quartet and string quintet.

To a much greater degree than his earlier works for wind and strings, Mozart's Clarinet Quintet engages the four-movement sonata cycle associated with learned instrumental writing in the late eighteenth century and incorporates conversational texture throughout. Earlier quartets for oboe, flute, or horn utilized a two- or three-movement structure and rarely trusted the strings with thematically significant musical materials.[5] In these and similar showpieces, the strings primarily accompany the solo wind instrument, which introduces all of the main themes and effects the transitions and modulations from one section or key to the next. This compositional style appropriately reflects the normal performance scenario for such a work, which would be intended to highlight the capabilities of the soloist. Whether in a benefit concert presented in a theater (the sort of concert that a

---

4   Mozart's Clarinet Quintet and Clarinet Concerto were composed for the basset clarinet (discussed elsewhere in this volume) with an extended range into the low register. Modern performers sometimes play these works on reproductions of Stadler's instrument, but it is also very common to play them on modern clarinets with minor adjustments to the passagework that utilizes the lowest register.

5   Carl Stamitz's Six Quartets for clarinet (or flute or oboe), violin, viola (or horn), and cello op. 8 (1773) use a three-movement structure. Of Mozart's own wind quartets, only the last flute quartet (K. 298) contains four movements; the finale of this work is quite short, though, lasting less than a minute in performance. The other three flute quartets, the Oboe Quartet, and the Horn Quartet also employ the strings primarily as accompaniment so that the listener's attention is continually on the solo wind player. The Clarinet Trio K. 498, on the other hand, provides an equitable distribution of materials in part because Mozart composed the viola part for himself to play and the piano part for his friend and patron Franziska von Jacquin.

virtuoso like Stadler would organize to fund a tour, for example) or in a private musical soiree in the salon of a music lover (the scenario for which the amateur flutist Ferdinand DeJean commissioned Mozart's flute quartets), works like these allowed a performer to demonstrate his or her prowess and good taste. The soloist might hire musicians to accompany himself or the ensemble might be made up of capable friends and family members. The popularity of such works is demonstrated by the fact that they were published and reprinted in large numbers throughout the late eighteenth and early nineteenth centuries.[6] In the Clarinet Quintet, however, Mozart designed a work intended to challenge all five players equally. Although Stadler was, by all accounts, a virtuoso technician and artist, the Clarinet Quintet contains very little writing that we would describe as "flashy" or showman-like today. Rather, all five parts participate in a rigorous, balanced conversational style reminiscent of the composer's string quintets.

The first movement demonstrates this collaborative style best. In the first presentation of both main themes, for example, the clarinet and strings work together to expose the main components of the melody, with the strings and clarinet imitating each other and emulating the polite back-and-forth of a friendly conversation. The work opens with the quartet playing a soft six-measure phrase in the tonic, answered by a contrasting two-measure response in the clarinet. When the strings repeat their opening phrase and the clarinet responds in the same way (mm. 9–14, 15–16), the violins pick up the clarinet's ornamental gesture and an imitative passage ensues, in which four of the five parts each take a turn in a highlighted phrase. This polyphonic transition effects the modulation from tonic (A major) to dominant. In a similar way, the second theme is presented first by the violin in E major, then repeated and slightly varied by the clarinet in the parallel minor. Throughout this sonata exposition, the clarinet is silent as often as it is playing, and although some passagework suggests the soloist's finesse, there is no long stretch of virtuosic display.

---

6   This style is also evident in popular piano trios of the period, which were often published as sonatas for the keyboard with accompaniment of a violin and cello, which may be optional (ad libitum) or required (obbligato). For a discussion of the correlation between style and texture in works like this, see Marie Sumner Lott, "Dussek's Chamber Music: Blurring the Boundaries: Between Private and Public Musical Life," in *Jan Ladislav Dussek (1760–1812): A Bohemian Composer "en voyage" through Europe*, ed. Roberto Illiano and Rohan Stewart-MacDonald (Bologna: Ut Orpheus, 2012), 281–328.

The development section begins with a role reversal, when the clarinet takes over the first violin's part in the six-measure primary theme and the violin plays the two-measure response (mm. 83–88, 89–90). When the second violin imitates the ornamental gesture, what had been a bit of imitation in the exposition becomes a more developed suggestion of fugue, with all four quartet members playing the full "subject" and countersubject in turn (mm. 89–98). This passage further demonstrates the Quintet's connection to a learned tradition of chamber music and separates it from the lighter style of Mozart's earlier wind and string works. The clarinet does not participate in this fugato, and when it enters in measure 99, the developmental process turns from imitation to a melodic and harmonic sequence that features the clarinet playing arpeggios that cover the entire three-octave range of the instrument. Notably, though, the clarinet's arpeggios in eighth notes accompany continued collegial exchanges of passage-work in sixteenth notes played by the strings. First the viola and cello are highlighted, then the two violins, and so forth, so that all five players participate in this lively, active, and modulatory section leading to the retransition's dominant prolongation in measures 111–17. These collegial exchanges exemplify the famous, perhaps even clichéd, characterization likening a quartet to "four intelligent people conversing among themselves."[7]

With the exception of the second-movement Larghetto, the other movements of the Quintet also divide the musical materials so that all players receive abundant attention and opportunities to shine, treating the clarinet as one among equals rather than a soloist with accompanying ensemble. The third movement's Menuetto, for example, uses a homophonic style in which the strings are equal partners in the presentation of the opening theme. Then in the contrasting second theme, the violin and clarinet pass a chromatic oscillating figure back and forth while the lower three strings engage in a playful hemiola effect. The first trio is performed by the strings alone, providing the reduction of texture typical of this section type (usually from four or

---

7   On the different types of conversation metaphors used to describe quartet playing, see Mara Parker, *The String Quartet, 1750–1797: Four Types of Musical Conversation* (Aldershot, UK, and Burlington, VT: Ashgate, 2002). For a recent stimulating discussion of Mozart's chamber music and its conversational elements, see Edward Klorman, *Mozart's Music of Friends: Social Interplay in the Chamber Works* (Cambridge: Cambridge University Press, 2016).

five voices to three, hence a "trio" section).[8] For the finale, Mozart provides an Allegretto con variazioni movement with a sixteen-measure
theme and six variations. Here, as in the earlier movements, the clarinet frequently blends into the texture of accompaniment or is silent
while the rest of the ensemble exposes and develops the theme. The
variations go through a series of standard procedures for this type of
movement, and in this way they exemplify the Classical approach to
the genre also evident in other works. The theme itself is a concise,
rounded melody in an *a b a'* format, and although the clarinet joins
the texture for cadences at the ends of phrases, the theme is presented
mainly by the strings. Each of the following variations introduces a
contrasting element, such as placing the theme in the minor mode
instead of major (variation 3) or in a slow tempo (variation 5), but
throughout the movement Mozart carefully balances variations that
place the clarinet at the center of attention with variations in which
it defers to the stringed instruments. The most clarinet-centric portions of the movement are variation 1, with large leaps to show off the
instrument's range and the player's ability to move smoothly from the
depths of the chalumeau register to the altissimo, and variation 4, with
sparkling arpeggio passagework for the clarinet. Variations 2 and 3,
on the other hand, focus on the strings. Variation 5 (marked *adagio*)
brings the ensemble together in a more conversational style in which
the clarinet and first violin alternate playing chromatic diminutions
that fill in the outlines of the theme in a style that recalls the second
movement of the Quintet. This finale displays several of the clarinet's
unique aspects while also demonstrating that the instrument fits well
in a context with other instruments, and is as capable as they are of
participating in the wide variety of styles available to the eighteenth-
century musician. Although variation sets had long been (and would
continue to be) associated with virtuosic display and showmanship,
this movement focuses on presenting compositional treatments of the
theme that are widely varied but still audibly related, as opposed to virtuosic showpieces that tend to bury the theme in ornamentation and
passagework that frequently renders it difficult to recognize.

Prior to Mozart's collaboration with Stadler, no works combined
the standard string quartet instrumentation with clarinet. Many publications of the 1770s through 1820s offered chamber music enthusiasts the option of playing clarinet or replacing it with some other
treble instrument (most often flute, oboe, or violin), much as Baroque

8   Erich Schwandt, "Trio," *Grove Music Online.*

trio sonatas had been published with the expectation that any treble instrument could play either of the melody parts. In other eighteenth-century and early nineteenth-century works published as sonatas with obbligato strings, the string parts are treated as an accompaniment to a solo clarinet part and not much more, and as easily replaceable by a piano, for example.[9] In K. 581 Mozart found the perfect middle ground between that tradition and what later commentators would call "true" chamber style. Yet very few composers followed his example; although the clarinet quartet (clarinet, violin, viola, cello) was a popular genre in the late eighteenth century,[10] Mozart's work stands out as the sole example of a quintet for clarinet and string quartet until the 1810s. Thus, his Quintet set the standard by which later works would be measured.

---

9   The Viennese firm Artaria published Mozart's "Kegelstatt" Trio K. 498 in 1788 with the following title and note on the cover page: "Trio for the Harpsichord or Fortepiano, with the accompaniment of a violin and viola composed by Mr. W. A. Mozart, op. 14. The Violin part can be played also with a clarinet." As was normal in this period, the publication does not include a full score, but consists of separate parts for the piano alone, a part for "violin or clarinet," and the viola part. See Henning Bey and Daniel Brandenburg, "Kritischer Bericht," in *Neue Mozart Ausgabe, ser.* VIII, vol. 22/2, *Klaviertrios* (Kassel: Bärenreiter, 2001), 43. The Quintet (K. 581) was not published in Mozart's lifetime. Artaria printed the parts in 1802 in a complete collection of Mozart's quartets, quintets, trios, and duets (plate number 1536). J. André (based in Offenbach) printed a rival edition in the same year, as op. 108 (plate number 1602). In 1809 Artaria published an alternate version of the Quintet as a piano sonata with obbligato clarinet or violin. See Manfred Hermann Schmid, "Kritischer Bericht," in *Neue Mozart Ausgabe,* ser. VIII, vol. 19/2, *Quintette mit Bläsern* (Kassel: Bärenreiter, 2007), 62–64.

10 In a chapter titled "The Classical Clarinet" in his book on the instrument, Eric Hoeprich lists twenty-seven composers who wrote clarinet quartets in this period, noting that this genre was much more popular than the quintet for clarinet and string quartet; see Hoeprich, *The Clarinet* (New Haven, CT: Yale University Press, 2008), 84. Many of these works remain difficult to access today; hopefully as more libraries and archives move to digitize their holdings, more of them will become widely available and be recorded. The clarinetist Dietrich Klöcker was a staunch champion of "off-the-beaten-path" clarinet music, but his recordings tended to focus on early Romantic works composed by the generation of Weber and Meyerbeer.

Weber, Meyerbeer, and Baermann Expand the Possibilities

As the clarinet became more familiar as a solo instrument and as an essential member of the orchestra in concert and theater works, improvements in its design also led to more daring treatments in the music composed for clarinetists building careers as solo artists. The next generation of composers and performers would expand on Mozart's and Stadler's innovations, and the explosion of compositions for clarinet at the beginning of the nineteenth century shows how quickly the instrument and its unique qualities was embraced by the musical world. A survey of music published for clarinet and strings between 1800 and 1900 reveals a predominance of three- and four-movement sonata cycles, but also a great many works based on popular and operatic tunes. Arrangements and medleys for a startling variety of ensembles and instrumentations made up a large proportion of the total sum of published sheet music during the nineteenth century. Duets for two clarinets or two flutes based on operas by Donizetti or Rossini were popular, and fantasies and variations were published for every instrument of the orchestra by firms who made their living satisfying the musical public's appetite for opera-inspired music scaled down to fit the middle-class living room and salon.

These clarinet works reflect wider trends in musical life of the early nineteenth century, which embraced virtuosic performance in theatrical concerts and salon appearances meant to astound attendees. This is not to say that virtuosity—the celebration of apparently unique, even super-human prowess on an instrument (or voice)—had not played an important role in earlier eras. But the Romantic period saw a new focus on virtuosity that aligned with a philosophical and artistic love of the unique, of the extraordinary, and of the artist-genius. Nineteenth-century art celebrated the supernatural, the macabre, and the mysterious, which made the virtuoso musician and his (or, rarely, her) skill the subject of extreme fascination.[11] Virtuosity and the instrumental genres that fostered it saturated musical life

---

11 Some commentators have called the early nineteenth-century piano style that bridges the Classical repertoire of the 1770s–1800s and the Lisztian pyrotechnics that would come in the 1840s the "post-Classical brilliant style." Jim Samson, *Virtuosity and the Musical Work: The Transcendental Studies of Liszt* (Cambridge: Cambridge University Press, 2003), provides a good overview and discussion of this style; see also Alex Stefaniak, *Schumann's Virtuosity: Criticism, Composition, and Performance in Nineteenth-Century Germany* (Bloomington: Indiana

in the nineteenth century, and we can clearly hear its influence in the clarinet chamber works of this era.

Many original works for clarinet were inspired by the playing of the virtuoso Heinrich Baermann (1784–1847), who was based at the Bavarian court in Munich from around 1806 to his retirement in 1839. In addition to being perhaps the most celebrated clarinetist of the first half of the nineteenth century, Baermann was, by all accounts, an affable host and a good friend to the composers and artists who had the good fortune to encounter him.[12] Baermann played a concert in Darmstadt in 1811 and met there the young Carl Maria von Weber and his friend Jakob Meyer Beer (who later styled himself Giacomo Meyerbeer), who were both studying with Abbé Vogler at the time. Baermann and Weber gave a concert together, and the three men struck up lasting friendships that resulted in orchestral and chamber works for clarinet.[13] Weber's Clarinet Quintet in B-flat Major, op. 34 (1811–15), holds a firm place in the modern clarinet repertoire, partly because it is widely understood as bridging the Classical style of Mozart's Clarinet Quintet and the late Romantic or even post-Romantic style of Brahms's work for the same instrumentation. Meyerbeer's Quintet in E-flat Major (1813) shares many compositional characteristics and

---

University Press, 2016). Carl Maria von Weber, whose Clarinet Quintet is discussed below, was an important proponent of this style.

12 According to Pamela Weston: "Weber called [Baermann] a 'truly great artist and wonderful man,' and Mendelssohn wrote … 'He is one of the best musicians I know; one of those who carry everyone along with them, and who feel the true life and fire of music, and to whom music has become speech.'" See Weston, "'Never More Beautiful Tones': The Great Heinrich Baermann," in *Clarinet Virtuosi of the Past* (London: Robert Hale, 1971), 128.

13 The two young composers became close friends in 1810 in Darmstadt (Weber was twenty-four and Meyerbeer nineteen years old at the time). Weber toured with Baermann from December 1811 through March 1812, and they met and played together on several subsequent occasions before Weber's premature death in 1826. Meyerbeer grew up in Berlin, where he may have heard and even performed with Baermann as a young man. When he spent three months in Munich in summer 1812, he and Baermann visited each other almost daily, attended the theater and concerts together, and performed together. *The Diaries of Giacomo Meyerbeer*, vol. 1, *1791–1839*, trans. Robert Letellier (Plainsboro, NJ: Associated University Presses, 1999).

formal features with the outer movements of its more famous cousin.[14] An examination of the two together here demonstrates the extent to which both composers were able to synthesize the same influences— instruction in the Classical style from Vogler, familiarity with the playing of Baermann, prior experience of composing and performing the post-Classical brilliant repertoire of their generation—into something altogether new and wholly representative of the early Romantic style.

Both Meyerbeer and Weber held Mozart up as an important influence and model. Weber's father, the founder and director of a traveling theater troupe, sought to promote his son as a "second Mozart," training him in performance and composition from an early age and billing him in concerts as a child prodigy. Weber would go on to make a living as a touring virtuoso pianist during his teens and twenties before eventually establishing himself as a successful theater director and opera composer, first in Prague (1813–16) and then in Dresden (1817–26). Meyerbeer, who was five years younger than Weber, came from an affluent Berlin family, so although he also performed from an early age, there was less pressure to affect the sensational aura of a wunderkind. Like many composers of his generation, he began his career as a piano virtuoso and frequently performed Mozart's piano concertos.[15] Thus, for both composers, virtuosic instrumental music was a cornerstone of their own training and early professional experience.

---

14 Meyerbeer's Quintet in E-flat, which remained unpublished in his lifetime, is actually titled "Sonate pour le Clarinette avec accompagnement de 2 Violons, Alto, & Violoncelle" in the surviving copyist's manuscript. The clarinetist Dieter Klöcker found the work among the papers of Heinrich Baermann's descendants and was the first to record the work in 1982. Bärenreiter published his modern critical edition in 2001. Klöcker also found an Adagio theme and variations movement probably by Meyerbeer among the Baermann family papers, which may be the "missing" slow movement of the Clarinet Quintet. Although he has recorded it together with the Allegro moderato and Rondo (thus proffering a three-movement quintet), the critical edition contains only two movements: a sonata form (Allegro moderato) and a Rondo (Allegretto scherzando).

15 Matthias Brzoska, "Meyerbeer, Giacomo," *Grove Music Online*. At the end of a nine-year study tour of Italy (1816–25), Meyerbeer achieved his first international success with the opera *Il crociato in Egitto*. The popularity of this work paved his way to Paris, and after the unprecedented success of his first French opera *Robert le diable* (1831), he divided his time between Berlin and Paris until his death at age seventy-three in 1864.

As in solo and chamber music composed for most instruments in the early nineteenth century, Weber's and Meyerbeer's Clarinet Quintets share a love of brilliant writing that would demonstrate the instrument's abilities and the performer's prowess. In the quintets, this takes the form of long stretches of music featuring virtuosic passagework—scalar runs and arpeggio patterns in sixteenth notes, chromatic roulades that traverse the full range of the instrument, ornamented lines filled with turns and grace notes—frequently used in transition and closing sections. The closing group from the exposition of Weber's first movement provides a concise example of all these features within just twenty-one measures (ex. 7.1). The technical feats in both Weber's and Meyerbeer's Quintets build on the innovations of Mozart and Stadler; dramatic leaps of two octaves or more from the lowest range of the clarinet to the altissimo register are common (see ex. 7.1, m. 77), as are sequences and arpeggios with "slur two, tongue two" articulation patterns. The string parts sometimes also imitate the clarinet's melodies and might develop motives from them, but rarely introduce new thematic material without the aid of the clarinet. In Meyerbeer's first movement, for example, the main head motifs for the primary and secondary themes are presaged by the cello (ex. 7.2a and ex. 7.2b) but immediately taken over by the clarinet.

Weber and Meyerbeer both take a mostly standard approach to form in their opening movements yet imbue sonata-form procedures with typically Romantic harmonic surprises and dramatic flourishes. In Meyerbeer's Quintet, for example, the primary theme closes with a definitive perfect authentic cadence in the tonic followed by an ensemble rest in measure 25. The melody that enters at the pick-up to measure 26 is a recomposition of the primary theme in C minor (vi), but the soft dynamic, lyrical opening, and static harmony in the accompaniment give it all the usual markers of a secondary theme rather than the roiling momentum of normal transitional material. The clarinet's three-measure trill over F major (V of V) harmony in measures 33–35 clarifies the role of this passage and leads to the actual secondary theme in B-flat already shown in example 7.2b. Weber also uses a minor-mode thematic variant to begin the transition from tonic in his opening movement. The eight-measure primary theme (mm. 17–24) cadences clearly in the tonic (B-flat) and is followed by an ensemble rest, as in the analogous moment in Meyerbeer's work. Weber's transition, though, begins with a startling G-minor chord marked *fortissimo* and notated in double and triple stops for the strings, followed by an arpeggio and an almost hesitant, tip-toe-like gesture that rests on D.

Example 7.1. Weber, Clarinet Quintet op. 34 (1811–15), mvt. 1, mm. 64–84, exposition closing group.

—(*continued*)

Example 7.1—*continued*

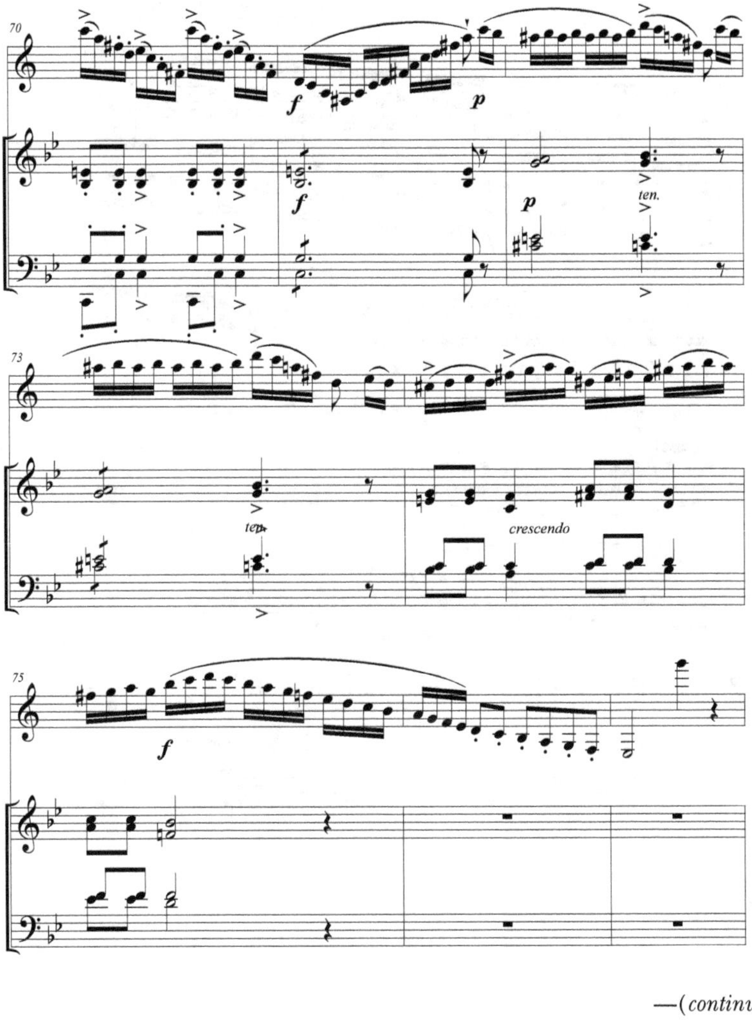

—(*continued*)

Example 7.1—*concluded*

Example 7.2a. Meyerbeer, Clarinet Quintet (1813), mvt. 1, mm. 1–8, primary theme.

Example 7.2b. Meyerbeer, Clarinet Quintet, mvt. 1, mm. 33–42, secondary theme.

After repeating this harmonic-melodic idea on F minor moving to C (V of V), the ensemble moves into a fast-paced, more normative transitional style that completes the modulation to F major.

Meyerbeer's Quintet contains a more striking harmonic surprise in the coda of the first movement. The recapitulation ends without a strong cadence on the tonic in measure 151, and the coda begins with a reprise of the primary theme over tense tremolo B♭s in the second violin. A stretto-like layering of the movement's primary and secondary themes and a gradual ensemble crescendo in measures 154–60 build toward a strong close on V in measure 163. The clarinet's trill over a three-beat rest in the strings invites ornamentation, and would seem to signal the return to tonic and a definitive, brilliant close to the movement (see ex. 7.3).[16] But at the downbeat of the next measure, a sudden *fortissimo* B-natural chord (♯V or, enharmonically, ♭VI) in shimmering sixteenth notes heralds one final iteration of the secondary theme's soaring lyrical motive shared by the cello and clarinet. Here, as elsewhere in the work, Meyerbeer demonstrates the theatrical flair that would make his music so effective on the operatic stage.

Meyerbeer's theatrical style and ability to convey drama without the aid of text are even more apparent in the witty Rondo that comprises the second half of the surviving Quintet. The work opens as though it will be a theme and variations, with a memorable rounded refrain (*a b a'*) in E-flat major. After a brief imitative section for the strings, the opening phrase of the refrain returns in the unexpected key of D major (VII), varied and ornamented to include faster triplet figurations. But the melody begins to fragment after the first four-measure phrase, with the strings interjecting clipped chords instead of their previous smooth syncopated pulse, and the clarinet repeats short motives instead of completing the phrase. The ensemble seems to confer in measures 39–43 when the strings respond to the clarinet as a group in unison, pointing the way to the dominant with a rising F–G–A gesture (see ex. 7.4). Immediately in measure 44, the clarinet introduces a new melody in B flat major (V) with a stately dotted rhythm and accented quarter-note pattern. The strings support the new musical idea with a solid pedal in the cello and punctuating chords in the other three voices, and a seven-part Rondo movement of alternating themes ensues.

---

16 Klöcker performs a cadenza-like extension here that we could also label an *Eingang*, or improvisatory lead-in to the next entrance.

Example 7.3. Meyerbeer, Clarinet Quintet, mvt. 1, mm. 160–69, coda.

—(continued)

Example 7.3—*concluded*

Weber's Clarinet Quintet op. 34 closes with a playful Rondo as well (Allegro giocoso); the movement is filled with fast sixteenth-note runs and passagework for the clarinet, resulting in a brilliant close to the work. As in Meyerbeer's Quintet, the strings play an important role in the finale. Reversing the procedures of earlier movements, where transition and closing sections invited an outburst of virtuosic playing from the clarinet, the transition sections in the Rondo tend to feature the strings, which gives the very busy clarinetist a moment to breathe and prepare for the next thematic section. The transition between the second refrain and the C section draws special attention to the string quartet by incorporating a fugato texture based on the B

Example 7.4. Meyerbeer, Clarinet Quintet, mvt. 4, mm. 36–46, witty dialogue.

section's theme. This twenty-one-measure passage moves the harmony from B-flat major (I) to D-flat (♭III), and allows all four of the stringed instruments to interact with each other and engage an important—and fun—melodic idea heard earlier in the movement. The section also introduces motivic development here at the mid-section of the work by exploring a minor-mode version of the theme (mm. 160–70) and combining it with the head motive from the refrain (mm. 170–76).

Weber uses a similar technique to provide a brief compositional climax at the end of the first movement. After the recapitulation finishes the business of restating the main themes of the movement in the tonic, including the brilliant-style closing group (mm. 180–91), the coda begins with a ten-measure passage for the string quartet alone. The strings introduce imitation here, starting with the first violin, which plays an augmented version of the motive first heard in the exposition's transition from tonic to dominant for the secondary theme. In typical fugal fashion, the theme moves through the four-part texture from top to bottom, then cycles through the ensemble again in its usual shorter note values. The quartet seems here to ignore the clarinet's interjection at measures 197–98, but works itself into a *fortissimo* unison frenzy at measures 200–202, repeating a short two-beat motive that eventually culminates in a half cadence on F (V) at the downbeat of measure 203. At this point, the clarinet takes over the texture once again with sparkling passagework to drive home the final cadence and close the work in the tonic.

In both of these instances, the string quartet takes on a standard persona or characterization associated with learnedness and sophistication that became increasingly common in writing about the ensemble and the genre after the turn of the nineteenth century. The scholar Klaus Aringer has proposed that Weber's Quintet represents a combination of opposing ideals or aesthetics because of its combination of the string quartet (associated with "true" or "pure" chamber style by previous commentators) and the solo wind instrument (associated with virtuosic showpieces).[17] Aringer suggests that in the Quintet Weber brings these two genres and sets of ideals together to represent his and Baermann's distinct roles in the creation of the work as an expression of the two men's friendship. In that reading of the work, these brief moments of compositional display may represent Weber and his personal identity as a composer, while the remainder of the piece represents Baermann and their interactions.[18] However, this reading is dependent on an understanding of the young Weber as

---

17 Klaus Aringer, "Carl Maria von Webers 'Klarinettenquintett'—Mozart als Vorbild?," in *"In Liebe zerflossenes Gefühl": Die Klarinette, Symposium im Rahmen der 30. Tage Alter Musik in Herne 2005*, ed. Christian Ahrens und Gregor Klinke (Munich: Katzbichler, 2008), 122–33.

18 Aringer's larger point in the article is to demonstrate that Weber did not take Mozart's K. 581 as a model in his composition of the Clarinet Quintet, or, put another way, that the differences in approach are due to the very different purposes of these works and their roles in social

primarily a "serious" composer by a later definition and ideology associated with Romanticism and Modernism, and it ignores his concurrent identity and experience as a virtuoso pianist himself and as a composer and director (not to mention consumer) of popular operas and the fantasies based on them.

The second movement (Fantasia: Adagio ma non troppo) of the Clarinet Quintet demonstrates Weber's experience as a composer and performer of the virtuoso vehicles of his day. This Fantasia is not based on a pre-existing tune, though Weber and Baermann had collaborated on that sort of work with the Variations for clarinet and piano op. 32 (1811), based on music from Weber's opera *Silvana.* Rather, it presents a doleful two-part aria for the clarinet. The opening A section in G minor is filled with falling scales and longing sighs, such as the appoggiatura at the downbeat of measure 8. The melody evokes the sensitive solo singing of a melancholy opera character with long, arch-shaped legato lines and slow rhythms that invite subtle dynamic effects. The notated grace notes provide *sprezzatura,* or nonchalance, associated with a free, seemingly effortless expression of emotion in a highly virtuosic style. The string quartet, meanwhile, is tasked with following the soloist and reflecting minute changes in tempo and pacing, much as an opera orchestra would, and Weber has provided a suitable accompaniment of long tones and quivering figurations that form a warm backdrop for the soloist. Like Chopin and other instrumentalists imitating operatic superstars, Weber maintains a quasi-vocal mirage in the Fantasia while also taking advantage of the clarinet's unique abilities to create an idiomatic approximation of the voice. This aspect of the Fantasia is most evident in two-octave leaps (m. 21), the combination of a three-octave leap with sudden changes of dynamic (mm. 35–37), and the cadenza-like chromatic scales at the end of the B and A' sections.

Although a variety of other works for clarinet and strings were composed, published, and performed between the composition of Mozart's Clarinet Quintet and Weber's, few if any of them can be said to have a strong presence in the modern clarinet chamber repertoire. That situation would change after the 1890s, when the aging composer Johannes Brahms came out of retirement to compose a group of chamber works for clarinet inspired by the playing of Richard Mühlfeld.

---

life at the time of composition, not to a lack of compositional ability or understanding of chamber music on Weber's part.

Brahms and Mühlfeld Commemorate a Legacy

In 1890 Johannes Brahms (1833–97) wrote to his longtime publisher and friend Fritz Simrock that he intended to retire from composition and that his String Quintet in G, op. 111, would be the last work he released to the world.[19] In March 1891, though, he made a visit to the court of Meiningen, where Duke Georg II, who was a great admirer of Brahms and his music, maintained one of Europe's best private musical establishments at the end of the century.

The court's music director brought to Brahms's attention the fine playing of a young clarinetist named Richard Mühlfeld (1856–1907). During this visit, the two men met and made music together, with Brahms quizzing his younger colleague on the clarinet's capabilities and limitations and listening raptly to his playing of Mozart's Clarinet Quintet and Weber's F Minor Concerto among other works.[20] Brahms left Meiningen with the promise of new compositions designed for Mühlfeld, and he began fulfilling that promise immediately during his annual summer retreat in Bad Ischl, when he composed the Trio for Clarinet, Cello, and Piano op. 114 and the Quintet for Clarinet and Strings op. 115. Both works were performed in a semi-private concert at Meiningen in November, then publicly premiered in Berlin in December at one of Joseph Joachim's famous quartet evening concerts. Brahms would go on to perform with Mühlfeld in several private and public concerts and to compose two clarinet sonatas (published together as op. 120) for his friend in 1894. After noting that there existed too few works available in the repertoire for an artist of Mühlfeld's caliber, he convinced the Vienna Tonkünstlerverein that it should sponsor a competition for new compositions "for the

---

19 Writing to chide his friend about the high retail cost of his scores and to send the four-hand piano arrangement of the String Quintet, Brahms opened his letter to Simrock (December 11, 1890): "The enclosed is the ending of the 1st movement ... With that scrap of paper you can take your farewell from my music." Trans. in Styra Avins and Josef Eisinger, *Johannes Brahms: Life and Letters* (Oxford: Oxford University Press, 1997), 674.

20 Pamela Weston includes probably the most detailed biography of Mühlfeld in English in *Clarinet Virtuosi of the Past*, 215–16; and Colin Lawson recounts it in *Brahms: Clarinet Quintet*, Cambridge Music Handbooks (Cambridge: Cambridge University Press, 1998), 31–32.

furtherance of wind-instrument music" in 1897 and increased the prize money from his own funds.[21]

The Clarinet Quintet that Brahms composed for Mühlfeld combines the best, most memorable features of both Mozart's and Weber's Quintets to create something wholly new in a work that commemorates the achievements of the eras that those two works represented for Brahms and his contemporaries.[22] It recalls the equitable dialogue of Mozart's work, sometimes going beyond dialogue to suggest a fusion of voices in service of a single expressive aim. In Brahmsian fashion, it utilizes a Classical four-movement form modeled, perhaps, on Mozart's own Quintet. The first three movements follow standard procedures, at least on the surface: a fast sonata form and slow movement are followed by a lighter scherzo-style movement. The work closes with a Theme and Variations finale movement, just as Mozart's Quintet had, which was unusual for Brahms's multi-movement works. Brahms's Quintet is also infused with Romantic features, though, drawn from Weber's dramatic style and strongly influenced by Brahms's more immediate artistic forebears: Robert and Clara Schumann, Frederick Chopin, and even Wagner.

In this way, Brahms's composition also provides a culminating point for his own career and for the musical legacy that he loved and celebrated throughout his working life. The Quintet shows many characteristics of a "late style" that indicates a composer wrestling with mortality, and it demonstrates Brahms's unique response to the ennui and nostalgia that dominated high culture at the end of the nineteenth century.[23] In fin-de-siècle Vienna (ca. 1880–1910), artists of Brahms's

21 The winner of the prize, awarded in March 1897, was Walther Rabl, for his Quartet for Clarinet, Violin, Cello, and Piano, published by Simrock as his opus 1 later that year. Brahms, whose health and vitality were rapidly declining because of liver cancer, attended the dress rehearsal for this work at the home of Karl and Leopoldine Wittgenstein so that he could hear Mühlfeld play. (He specifically requested to hear Weber's Quintet as well.) Brahms would die just a month later on April 3.

22 Of the works discussed here, the Brahms Quintet has received the most attention in scholarship, in part because it so neatly encapsulates Brahms's late style. Lawson provides an excellent movement-by-movement overview of the work as well as a concise discussion of relevant historical performance practices, contemporaneous compositions, and other matters in *Brahms: Clarinet Quintet.*

23 Margaret Notley, *Lateness and Brahms: Music and Culture in the Twilight of Viennese Liberalism* (Oxford: Oxford University Press, 2007). On

generation and within his social circle felt that their way of life was coming to an end with the dawn of the new century and the technological and social changes whirling around them.[24] On a personal level, Brahms's awareness of his own mortality was sharpened by the decline and deaths of several close friends in the 1880s, and his role in a changing social circle began to evolve into that of a beloved uncle or grandfather, rather than the gregarious bachelor about town that he had seemed in earlier decades.[25]

The Clarinet Quintet's expression of "lateness" or nostalgia manifests primarily in its persistent minor mode, the "Gypsy" lament style of the Adagio movement, and melodic reminiscences that create a cyclical form within the work. Because previous scholars have noted both the melancholy minor mode and the importance of the Adagio movement's lament style, I will focus here on the layers of musical connections that Brahms created through melodic reminiscences and allusions to other works, particularly in the finale's set of variations.[26]

Musical references at the end of a work or movement that recall earlier music within it mimic the act of reflecting on a moment or idea from the past. With these musical reminiscences, artists create thematic unity across the different portions of a work. Reminiscences at the ends of movements or works create "cyclicity" because the work seems to return to an earlier point in time (often its beginning) as though on a loop. In some cases, composers use this technique to

---

"late style" more generally (i.e., interpreting the common features or aesthetic apparent in the music of composers writing at the end of their lives), see Theodor Adorno's seminal essay "On Beethoven's Late Style" of 1937 (translated and reprinted in *Essays on Music*, ed. Richard Leppert, Berkeley: University of California Press, 1993) and Michael Spitzer, *Music as Philosophy: Adorno and Beethoven's Late Style* (Bloomington: Indiana University Press, 2006).

24 Carl E. Schorske, *Fin-de-siècle Vienna: Politics and Culture* (New York: Alfred A. Knopf, 1979).

25 I discuss the different opportunities for music making that this change in Brahms's social role created in *The Social Worlds of Nineteenth-Century Chamber Music* (Champaign: University of Illinois Press, 2015), 206–15.

26 Lawson, *Brahms: Clarinet Quintet* discusses the prevalence of minor mode. On the "Gypsy" lament, or *hallgató*, style of the Adagio, see Jonathan Bellman, *The style hongrois in the Music of Western Europe* (Boston: Northeastern University Press, 1993). For a thorough discussion of the importance of instrumental Adagios in music of the late nineteenth century, including this movement by Brahms, see Notley, *Lateness and Brahms*.

comment on the passage of time or on the important role that memory plays in the human experience. Brahms had used this approach, modeled after Beethoven and Schumann among others, in several earlier works. In some of these, he employed dramatic transformations to suggest, in the words of Walter Frisch, "not so much a return to where we started as ... an emblem of how far we have come," and in others he used a more direct thematic recall to point up the contrast between where the work started and where it ends.[27] Several of Brahms's cyclical works also contain reminiscences of musical features from works by other composers. Often called allusions or borrowings, these references allow composers to engage in dialogue with their artistic forebears and contemporaries, and they deepen the suggestion of memory and reflection in these works.[28]

In his earlier examples of cyclic forms, Brahms displays a characteristic youthful optimism and bravura. These works stake his claim to the mantel of great German artist alongside the works of Mozart, Beethoven, and Schumann. In them, he demonstrates his familiarity with the legacy of art music while also showing off new stylistic and formal approaches to the Classical tradition. In the later Clarinet Quintet, however, Brahms's recollection and recomposition of earlier moments in the work and beyond it lead to a nostalgic style. Each movement of the work ends quietly in the minor mode with no suggestion of the triumphant transformation heard in earlier cyclic works by the composer, which has led previous commenters to describe it and Brahms's other late works as "autumnal" in character.

The finale's telltale callback to the first movement's theme actually presents a recollection of a recollection. The first-movement Allegro brings back the opening two-measure introductory motive at several points in its second half, and each time that motive dissolves into a different continuation. (Brahms's characteristic developing variation technique is on full display in this movement.) The continual variance

---

27 Walter Frisch, "The Snake Bites Its Tail: Cyclic Processes in Brahms's Third String Quartet, op. 67," *Journal of Musicology* 22, no. 1 (2005): 158.

28 See Christopher Reynolds, *Motives for Allusion: Context and Content in Nineteenth-Century Music* (Cambridge, MA: Harvard University Press, 2003) and Jacqueline Sholes, *Allusion as Narrative Premise in Brahms's Instrumental Music* (Bloomington: Indiana University Press, 2018). On the experience of time in Romantic music, see Benedict Taylor, *Mendelssohn, Time, and Memory: The Romantic Conception of Cyclic Form* (Cambridge: Cambridge University Press, 2011).

of this opening gesture creates anticipation, as the listener awaits a complete recollection of the violins' phrase and the clarinet's original entry or answer. The introductory phrase returns in the paired violins at the end of the coda in measures 207–10 in a version that very closely replicates the opening of the movement, but when the clarinet enters the texture in measure 211, it eschews its original rising arpeggio and swelling lyrical theme to present instead a quiet, halting motive that emphasizes the half step between A♯ and B, then E♯ and F♯, before a subdued drop down through the tonic triad to rest on a quiet, sustained F♯ in the low register. The quiet close here and at the ends of the Quintet's other movements reinforces the work's reflective atmosphere and the seeming refusal to provide a triumphant or celebratory ending. That sentiment is amplified at the end of the finale, which closes by recalling the Allegro's ending, not its beginning, in the *un poco meno mosso* section (m. 193 to the end). Here as in other cyclical works, Brahms recomposes his material to offer a transformation of the first movement's beginning/ending. The first violin plays the Allegro's introductory motive alone, over throbbing Bs in the lower voices, joined here by the viola rather than second violin for the theme's sumptuous parallel sixths. Borrowing from the close of the first movement, though, the theme pauses in measure 197, then gives the halting four-note motive ending in half steps. The clarinet finally enters the texture at measure 201 with a variation on the opening motive that, as at the end of the first movement, does not develop into an expansive theme, but into an exploration of the four-note, half-step motive in a soft dynamic. The recollection of an earlier musical moment highlights the distance traveled, rather than the point of origin. In this expression of late-life nostalgia, it also emphasizes a quiet reflection on endings and on satisfactory, if bittersweet, closure.

But the Clarinet Quintet's finale also evokes earlier works by Brahms and by his artistic idols. The first and most obvious reference is to Mozart's own Clarinet Quintet, which also ends with a set of variations. Both composers adopt a five-variation approach to the overall form, with the work's tonic anchoring each variation until a shift to the parallel key (in variation 3 for Mozart and variation 4 for Brahms). For the fifth variation, both composers introduce a striking change. Mozart includes a luscious *adagio* variation filled with chromaticism and sensuous pauses in the dialogue between clarinet and first violin (mm. 85–105). Brahms adds a new kinetic element in variation 5 by changing the meter from a square $\frac{2}{4}$ to a dancing $\frac{3}{8}$. Pizzicato arpeggios in the cello provide a light backdrop to the playful interaction of the viola and clarinet, conveying a charming conversational style. In this movement as in his other mature sets, Brahms varies his theme in a restrained, Classical style by hewing closely to the underlying structure of the original theme and altering aspects of style and instrumentation, rather than piling on ornaments or diminutions so that the theme becomes unrecognizable. The theme itself is closely modeled on the style of Mozart, perhaps on the theme of K. 581 specifically. Both themes comprise two pairs of phrases with the second half repeated (|| AA' ||: BA'' :||). Brahms's theme moves to the submediant (G major) for its B phrase, and this harmonic gambit remains a consistent feature of each variation. That brief glimpse of major-mode lyricism in each variation is highlighted by a change of instrumentation or style, contributing to the autumnal quality of the work. In variation 2, for example, the first half of the theme is treated in a stormy style with the theme in the first violin enclosed by rapid arpeggio figures in the clarinet and cello. The inner voices' syncopated chords add urgency, especially in the group crescendos at measures 69–70 and 77–80. When the B phrase begins in G major at measure 81, the clarinet assumes the starring role with a swaying legato melody in eighth notes, and the syncopated chords in the rest of the ensemble take on a gentle throbbing quality. When the cello joins the clarinet in parallel octaves, the calming gesture expands, momentarily, into a cozy peaceful interlude. That atmosphere dissipates immediately in measure 89, however, with the *forte* B-minor chord and the clarinet's forceful statement of the variation's opening motive.

Elaine Sisman has shown that the theme and variations format was a touchstone for Brahms throughout his career, one in which he could "assess his relationship to his musical forebears and contemporaries," and works in this form contain his most pointed references to earlier compositions.[29] Despite completing several brilliant stand-alone sets of variations, Brahms used this format sparingly within multi-movement works, and only rarely in finales; he seems to have reserved it for especially significant or personal works.[30] For example, the Third String

---

29 Elaine Sisman, "Brahms and the Variation Canon," *19th-Century Music* 14, no. 2 (1990): 132.

30 Brahms set his other variations movements within larger works in slow tempi and used lyrical themes, usually based on historical models such as a medieval song or folksong. Brahms's variation technique was remarkably consistent, with the exception of the op. 67 String Quartet finale. In each of his other variations movements, he included three variations very closely modeled on the harmonic structure of the

Quartet (op. 67, 1876) ends with a compositionally virtuosic set of eight variations that, like those of the Clarinet Quintet, make reference to a work by Mozart and include a cyclical thematic return. Tellingly, the op. 67 finale is the only variations movement within a larger work that Brahms labeled as such, and it is the only one to conclude a multi-movement work before the Clarinet Quintet. His return to this sort of finale and to the music of Mozart as a model may have been prompted by his collaboration with Mühlfeld, and it offered the opportunity to re-evaluate his relationship to that idol.

Although Richard Mühlfeld clearly possessed flawless technique, Brahms and his contemporaries responded most effusively to the soulful, singing quality of his tone and the depth of his musical inflection. In Mühlfeld's thoughtful interpretations of works by revered masters such as Mozart and Weber, Brahms perceived a kindred spirit that inspired him to continue his own exploration of the Classical style. In the Clarinet Quintet's finale, he revisited the central tenets of his own compositional philosophy, based on techniques learned from decades of studying and performing the music of Mozart and others. In this way, Muhlfeld and Brahms provide a suitable transition: The Quintet (and other clarinet works created by this duo) commemorated the achievements of earlier generations while also inspiring new generations to compose in the format. Like the finale of the Quintet itself, this work brings to full circle the task, originating with Stadler and Mozart, of creating a genre to display the clarinet's best qualities.

---

theme, a fourth variation that changes mode, and a fifth variation that introduces a stylistic change such as a new pastoral element.

8

IMPORTANT CLARINETISTS SINCE 1900

A Concise Introduction

Jane Ellsworth

The panorama of clarinet artistry in the twentieth and early twenty-first centuries is spectacular. How can one possibly select just a few individuals to highlight in an essay such as this, when there are hundreds of players whose achievements might warrant their inclusion? Any survey of important clarinetists must necessarily be selective, and to some extent personal. Therefore, besides their excellence as performers, the individuals discussed in this chapter have made additional significant contributions to the field in one or more of the following areas.

1   Recording: Performers from the early history of recording technology, and later individuals whose recording activities were notable in terms of quality, quantity, and repertoire.

2   Repertoire expansion: Serving as the dedicatees or commissioners of clarinet repertoire from important composers; premiering new works or rediscovering lost or forgotten clarinet repertoire.

3   Ensembles: Founders and/or members of important chamber ensembles.

4   Breaking barriers: Members of historically underrepresented groups in the profession who have made significant careers as clarinetists.

5   Popularizers: Clarinetists who have especially contributed to the visibility of the clarinet with the general public.

Even these criteria could potentially allow for the inclusion of many more clarinetists than those who appear in this chapter. For readers disappointed that their favorite clarinetist has been excluded, there are several sources one may consult to read about these individuals. First and foremost among this biographical literature are the numerous books by Pamela Weston (1921–2009).[1] She also contributed over thirty articles on clarinetists to *The New Grove Dictionary of Music and Musicians*, as well as many reports in the journals of the International Clarinet Association and the Clarinet & Saxophone Society of Great Britain. To avoid duplication, I have chosen—with a few exceptions—to omit players who are already discussed in Weston's *Clarinet Virtuosi of Today* (1989), a number of whom are still at the forefront of the profession as of this writing.

While many general books about the clarinet contain brief biographical sketches of historical clarinetists, one must look to journal articles, along with academic theses and dissertations, to find in-depth biographies of specific players. Among the most useful is "A Biographical Dictionary of Twentieth-Century American Clarinetists" (2011) by Tracey Lynn Paddock, a large thesis which is nevertheless limited to a particular nationality.[2] Several dissertations have been written that focus on single clarinetists.[3] A few clarinetists, including Benny

---

1   Weston's books are *Clarinet Virtuosi of the Past* (London: Robert Hale, 1971); *More Clarinet Virtuosi of the Past* (London: the author, 1977); *Clarinet Virtuosi of Today* (Wakefield, UK: Egon Publishing, 1989); *Yesterday's Clarinettists: A Sequel* (Ampleforth, UK: Emerson Edition, 2002); and *Heroes and Heroines of Clarinettistry* (Victoria, BC, and Bloomington, IN: Trafford, 2008).

2   Tracy Lynn Paddock, "A Biographical Dictionary of Twentieth-Century American Clarinetists" (DM treatise, Florida State University, 2011). Richard Stoltzman and Robert Spring have been the subject of dissertations, which are cited later in these notes.

3   See, for example, Adria Sutherland, "Partnerships and Creation: A Brief History of Clarinetist-Composer Partnerships and How They Contributed to Clarinet Literature, and the Influence of Robert Spring on Contemporary Compositional Output for the Clarinet"

Goodman, Guy Deplus, and Stanley Drucker, have been the subject of monographs.[4] Some well-known clarinetists have written about their profession, such as Jack Brymer (three books), Richard Temple Savage, and Basil Tschaikov.[5]

Needless to say, all of the clarinetists mentioned in this chapter have contributed to more than one of the categories mentioned above. I will introduce each performer's biography in a category in which their activities have been especially significant, referring to them again in other categories as appropriate. Where a clarinetist's main biography appears, his or her name is given in bold type.

Repertoire Expansion

One of the most important relationships in music is that between a composer and the performer for whom he or she writes. Performers can help composers understand the capabilities of an instrument, and composers can help performers reach toward extending those capabilities. Many such fruitful relationships have enriched the clarinet repertoire, going back to the early days of the instrument's use.[6] A good number of the standard clarinet works of the twentieth century have of course been dedicated to specific players, but it is also true that numerous clarinetists have actively commissioned works from major composers. Perhaps the most famous of these was **Benny Goodman** (1909–86).

(DMA project, University of Kentucky, 2018). Other dissertations of this type are mentioned in footnotes below.

4   For Benny Goodman, see n. 7 below; Bruno Martinez, *L'ascèse et la flamme: entretiens avec Guy Deplus* (*Asceticism and the Flame: Interviews with Guy Deplus*) (Paris: Éditions MF, 2013); Mitchell Estrin, *Stanley Drucker: Clarinet Master* (New York: Carl Fisher, 2018). The important Swiss-French-American player and pedagogue Daniel Bonade (1896–1976) has also been the subject of a biography: Carol Anne Kycia, *Daniel Bonade: A Founder of the American Style of Clarinet Playing* (Captiva, FL: Captiva Publishing, 1999).

5   Jack Brymer, *Clarinet* (London: MacDonald and Jane's, 1976), *From Where I Sit* (London: Cassell, 1979), and *In the Orchestra* (London: Hutchinson, 1987); Richard Temple Savage, *A Voice from the Pit* (Newton Abbot: David and Charles, 1988); Basil Tschaikov, *The Music Goes Round and Around* (Peterborough: FastPrint, 2009).

6   For an overview, see Pamela Weston, "Players and Composers," in *The Cambridge Companion to the Clarinet*, ed. Colin Lawson (Cambridge: Cambridge University Press, 1995), 92–106.

Goodman was probably the most widely documented clarinetist of his era.[7] Known primarily as a jazz clarinetist, he was nonetheless classically trained; throughout his lifetime he took lessons from such prominent clarinetists as Simeon Bellison, Reginald Kell, Gustave Langenus, Eric Simon, and David Weber.

Goodman's first commission was assisted by the violinist Joseph Szigeti. It may seem odd that a classical violinist would want to collaborate with a jazz clarinetist in the 1930s; but Szigeti had developed an interest in jazz as a teenager, and became so enamored of it that he frequented jazz clubs whenever he was in New York—including a memorable night at the Roosevelt Grill in 1935 where he met and befriended Goodman. As a result, Szigeti began to approach composers about writing a work that he and Goodman could play together. After the English composer William Walton declined the commission to write a concerto for them in 1936, Szigeti wrote to his fellow Hungarian Béla Bartók, who composed *Contrasts* for clarinet, violin, and piano (1938).[8] Although it was originally planned as a short, two-movement work in order to fit on a 78 rpm record, Bartók eventually added a slow movement, and in this form it has become a standard piece in the clarinet repertoire.

Goodman also commissioned concertos. The first of these was by Darius Milhaud in 1941; it was the result of much negotiation of terms, and in the end Goodman never played it, because of its difficulty. Paul Hindemith's Concerto was commissioned in the same year as Milhaud's, but its completion was delayed because Goodman worried that the public might disapprove of his association with a German composer in wartime. It was finished in 1947, and Goodman finally premiered it in 1950. The war also affected the fate of a concerto composed for

---

7   A sample of sources for further reading includes James Lincoln Collier, *Benny Goodman and the Swing Era* (Oxford: Oxford University Press, 1989); Ross Firestone, *Swing, Swing, Swing* (New York: W. W. Norton, 1993); D. Russell Connor and Warren W. Hicks, *BG on the Record: A Bio-discography of Benny Goodman* (New Rochelle, NY: Arlington House, 1970); and John Snavely, "Benny Goodman's Commissioning of New Works and Their Significance for Twentieth-Century Clarinetists" (DMA thesis, University of Arizona, 1991).

8   The text of Szigeti's letter is given in Vera Lampert, "Benny Goodman and Bartók's *Contrasts*: An Extraordinary Collaboration," *The Musical Quarterly* 101, no. 1 (2018): 6–34. The article also presents an excellent overview of the relationships between Szigeti, Goodman, and Bartók.

Goodman by Benjamin Britten, begun in 1941 when Britten was resid-
ing in the United States. As Britten attempted to return to the United
Kingdom in 1942, United States customs authorities confiscated the
manuscript of the concerto that Britten carried with him, fearing that
it contained some kind of a code. The manuscript was later returned to
the composer, but he did not finish the work.[9] Other commissions by
Goodman included Morton Gould's *Derivations* for clarinet and dance
band (1955) and Malcolm Arnold's Second Clarinet Concerto (1974).

Frederick Thurston (1901–53) was one of the most important English clarinetists of the first half of the twentieth century. After a period
of study with Charles Draper at the Royal College of Music, Thurston
went on to perform in numerous London orchestras, most importantly the BBC Symphony Orchestra, with which he played as principal
clarinetist from its founding in 1930. Although he never directly commissioned new works from composers, his artistic stature was such that
many major works were written for him, particularly by English composers. These included sonatas by Arnold Bax and Herbert Howells,
as well as John Ireland's *Fantasy-Sonata* and the Sonatina by Malcolm
Arnold; quintets for clarinet and strings by Gordon Jacob and Arthur
Bliss; concertos by Arnold, Iain Hamilton, Gerald Finzi, and Alan Raw-
sthorne; and the Concertino no. 1 by Elizabeth Maconchy.[10]

The Swiss-German clarinetist **Eduard Brunner** (1939–2017) was
principal clarinetist of the Bavarian Radio Orchestra for thirty years,
retiring in 1993.[11] His interest in contemporary music attracted the

---

9   The manuscript consisted of a single, nearly complete movement.
     Colin Matthews orchestrated this in 1989, and the first performance
     of it was given in 1990 by Michael Collins. Matthews added additional
     movements from material in Britten's unpublished archive in 2007;
     the complete work has been recorded by Collins.

10   Further information about Thurston's life may be found in Weston,
     Clarinet Virtuosi of the Past, 271–74; Andrew Smith, "Portraits 4:
     Frederick Thurston," *Clarinet & Saxophone* 12, no. 1 (March 1987):
     19–21; Pamela Weston et al., *Frederick Thurston: A Centenary Celebration*
     (London: Clarinet & Saxophone Society of Great Britain, 2001);
     Colin Bradbury, "Frederick Thurston," *Clarinet & Saxophone* 26, no.
     2 (Summer 2001): 16–21; and Aileen Marie Razey, "The Inspiration
     behind the Compositions for Clarinetist Frederick Thurston" (DMA
     diss., University of North Texas, 2018).

11   Information about Brunner's life and activity may be found in
     Antonio Galindo Agunduz, "Conflict in Contemporary Music
     Interpretation. Brunner-Lachenmann: A Case Approach" (master's
     project, University of Gothenberg, 2011); and in liner notes to Isang

attention of many composers, including Pierre Boulez, Edison Denisov, Jean Françaix, Sofia Gubaidulina, Paul Hindemith, Giya Kancheli, György Kurtág, Helmut Lachenmann, Krzysztof Meyer, and Isang Yun.

Not all twentieth-century expansion of the clarinet repertoire has involved the creation of new works; there has also been the rediscovery of older repertoire that has been lost or forgotten. No clarinetist has been more central to this activity than **Dieter Klöcker** (1936–2011).[12] Under the influence of his first teacher, Karl Kroll (whose son Oskar, also a clarinetist, wrote an important book on the clarinet before losing his life in World War II), Klöcker developed an interest in old music editions. In the 1960s, while playing in regional orchestras in Germany, Klöcker began to search for forgotten and unpublished works from the eighteenth and early nineteenth centuries in many European libraries and private collections. He discovered works that were known but thought to have been lost, and others that were incomplete but worthy of restoration. Occasionally his enthusiasm led to controversy—for example, asserting Mozart as the author for some quartets for clarinet and string trio he had discovered, erroneously attributing several clarinet concertos to Haydn, or inserting a movement by one composer into the work of another without identifying it. Nevertheless, he was outstandingly successful in introducing new and lesser-known eighteenth- and nineteenth-century composers to the public, such as Louis Ferdinand, Archduke Rudolph, Antonio Cartellieri, Conradin Kreutzer, Theodor von Schacht, Friedrich Witt, and many others.

Other twentieth-century clarinetists who had an important impact on the expansion of the clarinet repertoire deserve to be mentioned at least briefly. Aage Oxenvad (1884–1944) was most famously the dedicatee of the Clarinet Concerto by Carl Nielsen, but other Danish composers wrote for him as well, including Harald Agersnap, Jørgen Bentzon, Herman Koppel, and Rudolph Simonsen. The English clarinetist Gervase de Peyer (see below) had works written for him by

---

Yun, *Clarinet Concerto,* Camerata CMT 1084, 1982; Isang Yun, *Clarinet Quintets,* CPO 999 428, 1996; and Helmut Lachenmann *Accanto,* Wergo WER 6738, 1977.

12 Pertinent sources of information include Heribert Haase, "Dieter Klöcker: A Profile," *The Clarinet* 12, no. 3 (Spring 1985): 38–42; Luigi Magistrelli, "An Interview with Dieter Klöcker," *The Clarinet* 23, no. 2 (February–March 1996): 40–42; Dieter Klöcker, "Discovering the Mozart Quartets," *The Clarinet* 14, no. 3 (May–June 1987): 18–19; and Jane Ellsworth, "Haydn Clarinet Concertos: A Case of Wishful Thinking," *The Clarinet* 29, no. 3 (June 2002): 50–53.

Joseph Horovitz (a Concertante for Clarinet and Strings and a Sonatina); Kenneth Leighton, John McCabe, and Robert Simpson (all three wrote clarinet-cello-piano trios for him); Alun Hoddinott (Sonata); and Thea Musgrave, Berthold Goldschmidt, and William Mathias (all of whom wrote concertos for him). He also gave first performances of works not specifically written for him, such as concertos by Arnold Cooke (no. 1) and Ivor Keys, and Robert Simpson's Clarinet Quintet. Elsa Ludewig-Verdehr and the Verdehr Trio all but created the repertoire for clarinet, violin, and piano (see details below).

Recordings

Recordings provide evidence of a musician's artistry, allowing the musician to leave a legacy of work for future audiences. An excellent survey of clarinet recordings to about 1990 is Michael Bryant's chapter in *The Cambridge Companion to the Clarinet* (1995).[13] Richard Gilbert's clarinet discographies and the CHARM database can also serve as guides to the subject.[14]

The earliest clarinet recordings date from the end of the nineteenth century, when Henry Giese, William Tuson, and several other American clarinetists recorded short works on cylinders.[15] Very little is known about these musicians, except that some of them played in distinguished bands; Henry Giese was also a member of the New York Symphony under Walter Damrosch. Readers wishing to explore these

---

13 Michael Bryant, "The Clarinet on Record," in *The Cambridge Companion to the Clarinet*, ed. Colin Lawson (Cambridge: Cambridge University Press, 1995), 199–212.

14 Richard Gilbert, *The Clarinetists' Solo Repertoire: A Discography* (New York: The Grenadilla Society, 1972); *The Clarinetists' Discography II* (New York: The Grenadilla Society, 1975); *The Clarinetists' Discography III* (Harrington Park, NJ: RG Productions 1991); *Supplement to The Clarinetists' Discography III* (Harrington Park, NJ: RG Productions, 1996); *The 20th Century and Beyond: A Clarinet Discography* (Grenadilla Music, 2009, compact disc). CHARM (Centre for the History and Analysis of Recorded Music) is a searchable discographical research tool: https://charm.rhul.ac.uk/index.html.

15 Stan Stanford, "Clarinet Recordings (Historic)," in *Encyclopedia of Recorded Sound*, ed. Frank Hoffman (New York: Routledge, 2005), 2:189–90; "Edison Clarinet Recordings in America 1889–1924," *The Clarinet* 38, no. 1 (December 2010): 38–41; "Clarinet Recordings in America 1890–1920," *The Clarinet* 41, no. 2 (March 2014), 79–83.

early recordings can find opportunities online or on compact discs.[16] Many of the early recorded works were of a popular nature, and it was not until after recording equipment crossed the Atlantic that consideration began to be given to core classical repertoire.

One of the earliest recordings of works from the standard clarinet repertoire was made by the English clarinetist **Charles Draper** (1869–1952). Draper's life and achievements have been well documented.[17] He studied with Henry Lazarus and Julian Egerton at the Royal Academy of Music in London, and was subsequently a member of Queen Victoria's private band and Thomas Beecham's New Symphony Orchestra. Under the influence of Manuel Gomez, Draper was an early proponent of the Boehm clarinet in England. Draper was comfortable in the recording environment. At the outset he recorded popular music, but he soon began to pioneer recordings of canonic works such as Weber's Concertino (1909, abridged), Brahms's Quintet (two movements, abridged, 1917; complete, 1929), Mozart's Quintet (1926 and 1928), Schubert's Octet (1928) and *The Shepherd on the Rock* (in English, 1928), and Beethoven's Septet (1930).

Another English clarinetist who made early recordings was **Reginald Kell** (1906–81).[18] After two years of study with Haydn Draper at the Royal Academy of Music, Kell started to play in London orchestras.

---

16 An important online resource is the website of Stan Stanford, who has exhaustively researched early clarinet recordings: http://www.clarphon.com/. Compact disc recordings include *The Acoustic Era: Clarinet Recordings 1898–1918*, North Pacific Music 2365, 2011; *Masters of the Clarinet*, Archeophone Records ARCH 5451, 2010; and *Historical Recordings*, vols. 1 and 2, Clarinet Classics CC0005, 1993, and CC0010, 1994.

17 Weston, *Clarinet Virtuosi of the Past*, 264–71, *More Clarinet Virtuosi of the Past*, 87–88, and *Yesterday's Clarinettists*, 62; Arnold Draper, "A Musical Family: The Welsh Connection," *Clarinet & Saxophone* 22, no. 1 (Spring 1997): 11–13, and no. 2 (Summer 1997): 19–21.

18 Further information about Kell may be found in James Sclater, "Reginald Kell: Clarinetist Without a Country," *The Clarinet* 28, no. 2 (March 2001): 58–63, no. 3 (June 2001): 34–39, and no. 4 (September 2001): 58–63; and 29, no. 1 (December 2001): 40–45. See also Paddock, "A Biographical Dictionary of Twentieth-Century American Clarinetists," 166–67; John Denman et al.; "Tributes to Kell," *The Clarinet* 9, no. 2 (Winter 1982): 6–11 (includes a partial discography); Stephen Trier, obituary of Reginald Kell, *Clarinet & Saxophone* 6, no. 4 (October 1981): 20; and Andrew Smith, "Portraits 2: Reginald Kell," *Clarinet & Saxophone* 11, no. 3 (September 1986): 39–42.

He was an early adopter of vibrato, which at the time was generally not used by English clarinetists; his use of it received mixed reviews, with the criticism coming mostly from other clarinetists. Kell was completely at home in the recording studio, and in 1937 began recording most of the major works in the repertoire: Brahms's Quintet with the Busch Quartet, Ravel's *Introduction and Allegro*, Holbrooke's Quintet (Holbrooke was his brother-in-law), Weber's Concertino, Mozart's Concerto, Schumann's *Fantasiestücke* op. 73, and trios by Mozart, Beethoven, and Brahms. He re-recorded many standard works after the technology changed to long-playing (LP) records in 1948.

In America, an early recording of the standard repertoire was made by **Simeon Bellison** (1883–1954) when he recorded Mozart's Quintet in 1936.[19] Born in Russia, Bellison was first clarinet of the Imperial Opera in St. Petersburg from 1915 until the Russian Revolution in 1917. In 1918 he organized a world tour of his chamber ensemble, called Zimro (see below). Bellison eventually arrived in America, joining the New York Philharmonic as first clarinet in 1920 and taking American citizenship in 1921.[20] Besides the Mozart Quintet, Bellison also recorded Khachaturian's Trio, the Quintet and Trio by Brahms (the recordings are preserved at the Library of Congress), a collection of transcriptions for clarinet and piano of music by Mozart, Beethoven, Tchaikovsky, and Baermann (recorded in 1940 on LP), and much else. At least three compact discs of his historic recordings have been released.[21]

The Frenchman **Louis Cahuzac** (1880–1960) began recording in the 1930s. Cahuzac was one of the most distinguished soloists of his day. He passed auditions for the Paris Opéra and the Concerts Colonne in 1901 and remained with them for thirty years, during which time he also played in other orchestras and ensembles and toured Europe extensively.[22] Cahuzac's first recording was of Weber's Concertino (with piano) in 1930. Although Nielsen's Clarinet Concerto

---

19 Mozart, Clarinet Quintet K. 581, with Simeon Bellison and the Roth String Quartet, Columbia LX 8328-8331, 1936; and Grenadilla LP GS 1003, 1950.
20 Weston, *More Clarinet Virtuosi*, 45–47, and *Yesterday's Clarinettists*, 33–35.
21 *The Simeon Bellison Clarinet Legacy*, Tantara Records TCD 0110BLN-HS, 2010, 2 compact discs; and *Simeon Bellison: His Arrangements for Clarinet*, performed by Michelle Zukofsky, Summit DCD 503, 2008, compact disc.
22 Philippe Cuper, "Louis Cahuzac, the 20th Century Clarinetist," *The Clarinet* 28, no. 1 (December 2000): 46–57; Malcolm McMillan, "The

(1928) was written for Aage Oxenvad, Cahuzac was the first to record it, in 1947. He also recorded Mozart's Quintet (1948), Herman Koppel's Concerto (1948), and Mozart's Concerto (1948 and 1952). Cahuzac is renowned for having played without vibrato (unusual for a French player at the time).

Since about 1950 there have been a number of clarinetists who have been especially prolific in the recording studio. Dieter Klöcker, already mentioned above, was one of these. Starting in the late 1950s, he recorded both as a soloist and with his ensemble, the Consortium Classicum (see below). The series of box sets issued by EMI Electrola of music by lesser-known contemporaries of Haydn, Mozart, Beethoven, and Schubert and a collection of rarely heard works in the sinfonia concertante genre were major milestones. The extensive *Courts and Residences* series, begun in 1972, contained many works that had not been heard since the time of their composition; it is now available as a twenty-compact-disc collection. Overall Klöcker's recorded repertoire ranged from Telemann to Hindemith.

Gervase de Peyer (1926–2017) has been mentioned above as the dedicatee of a number of compositions, but he was extraordinarily prolific in the area of recording as well. A student of Frederick Thurston, de Peyer was a founding member of the Melos Ensemble (see below) in 1950, and principal clarinet of the London Symphony Orchestra from 1955 to 1972. After that he moved to the United States as the clarinetist with the Chamber Music Society of Lincoln Center, returning to England in 1989.[23] Because de Peyer's discography is so extensive, a list of recordings here must be selective. He began recording in 1950 with the Suite by Handel for two clarinets and horn, the other players being Thurston and Dennis Brain. He recorded much of the standard concerto repertoire with works by Spohr, Weber, Copland, and Crusell; of his two recordings of Mozart's Concerto—with Antony Collins in 1956 and with the Swiss conductor Peter Maag in 1960— he preferred the second. De Peyer also recorded concertos by Hoddinott (1971), Musgrave (1974), and Mathias (1977), the Quintet by Bliss (1963), the Sextet by Ireland (1972), and Phyllis Tate's Sonata for Clarinet and Cello (1966). The monophonic recording of Brahms's Sonatas with Hephzibah Menuhin (1958) was released only in Japan, but he recorded them again with Daniel Barenboim in 1968. Many of

French Clarinet Tradition and Louis Cahuzac," *Classic Record Collector* (Autumn 2009): 29–34.

23 Weston, *Clarinet Virtuosi of Today,* 89–95; June Emerson, obituary of Gervase de Peyer, *The Guardian,* April 24, 2017.

de Peyer's recordings have been re-issued on compact discs, and an eleven-disc set of the Melos Ensemble appeared in 2011. In the 1980s he recorded many of the best works in the clarinet and piano repertoire with his long-standing duo partner Gwyneth Pryor.

Chamber Ensembles

Several chapters in this book have already considered the place of the clarinet in orchestras, and of course many important twentieth-century clarinetists spent part or all of their careers as orchestral players. Here, however, we consider clarinetists who have been founders and/or members of long-standing chamber ensembles. An early precedent for such a relationship existed in mid-nineteenth century Boston, when Thomas Ryan (1827–1903) served as clarinetist of the Mendelssohn Quintette Club, a chamber ensemble that performed concerts across America for more than forty-five years from about 1849 to 1895.[24] In the early twentieth century Simeon Bellison, already mentioned above, organized a world tour of a chamber ensemble he had formed in 1918 called Zimro, consisting of clarinet, string quartet, and piano. The group, whose members were all Jewish, was supported by the Russian Zionist Organization and performed in Russia, Siberia, China, Hong Kong, Singapore, Japan, Indonesia, and Canada, before arriving in the United States and finally settling in New York in November 1919. It performed arrangements of Jewish folk music and works written by Jewish composers; it was for it that Prokofiev wrote the *Overture on Hebrew Themes*. Zimro performed as a group until 1921, when it disbanded.[25]

The busy career of Dieter Klöcker included, in addition to the work already mentioned, the founding of an ensemble called the Consortium Classicum to record the chamber works he uncovered. Performing on modern instruments, the group had a variable instrumentation of winds and strings. Between about 1965 and Klöcker's death in 2011 the Consortium Classicum concertized and produced

---

24 Thomas Ryan, *Recollections of an Old Musician* (New York: E. P. Dutton, 1899); Richard Mace Dowell, "The Mendelssohn Quintette Club of Boston" (PhD diss., Kent State University, 1999).

25 Nelly Kravetz, "I Must Be the Only Jewish Composer! Prokofiev and Jewish Music," trans. Simon Morrison, *Three Oranges Journal* (journal of the Serge Prokofiev Foundation), accessed July 3, 2020, http://www.sprkfv.net/journal/three26/jewishmusic1.html.

dozens of excellent recordings of rare chamber music from the late eighteenth and nineteenth centuries.

The Melos Ensemble was an English group formed in 1950. As with the Consortium Classicum, the intention was to perform the repertoire of larger chamber music for mixed winds and strings; but in the case of the Melos Ensemble the instrumentation also included piano and harp, and the repertoire included both old and new music. One of the founding members was the group's clarinetist, Gervase de Peyer, who performed with the group for twenty-four years. In addition to live concerts and tours, the Melos Ensemble made over fifty recordings, including much of the clarinet's chamber repertoire. This included the Clarinet Quintets of Mozart, Brahms, Weber, and Arthur Bliss; the Beethoven Septet, the Schubert Octet, and the Berwald Septet; Ravel's *Introduction and Allegro*; sextets by John Ireland and Lennox Berkeley; and much else. It was for the Melos Ensemble that Benjamin Britten wrote the chamber orchestra sections that accompany the English texts in his *War Requiem* of 1962. After de Peyer left the ensemble, the clarinet position was taken by Thea King, who performed with it from 1974 to 1993.[26]

Several chamber ensembles with an important clarinetist member have specialized in twentieth-century music. The English clarinetist **Alan Hacker** (1938–2012) was a founding member of the Pierrot Players (later called The Fires of London), a group he played with from 1967 until 1976, under the direction of the composers Harrison Birtwistle and Peter Maxwell Davies, premiering such works as Maxwell Davies's *Eight Songs for a Mad King*. Hacker had studied with a number of different clarinet teachers as a young man, and at age nineteen was named principal clarinet of the London Symphony Orchestra. He suffered a spinal thrombosis in 1966 and was subsequently confined to a wheelchair, a circumstance which did not prevent him from pursuing his clarinet career. In addition to his activities with The Fires of London, Hacker founded several of his own groups, including a period-instrument ensemble called The Music Party (1971; see also chapter 9 in this volume) and the Whispering Wind Band (1976). He also had a career as a conductor.[27]

In America, the clarinetist Richard Stoltzman (see below) was a founding member of the group Tashi (Tibetan for "good fortune"). Founded in 1972, Tashi was originally a quartet consisting of violin,

26 Noël Goodwin, "Melos Ensemble," *Grove Music Online*.

27 Weston, *Clarinet Virtuosi of Today*, 121–25.

clarinet, cello, and piano, and although its sometimes expanded in instrumentation to perform a variety of old and new repertoire, its original purpose was to perform Messiaen's *Quartet for the End of Time* and other works for that combination. The group had compositions written for it by Toru Takemitsu, Charles Wuorinen, and others, and made a number of recordings.

Another American, **Elsa Ludewig-Verdehr** (b. 1936), formed the Verdehr Trio (clarinet, violin, and piano) with her husband, the violinist Walter Verdehr, and a number of different pianists over the years of its existence (1972–2015). The group was based at Michigan State University, where the Verdehrs were members of the faculty. At the beginning the trio had just a handful of existing works to perform, so it embarked on a long-term project of commissioning new compositions—ultimately more than 200 of them, from a wide range of composers including Karel Husa, Thea Musgrave, Gian Carlo Menotti, William Bolcom, Peter Schickele, Wolfgang Rihm, Michael Daugherty, and many others. The Verdehr Trio toured actively, playing hundreds of concerts all over the world. The Verdehrs are currently writing a memoir about their trio's career and commissions.[28]

Breaking Barriers

In the world of European classical music, the clarinetist's profession has historically been the domain of white males of European descent. As the instrument's use spread outside Europe, and outside classical music, however, a more diverse set of people gradually took up the instrument. Nevertheless, it was not until the early twentieth century that jazz brought black clarinetists to prominence, and not until relatively late in the twentieth century that female and non-white clarinetists were accepted into the upper echelons of classical music performance as soloists, orchestral players, and chamber musicians. As

---

28 Ibid., 183–89; Maxine Ramey, "40 Years of the Making of a Medium," *The Clarinet* 40, no. 4 (September 2013): 36–38; Stephanie Powell, "The Verdehr Trio Announces Retirement," *Strings Magazine,* September 12, 2015, https://stringsmagazine.com/the-verdehr-trio-announces-retirement/; "Masters of a Medium: Eastman Honors The Verdehr Trio," September 26, 2019, https://www.esm.rochester.edu/blog/2019/09/masters-of-a-medium-eastman-honors-the-verdehr-trio/. A listing of works commissioned by the trio may be found on its website: http://www.verdehr.com/repertoire.htm.

in all areas of society and culture, breaking the barriers of race, gender, and ethnicity has not been easy for clarinetists, and the process has been slow. But as of the publication date of this book, two decades into the twenty-first century, some progress has been made that is worth celebrating.

Female clarinetists in any setting were a relative rarity in the nineteenth and early twentieth centuries. The English clarinetist Pauline Juler (1914–2003) began a solo career in the 1930s, only to retire upon marriage in the late 1940s. It wasn't until the 1950s that a larger number of female clarinetists started to appear on the concert stage and in the recording studio, most notably Thea King (1925–2007), whose many professional activities included the principal clarinet positions with the London Mozart Players and the English Chamber Orchestra as well as a large number of recordings. The first female principal clarinet of a major symphony orchestra—Michele Zukovsky (b. 1942), of the Los Angeles Philharmonic—was named in 1961. The first female prizewinner on clarinet at the Paris Conservatoire was Edwige Caquet, in 1974.[29]

These dates remind us that it is only recently that women have been able to gain a foothold in the profession. And the struggle has not ended. In 1983 the conductor Herbert von Karajan locked horns with the members of the Berlin Philharmonic when he appointed the clarinetist **Sabine Meyer** (b. 1959) to the orchestra. The orchestra refused to accept Meyer, despite Karajan's insistence (he threatened to cancel concerts and recording commitments because of the orchestra's recalcitrance), and eventually she was voted out by her colleagues.[30] She is now one of the most distinguished solo clarinetists and teachers in the world, with a large discography and a legacy of former students who have themselves gone on to important careers.[31]

If classical music has historically been unreceptive of female clarinetists, jazz has been even more so. A groundbreaking performer in

---

29 An overview of female clarinetists can be found in Manchusa Loungsangroong, "First-Wave Women Clarinetists Retrospective: A Guide to Women Clarinetists Born before 1930" (DMA diss., Ohio State University, 2017).

30 "Karajan and Orchestra Clash over Clarinetist," *New York Times*, January 8, 1983; "Schlag ins Konto," *Der Spiegel,* January 10, 1983.

31 More information about Sabine Meyer's biography can be found in Pamela Weston, *Clarinet Virtuosi of Today*, 215–19, and in a recent book-length biography (in German): Margarete Zander, *Sabine Meyer: Weltstar mit Herz* (Hamburg: Edel, 2013).

this area is **Anat Cohen** (b. 1979). Born in Tel Aviv, and educated there and in the United States, Cohen specialized from early on as a jazz player. She moved to New York City in 1999 and performed for ten years with the all-female Diva Jazz Orchestra, as well as with various Brazilian music groups. In 2007 she first appeared at the Newport Jazz Festival, and in 2009 she made her debut at the famed Village Vanguard. Cohen has an extensive discography. She recorded four albums with her brothers Yuval (saxophone) and Avishai (trumpet) as part of the 3 Cohens Sextet, and has to date recorded fifteen additional albums as a bandleader or co-leader, with the Anat Cohen Tentet, the Trio Brasiliero, and others. Cohen has been named "jazz clarinetist of the year" by the Jazz Journalists Association every year since 2007, as well as in readers' and critics' polls in *Downbeat* magazine. She is also an award-winning soprano and tenor saxophonist.[32]

Black musicians have also faced obstacles in accessing the world of classical music. Perhaps the earliest black clarinetist to gain prominence was **Rudolph Dunbar** (1907–88). Born in British Guiana, Dunbar studied clarinet at the Juilliard School (then called the Institute of Musical Art) starting in 1919. In 1924 he went to Europe, where he studied clarinet in Paris with Louis Cahusac and conducting in Vienna with Felix Weingartner. His Paris recital debut in 1930 at the Salle d'Iéna, where he played works by Weber and Chopin, received glowing reviews; the *Revue internationale de musique et de danse* quoted many of them, and its critic stated, "Mr. Dunbar possesses a thorough knowledge of his instrument and plays with a brilliant technic [*sic*] and unusual musical understanding. His playing was one of the rarest treats heard in Paris for some time."[33] In 1931 he moved to London, where he performed and broadcast with dance bands and orchestras (he was a skilled jazz musician) and conducted stage shows. After returning to New York in 1938 he published his book *Treatise on the Clarinet, Boehm System* (1939). Beginning in the 1940s Dunbar's career shifted mostly to conducting; he was the first black musician to conduct the London Philharmonic Orchestra (1942) and the Berlin Philharmonic (1945, in its first postwar concert). In addition, he served as a wartime correspondent for the Allied forces. For the remainder of his life Dunbar

---

32 https://www.anatcohen.com/biography; Bradley Bambarger, "A Smile in Her Sound: Jazz Clarinetist Anat Cohen Keeps Winning Hearts and Minds Worldwide," *The Clarinet* 39, no. 4 (September 2012): 42–44.

33 Quoted in "W. Rudolph Dunbar: Pioneering Orchestra Conductor," *The Black Perspective in Music* 9, no. 2 (Autumn 1981): 195.

continued to conduct orchestras around the world, especially championing the music of black composers.[34]

Marcus Eley was one of the first African-American clarinetists to become prominent. Eley has performed as a concerto soloist and recitalist around the world, championing the music of black composers. In 2012 he released a compact disc, "But Not Forgotten: Music by African-American Composers for Clarinet and Piano."[35] Following Eley, **Anthony McGill** (b. 1979) was the first African-American clarinetist to hold principal positions with major orchestras, including the Cincinnati Symphony (2000–04), the Metropolitan Opera orchestra (2004–14), and the New York Philharmonic (from 2014). McGill first came to the general public's attention when he performed at the 2009 inauguration of the former United States President Barack Obama. Since then, in addition to his orchestral positions, he has performed frequently as a soloist and has made several recordings of the standard clarinet repertoire (including Debussy's *Première rhapsodie*, the Poulenc Sonata, concertos by Nielsen and Copland, the Brahms and Mozart Quintets, and other works). McGill also teaches at the Juilliard School, the Curtis Institute of Music (his *alma mater*), and the Conservatory of Music at Bard College. McGill's "Take Two Knees" video, posted on YouTube during the racial unrest in the United States following George Floyd's murder in 2020, further propelled him into the public eye and inspired other artists to respond with similar videos.[36]

In 2017 another major American orchestra appointed a principal clarinetist of color: **Afendi Yusuf** (b. 1989), who was hired by the Cleveland Orchestra. Yusuf was born in Addis Ababa, Ethiopia, and moved to Canada with his family at the age of eleven. He started playing clarinet in middle school, having had no former exposure to classical music; he went on to study the instrument at Wilfrid Laurier University and the Glenn Gould School in Toronto, and later gained a master's degree at the Colburn School in Los Angeles. In addition to his orchestral position, Yusuf teaches at the Cleveland Institute of Music and performs at the Marlboro Music Festival. He has recorded the Brahms Trio op. 114 for the Steinway & Sons label.[37]

---

34 Dominique-René De Lerman (rev. Jonas Westover), "Dunbar, W. Rudolph," *Grove Music Online*.

35 http://www.marcuseley.com/.

36 http://www.anthonymcgill.com/.

37 https://www.clevelandorchestra.com/about/musicians-and-conductors/meet-the-musicians/t-z-musicians/afendi-yusuf/;

Other clarinetists of color have begun to come to the fore in recent years. **Mariam Adam** is of Egyptian and Mexican descent. She was a founding member of the groundbreaking Imani Winds, a wind quintet with which she performed for more than fifteen years. Now based in Paris, she makes her career as a recitalist and chamber musician, and is a clarinetist with the Chineke! orchestra in London. Adam has recorded seven discs with the Imani winds, and has also recorded an album of works for clarinet and piano as part of the TransAtlantic Ensemble and, most recently, an album called *AdZel Duo* with her fellow clarinetist Stephanie Zelnick. An advocate for crossover styles as well as classical music, Adam has also collaborated on recordings with Chick Corea, Wayne Shorter, Steve Coleman, and others.[38]

The Syrian clarinetist and composer **Kinan Azmeh** (b. 1976) crosses stylistic boundaries between classical and popular music, between the music of Europe and the Middle East, and between notated music and improvisation. Now based in New York, Azmeh has performed as a soloist with the New York Philharmonic, the Seattle Symphony, the Bavarian Radio Orchestra, and many others. He founded and plays with the ensemble Hewar (the Arabic word for "dialogue"), consisting of a core group of clarinet, voice, and oud that performs with other collaborators; it has produced three recordings. Azmeh's album *Uneven Sky*, on which he plays his own compositions for clarinet and orchestra as well as works written for him by several other Syrian composers, was awarded the OpusKlassik Award in 2019. Azmeh also performs with the group CityBand and with Yo-Yo Ma's Silk Road Ensemble.[39]

Popularizers

All of the clarinetists mentioned so far can be said to have popularized the clarinet, insofar as they put themselves before the public on the concert stage or through the medium of recording. Perhaps more accurately, they put themselves before "a" public—a specialized audience primarily of clarinet lovers and a few others—rather than "the"

https://www.cleveland.com/musicdance/2017/09/afendi_yusuf_primed_to_get_dow.html.

38 https://www.mariamadam.com; Berginald Rash, "In Discussion: The Clarinetists of Chineke!," *The Clarinet* 47, no. 4 (September 2020): 56–59.

39 https://kinanazmeh.com/; Boja Kragulj, "Interview with Kinan Azmeh," *The Clarinet* 44, no. 3 (June 2017): 34–35.

public. It is likely that no clarinetist will ever gain the universal fame of Elvis, whose surname needn't even be mentioned to spur the reader's recognition; yet in recent decades there have been a few clarinetists who have come nearer to reaching "the" public, or at least a larger segment of it. One of these is surely Benny Goodman (see above), whose general fame as a jazz clarinetist can hardly be disputed. More recently, it may be argued that at least two others have also bridged the gap between specialized audiences and the general public.

One of these is the American clarinetist **Richard Stoltzman** (b. 1942), who—perhaps not coincidentally—has said that one of his main influences was Goodman.[40] Stoltzman has made his career as a soloist and chamber musician, never holding an orchestral position and only briefly holding a teaching one. While he has performed mainly in the area of classical music, his early interest was in jazz, and he has continued to perform in that style as well. In 1976 he was awarded an Avery Fisher Recital Award (now known as the Avery Fisher Career Grant), a large monetary award given to young instrumentalists with the potential for a solo career, and ten years later he received the Avery Fisher Prize in recognition of his success. Two of Stoltzman's many recordings have won Grammy Awards.

Stoltzman's role in popularizing the clarinet with the general public can be attributed to two main factors: his enormous discography, and his interest in performing popular and jazz styles alongside classical music. For example, his first crossover recording, *Begin Sweet World* (1986), made with his long-time friend and like-minded collaborator Bill Douglas, included original pop- and jazz-style compositions and clarinet transcriptions of light classical works, such as the "Pie Jesu" section of Fauré's Requiem and "La fille aux cheveux de lin" from Debussy's *Preludes*. An article in *Billboard* at the time of the release described the unusual promotional push the album was receiving, and quoted Stoltzman as acknowledging that some of the works "sound like they belong with the new age records" in the music store.[41] In the late 1980s and 1990s Stoltzman released albums in the same vein about once a year, including *Innervoices* (1989) with the pop singer Judy Collins; *Brasil* (1991); *Hark!* (1992), a Christmas album; *Dreams*

---

40 Amy Alizabeth Turnbull, "Richard Stoltzman: Defying Categorization" (DMA essay, University of Iowa, 2011), 15. More information about Stoltzman may also be found in Weston, *Clarinet Virtuosi of Today*, 290–97.

41 Jim Bessman, "Clarinetist Has Crossover Dreams," *Billboard*, June 28, 1986.

(1994); *Visions* (1995); *Spirits* (1996); *Aria* (1997); *Danza Latina* (1998); *Open Sky* (1998); and *WorldBeat Bach* (2000). All the while Stoltzman continued to record the standard clarinet repertoire, as well as new music by composers such as William McKinley, Margaret Brouwer, Carl Vollrath, and many others.[42] While the crossover recordings elicited a mixed reception from the clarinet community, they nevertheless reached out to the general public with some success.

Most recently, the Swedish clarinetist **Martin Fröst** (b. 1970) has brought the clarinet to the public in new ways. Virtuosi have always appealed to the public at large, and Fröst is a virtuoso of the highest order, with a complete command not only of finger technique but also of double tonguing and circular breathing—techniques that are still not generally common on the clarinet. But even more it is Fröst's artistic vision and rethinking of the concert experience that has appealed to a wide audience. For example, he regularly incorporates movement and choreography into his performances. In 1998 the composer Anders Hillborg wrote a concerto for Fröst called *Peacock Tales*, in which the soloist dances and mimes extensively while playing. Fröst has also created concerts that feature choreography, narration, and both solo and orchestral music centering on a specific theme; for example, his "Genesis" project (2015) presents a loose history of music and involves orchestra, children's choir, and Fröst himself as soloist and narrator. His latest project, entitled "Retrotopia," mixes traditional classical music by Mozart and Beethoven with new works, including Jesper Nordin's *Emerge*, which employs a motion-sensor technology called "Gestrument" allowing Fröst to control a virtual orchestra through his movements. These and other multimedia projects have been undertaken with the Royal Stockholm Philharmonic, of which Fröst has recently been appointed Chief Conductor.

Fröst could equally well be included in other categories in this chapter. Not only has he recorded standard repertoire (all of the clarinet works of Brahms, concertos by Mozart, Weber, Crusell, Nielsen, and Copland, the Quintets by Mozart and Weber, Messiaen's *Quartet for the End of Time*, and others), but he has also championed recent and new music. He has recorded clarinet concertos by Vagn Holmboe, Christopher Rouse, Karin Rehnqvist, and Kalevi Aho (the latter two written for him), as well as other works composed for him by Anders Hilborg,

---

42 A useful listing of Stoltzman's recordings through 2009 is found in Turnbull, "Richard Stoltzman," appendix B. He has produced several recordings since the publication of Turnbull's dissertation.

his brother Göran Fröst, and others. In addition, transcriptions of art and folk song are part of his recorded and performing repertoire.

ᛒ ᛒ ᛒ

In this chapter, I have attempted to assemble a representative sampling of influential clarinetists who illustrate the broad sweep of the profession in the twentieth and early twenty-first centuries, including individuals who not only were or are excellent musicians, but have also contributed in other ways to the musical and cultural impact the instrument has had since 1900. The legacy of clarinet artistry extends well beyond the performers written about here, however; dozens of additional clarinetists deserve to be mentioned, including many who are currently active. These players, in addition to as-yet-unknown young artists, will continue to shape the instrument's history and reception into the future, in innovative and exciting ways.

9

RE-CREATING HISTORY?

The Early Clarinet in Theory and Practice

Colin Lawson

Clarinetists around the world have recently been discovering that engagement with early instruments can radically expand their musical horizons. Taking account of original conditions of performance (insofar as they can be determined) has the capacity to bring significant new perspectives to a player's artistic life. Different historical clarinets present satisfying technical challenges, and their range of response can be a visceral experience, both physically and aesthetically. In particular, one might want to argue that the nuances available from most early clarinets (or copies) are well-nigh impossible to match on the modern instrument. Perhaps the very design of the familiar Boehm instrument encourages a tonal homogeneity that has diminished the clarinet's rhetorical potential.

As historical performance has become more widespread, the remarkable popularity of the modern clarinet is gradually being matched by its historical counterparts. Furthermore, it has become increasingly difficult to sustain the argument that period instruments are somehow more difficult to play within their own idiomatic repertoire. At the same time, it must be admitted that some fluent players of Boehm-system clarinets have been content to overload their early clarinets with anachronistic mechanisms and to pay scant attention to matters of style. Indeed, each period clarinetist, unwittingly or otherwise, establishes an individual position on a spectrum that ranges from historical fidelity to practical expediency. Some clarinetists have a genuine love of old instruments, while others have wanted to get as close as possible to the aesthetic of modern instruments—disguised in boxwood.

In any case, opportunities now exist to commission copies of various types of early clarinets and to perform a range of repertoire using instruments that come close to what a composer would have known. Given sufficient dedication, any experienced and open-minded player can achieve technical command over a wide range of clarinets.

Investigating the Past: The Evolving Panorama

More than a century ago the French instrument maker and musical pioneer Arnold Dolmetsch remarked in his seminal book, "we can no longer allow anyone to stand between us and the composer."[1] The movement he helped to found has been well documented in Harry Haskell's *The Early Music Revival,* an account of the activities of musicologists, editors, publishers, makers, collectors, curators, dealers, librarians, performers, teachers, and record producers.[2] Since the 1980s the philosophy of historical performance has been subject to vigorous discourse, including considerable debate about the notion of "authenticity." For example, in 1983 the viol player and Bach scholar Laurence Dreyfus described the "authentic" musician as someone who acted willingly in the service of the composer, denying any form of glorifying self-expression, but who attained this by following the textbook rules for scientific method with a strictly empirical program to verify historical practices. He was suspicious that these, when all was said and done, were magically transformed into the composer's "intentions."[3]

Nicholas Kenyon's 1984 symposium on "The Limits of Authenticity" in the journal *Early Music* took the role of expression as a central agenda for discussion. Richard Taruskin's contribution viewed the need to satisfy a composer's intentions as a failure of nerve, if not an infantile dependency, a topic that both he and the philosopher Peter

---

1   Arnold Dolmetsch, *The Interpretation of the Music of the XVIIth and XVIIIth Centuries* (London: Novello, 1915), 471.

2   Harry Haskell, *The Early Music Revival* (London: Thames & Hudson, 1988).

3   Laurence Dreyfus, "Early Music Defended against Its Devotees: A Theory of Historical Performance in the Twentieth Century," *The Musical Quarterly* 69, no. 3 (1983): 299.

Kivy were later to develop.[4] Within this climate the once-favored term "authenticity" gradually fell from grace. Translated from the German *Werktreue*—faithfulness to the musical text—it came for a time to signify an impossible (if not undesirable) dream. Throughout the twentieth century period performance faced many critics, such as the conductor Leopold Stokowski, who much preferred to rely on tradition rather than on primary sources. Pierre Boulez, Colin Davis, and Neville Marriner were among those to have been similarly dismissive. From within the clarinet community, Basil Tschaikov, a former member of Sir Thomas Beecham's Royal Philharmonic Orchestra, was somewhat disparaging, although as overtly critical of marketing strategies as of the musical product: "There are those who play Mozart in a style that purports to be 'authentic' and on what pretend to be 'original instruments,' though they are reproductions with improved intonation without which they would be unacceptable to a modern audience."[5]

Following the debates of the early 1980s, new philosophical approaches emerged. Performances moved from "authentic" to "historically informed," and recently to what might be more appropriately described as "historically intelligent." Promoters of the cause have numbered international conductors such as Mark Elder, Ivan Fischer, Charles Mackerras, Simon Rattle, Edo de Waart, and many more; they have upheld a variety of positions on the significance of historical evidence beyond the mere use of period instruments.[6] But during the course of little more than a generation, historical performance has truly become part of mainstream musical life and is pursued with skill and dedication by an ever-increasing circle of performers across the orchestral spectrum.

---

4   The symposium was subsequently revised and developed in Nicholas Kenyon, ed., *Authenticity and Early Music* (New York: Oxford University Press, 1988). See also Richard Taruskin, *Text and Act* (New York: Oxford University Press, 1996) and Peter Kivy, *Authenticities: Philosophical Reflections on Musical Performance* (Ithaca, NY: Cornell University Press, 1995).

5   Basil Tschaikov, *The Music Goes Round and Around* (Peterborough: Fastprint, 2009), 401.

6   It was notable that in a recent Glyndebourne season of *La clemenza di Tito* with the period instruments of the Orchestra of the Age of Enlightenment, the conductor Robin Ticciati made use of a normal-range clarinet for the obbligato to Sesto's aria "Parto, parto" rather than the B-flat basset clarinet clearly indicated by the contours of Mozart's writing.

Nevertheless, the challenge of re-creating earlier performances remains formidable and elusive, given that musicians work within the evanescent medium of sound. As one of Mozart's contemporaries wrote in 1789, some musical effects cannot be described; they must be *heard*.[7] Although biographies and histories of music can provide much information about historical context, words are essentially inadequate to communicate certain aspects of art, whether encapsulating tone quality or articulating those tiny differences in emphases and timing that distinguish a great performance from a merely good one.

Old instruments are key to this, not least because they represent tangible evidence; and, as one celebrated conductor put it, "they have more colour, shape and less weight than modern instruments. They are more tangy, more piquant. We can play full out with the greatest passion, and still sound like Mozart."[8] Yet the mere use of period instruments in re-creating the music of the past can never be the whole picture. Historical awareness also involves musical understanding, cultural and social context, acoustical considerations, and concert-giving situations; yet not all practitioners have been prepared to take such issues into account. The value of a wide range of knowledge to complement intuition and artistry has long been recognized by generations of composers and performers.

For today's specialist in period performance, the acquisition of instruments and even the technique to play them can only be the starting point; the whole exercise will be severely limited unless linked to a cultivation of appropriate styles. Much of the documentary evidence upon which historical performance is based retains an astonishing relevance for today's music students, not least clarinetists. In 1752 the flutist Quantz set out to train a skilled and intelligent musician, remarking that the majority of players had fingers and tongues, but that most were reluctant to use their brains. At the same time C. P. E. Bach warned that players whose chief asset was mere technique were clearly at a disadvantage. Both writers emphasized that if players are not themselves moved by what they play, they will never move others, which should be their real aim. In today's different musical climate it is easy to become embarrassed by such sentiments, but in Mozart's day—well before the enthusiasm for virtuosity as an end in itself during the

---

7   D. G. Türk, *Klavierschule* (Leipzig & Halle, 1789), trans. R. H. Haggh as *School of Clavier Playing* (Lincoln: University of Nebraska Press, 1982), 337.

8   Helen Wallace, *Spirit of the Orchestra* (London: The Orchestra of the Age of Enlightenment, 2006), 30.

nineteenth century, or the veneration for accuracy that developed during the age of recording—the communication of emotion was an absolute priority.[9]

Quantz described music as "nothing but an artificial language, through which we seek to acquaint the listener with our musical ideas."[10] This analogy with oratory implies, among other things, a range of articulation far removed from the goals of many modern clarinetists, who arguably have moved further in the direction of a smooth, seamless approach than most flutists, oboists, or bassoonists. There was clearly much that earlier composers did not trouble to write in their scores, for they simply expected contemporary conventions to be observed. Some of these conventions no longer exist, while others have undergone significant changes of meaning. Elements of this language will always remain foreign, but musicians can learn to converse freely within it and so bring a greater range of expression to performance, rather than merely pursuing some kind of unattainable "authenticity." For example, the mere fact that in Mozart's day detached, articulate playing was the norm is a salutary reminder that playing styles have changed out of all recognition.

Even such a basic matter as tempo flexibility can scarcely be deduced from composers' own comments, which take for granted the musical taste of their times, not ours. As Robert Philip has observed, we would be unable to deduce from notated scores the degree of flexibility of Elgar's tempi, the prominence of Joachim's vibrato, the lightness of rhythm of Bartók's piano playing, the reedy tone of French bassoons and clarinets in Stravinsky's Paris recordings, or the nature of Rachmaninov's rubato.[11] For students of Brahms's Clarinet Quintet op. 115 it is revealing that, according to a colleague, Brahms's violinist Joachim had an unpredictable approach to tempo: "to play with him is damned difficult. Always different tempi, different accents."[12]

9   J. J. Quantz, *Versuch einer Anweisung die Flöte traversiere zu spielen* (Berlin, 1752), trans. E. R. Reilly as *On Playing the Flute* (London: Faber and New York: The Free Press, 1966), 125; C. P. E. Bach, *Versuch über die wahre Art das Clavier zu spielen*, 2 vols. (Berlin, 1753–62), trans. W. J. Mitchell as *Essay on the True Art of Playing Keyboard Instruments* (New York: Schott, 1949), 152.

10   Quantz, *On Playing the Flute*, 120.

11   Robert Philip, *Early Recordings and Musical Style* (Cambridge: Cambridge University Press, 1992), 236.

12   Julius Levin, "Adolf Busch," *Die Musik* 18, no. 10 (July 1926): 746.

The very ambiguity of primary evidence means that there will always be more questions than answers. We have already observed that treatises for the violin, flute, and keyboards offer philosophical insights into the art and craft of music and make essential reading for any player wishing to develop a historical perspective. Musical styles are many and various, with national idiom an important element, distinguishing the music of Beethoven, Cherubini, and Rossini, for example. Specific areas for detailed study include articulation, melodic inflection, accentuation, tempo, rhythmic alteration, ornamentation, extempore embellishment, and improvisation. In addition, the interpretation of notation implies a knowledge of conditions and practices for which even an autograph score may offer no clues. These may include such central issues as pitch and temperament, constitution of original programs, orchestral disposition and placement, and the role (if any) of the conductor.[13] Sometimes pieces exist in contemporary yet contradictory versions that make a nonsense of today's obsession with *Urtext*. As performance standards have risen sharply, it has become less fashionable to claim that "early music" groups are filled with performers who failed to make the grade in the mainstream musical world. It must be admitted that technical facility was grossly undervalued in the early music market a few years ago, but what makes the criticism bite is that historical performers originally prided themselves on being more adventurous and readier to question received opinions.

Period clarinets became prevalent during a time of intense musical curiosity. Has the momentum of that time been maintained? In some quarters the original pioneering spirit inherent within historical performance has been rather diluted as early instruments have become ubiquitous in concert halls and studios throughout the world. Yet overall the musical results have been dramatic, and it can reasonably be claimed that that there is no worthwhile, thoughtful, intellectually stimulating, and musically adventurous performance going on today that has not been touched by the period instrument movement.

What are historically aware musicians attempting to achieve? In the mid-1990s the distinguished paleoclimate scientist, instrument collector, and clarinetist Sir Nicholas Shackleton answered the question by asserting that "our primary objective in playing historic instruments is to gain a better feeling for what earlier music actually sounded like

---

13 For an overview of these issues, see Colin Lawson and Robin Stowell, eds., *The Historical Performance of Music* (Cambridge: Cambridge University Press, 1999).

when heard in favourable circumstances."[14] As we have already hinted, each player (regardless of instrument) has an individual approach to balancing practicalities with historical accuracy, insofar as it can be determined. Meanwhile, faced with the vague promise of "original instruments," the consumer of recordings generally remains aloof from such issues. It need hardly be said that the virtuosi associated with great composers such as Mozart, Weber, and Brahms were not subject to the discipline of the microphone, which has imposed a veneration for accuracy permeating not only today's concerts but also preliminary rehearsals, whether on period or on modern instruments.

The influential careers of such clarinetists as Anton Stadler, Heinrich Baermann, and Richard Mühlfeld serve as a reminder that it is the exceptional (and often unrepresentative) rather than the ordinary in musical history which tends to capture our attention. This represents a striking contrast with the standardization that has become rife in many aspects of our musical lives, for example in artistic interpretation or the copying of instruments. In addition, today's musical tastes are bound to be a pervasive influence, together with a selectivity of evidence that simply ignores uncomfortable elements, such as the appalling orchestral conditions in Beethoven's Vienna. The vexed question of an earlier composer's intentions—or even their expectations—invites intense speculation. When they express them, composers may do so disingenuously or they may be honestly mistaken, owing to the passage of time or a not necessarily consciously experienced change of taste. Brahms relished conducting both the forty-nine-strong orchestra at Meiningen and the hundred-strong Vienna Philharmonic. One can listen to Stravinsky's five recordings of *The Rite of Spring* and then attempt to decide how he meant it to go, referring in addition to his published reviews of five other performances. Only at the age of eighty did Stravinsky finally admit that nothing in this life is stable: "if the speeds of everything in the world and in ourselves have changed, our tempo feelings cannot remain unaffected ... The metronome marks one wrote forty years ago were contemporary then. Time is not alone in affecting tempo—circumstances do too, and every performance is a different equation of them."[15] Stravinsky's beliefs might lead one to

---

14 Nicholas Shackleton, "The Development of the Clarinet," in *The Cambridge Companion to the Clarinet*, ed. Colin Lawson (Cambridge: Cambridge University Press, 1995), 17.

15 Igor Stravinsky, *Dialogues*, originally published as *Dialogues and a Diary* (1963; repr., Berkeley and Los Angeles: University of California Press, 1982), 122.

question whether any composers expect to have any influence over how their music is performed after they have written it, or what moral obligation there might be to fulfill their original intentions. Are we more likely to understand a composer's piece of music if we restrict ourselves to the means originally available, or does such a restriction inhibit our full expression of the piece? Is an early clarinet indeed a restriction or a liberation?

From Library to Concert Hall: The Emergent Early Clarinet

There is plenty of reading material for clarinetists with an interest in researching the history of their instrument. The clarinet was regularly featured in early nineteenth-century European periodicals such as the *Allgemeine musikalische Zeitung* and *Cäcilia*. A couple of generations later, the first edition of *Grove's Dictionary of Music* included a wide-ranging article on the clarinet, which enumerated its various characteristics and difficulties, noting its tendency to sharpness when warm and its susceptibility to squeaks.[16] There were complete books devoted to the clarinet in Italian (1887) and German (1904), and then in 1916 came an important historical survey from the English amateur Oscar Street, who observed that Mozart's Clarinet Concerto had not been played at a Philharmonic concert since its London premiere in 1838.[17] Adam Carse's general book on wind instruments from 1939 contains a celebrated (if then accurate) description of the chalumeau as "this will'o th' wisp amongst wind instruments."[18] Much context for playing early clarinets can be derived from the postwar literature that followed. Geoffrey Rendall's *The Clarinet: Some Notes upon Its History and Construction* incorporates illustrations of various old and unfamiliar instruments.[19] But a true watershed was Anthony Baines's distinctive

---

16 *Grove's Dictionary of Music* (London: Macmillan and Co., 1879).

17 Riccardo Gandolfi, *Appunti intorno al clarinetto compilati ad uso delle scuole del R. Instituto musicale di Firenze* (Florence: Galetti e Cocci, 1887); Wilhelm Altenburg, *Die Klarinette* (Heilbronn: Schmidt, 1904); Oscar W. Street, "The Clarinet and Its Music," *Proceedings of the Musical Association* 42 (1916): 89–115.

18 Adam Carse, *Musical Wind Instruments* (London: Macmillan, 1939), 150.

19 Geoffrey Rendall, *The Clarinet: Some Notes upon Its History and Construction* (London: Williams and Norgate, 1954).

and far-sighted *Woodwind Instruments and Their History*, which dealt separately with the mechanical and practical aspects of playing modern and historical woodwinds.[20] Meanwhile, *The Galpin Society Journal* contained from its beginnings in 1948 a steady stream of articles of interest to clarinetists, reflecting the society's overall aspiration to further research into the history, construction, development and use of musical instruments. Oskar Kroll, who had already undertaken groundbreaking research into the chalumeau, wrote a book on the clarinet which was published in 1965 and translated into English shortly afterward, though in preparation as early as 1939; he brought an important German perspective to the instrument's history and repertoire.[21] Pamela Weston's *Clarinet Virtuosi of the Past* and *More Clarinet Virtuosi of the Past* introduced a new biographical and critical perspective on earlier performers.[22] Jack Brymer's *Clarinet* (London: Macdonald and Jane's, 1976) included valuable historical information for the general reader and some significantly enthusiastic remarks about the early clarinet, reflecting its gradual emergence in the concert hall.[23] The journal *Early Music* has since 1973 been an important forum, venturing regularly into single-reed territory and offering much insight into performance practice issues.

Nicholas Shackleton's overview of the clarinet for *The New Grove Dictionary* (1980, 2001) proved to be a revelatory piece of work.[24] His scientific descriptions of the clarinet's structure, compass, and intonation preface a detailed organological history, in which—significantly—nationalities of instrument are distinguished primarily by their mechanism and design rather than their musical impact. His observations on acoustics, mode of operation, and fingering comprise a brilliant yet accessible account of how the clarinet actually works. Shackleton's few remarks on the subject of tone are full of insight and are perhaps now the most cited parts of the article. He draws attention to the richness of the chalumeau register of the Bohemian clarinet of Mozart's time, while observing that eighteenth-century English

---

20 Anthony Baines, *Woodwind Instruments and Their History* (London: Faber, 1957).
21 Oskar Kroll, *The Clarinet*, rev. Diethard Riehm, trans. Hilda Morris, ed. Anthony Baines (London: Batsford, 1968).
22 Pamela Weston, *Clarinet Virtuosi of the Past* (Corby: Fentone, 1971); *More Clarinet Virtuosi of the Past* (London: the author, 1977).
23 Jack Brymer, *Clarinet* (London: Macdonald and Jane's, 1976).
24 Nicholas Shackleton, "The Clarinet of Western Art Music," §II of "Clarinet," *Grove Music Online.*

clarinets were probably tonally similar to Continental instruments of two or more decades earlier. The clarinet has remained a popular subject for university disssertations; David Ross's dissertation is worth investigating for its many descriptions of surviving old clarinets.[25] His attempt to articulate the tonal characteristics of the Lotz clarinet in Geneva is especially notable. Melanie Piddocke offers further insights into Stadler's associate, the instrument maker Theodor Lotz.[26] Albert Rice's *The Baroque Clarinet* takes an essentially bibliographical approach to an under-researched area.[27] Rice proceeded to reflect his impressive organological interests in *The Clarinet in the Classical Period* and *From the Clarinet d'Amour to the Contra Bass.*[28]

Facsimiles of various clarinet tutors are currently in print and are listed, together with much of the earlier literature discussed here, in *Bibliography of the Early Clarinet.*[29] *The Cambridge Companion to the Clarinet* contains an important illustrated survey by Shackleton on the development of the clarinet.[30] A complementary chapter by the present author devoted to playing historical clarinets was afterward expanded into *The Early Clarinet: A Practical Guide.*[31] This latter volume ranges across context, historical considerations, equipment, practical advice, the language of musical style, and case studies. Eric Hoeprich's ambitious *The Clarinet* reflects the perspective of an early clarinet specialist, maker, and researcher; his stated objective is

---

25 David Ross, "A Comprehensive Performance Project in Clarinet Literature with an Organological Study of the Development of the Clarinet in the Eighteenth Century" (DMA disseration, University of Iowa, 1985).

26 Melanie Piddocke, "Theodor Lotz: A Biographical and Organological Study" (PhD diss., University of Edinburgh, 2012).

27 Albert Rice, *The Baroque Clarinet* (New York: Oxford University Press, 1992).

28 Albert Rice, *The Clarinet in the Classical Period* (Oxford: Oxford University Press, 2003) and *From the Clarinet d'Amour to the Contra Bass: A History of the Large Size Clarinets, 1740–1860* (New York: Oxford University Press, 2009).

29 Jo Rees Davies, *Bibliography of the Early Clarinet* (Brighton: Clarinet & Saxophone Society of Great Britain, 1986).

30 Nicholas Shackleton, "The Development of the Clarinet," in *The Cambridge Companion to the Clarinet, ed. Colin Lawson* (Cambridge: Cambridge University Press, 1995), 16–32.

31 Colin Lawson, *The Early Clarinet: A Practical Guide* (Cambridge: Cambridge University Press, 2000).

to touch on most of the important aspects of the clarinet from the past to the present, giving an overview of its physical development, of approaches to playing the instrument, and of the music. ... To study the clarinet is also to study the inventiveness, imagination and the industry of the people involved in playing, making and composing for it. It provides an impressive testimony to what has been accomplished by a great many people over a long period of time.[32]

It need hardly be observed that musical instruments are not primarily visual objects—and the early clarinet was soon destined to make the journey from the library to the concert hall. Historical performance after 1945 had centered upon Amsterdam, The Hague, London, and Vienna, and was predominantly occupied with Baroque repertoire. Only as the movement progressed into Classical and Romantic repertoire did the early clarinet gradually become a focus of attention around the world. A period performance of Beethoven's Trio op. 11 with the Concertgebouw Orchestra's principal clarinet Piet Honingh found its way onto LP by 1969. Honingh played a five-key clarinet of circa 1820 by Jung of Marseilles and was partnered by his fellow pioneers Anner Bylsmer (cello) and Stanley Hoogland (fortepiano). The 1970s witnessed a number of projects from such adventurous players (all born in the 1930s) as Hans Deinzer, Alan Hacker, and Hans-Rudolf Stalder. In Britain Hacker's work became especially well known through recordings with his own period ensemble The Music Party, founded in 1971. Its repertoire often featured string accompaniment, but the group's sound world was always characterized by Hacker's colorful, virtuosic clarinet playing. It also tackled Mozart's *Gran Partita* Serenade K. 361/370a, his Serenade K. 375, the Quintets for Piano and Wind by both Mozart and Beethoven, Beethoven's Septet op. 20, and Handel's *Ouverture* for two clarinets and horn. The group made discs of Weber's Clarinet Quintet op. 34 and Hummel's Clarinet Quartet (1973); Weber's *Grand duo concertant* op. 48, Schumann's *Märchenerzählungen* op. 132, and Glinka's *Trio pathétique* (1976); and Haydn's eight *Notturni* Hob. II:25–32 (1976). A significant offshoot, the Classical Orchestra, was founded in 1978 and was conducted by Hacker in Mozart's Symphony no. 39 K. 543, Mendelssohn's *Hebrides* Overture, Beethoven's Second, Third, and Seventh Symphonies, what was probably the first English performance of Beethoven's Ninth Symphony using period

---

32 Eric Hoeprich, *The Clarinet* (New Haven, CT: Yale University Press, 2008), xix-xx.

instruments, and Mozart's Clarinet Concerto K. 622, in which he also played the solo part. Hacker did not shrink from commissioning the maker Brian Ackerman to convert original English clarinets into basset instruments, which involved some radical interventions.

Hans-Rudolf Stalder, principal clarinet in the Tonhalle Orchestra in Zurich from 1955 to 1986, was a hugely influential figure as teacher and performer. He introduced the chalumeau into the studio in music by Graupner, explored *Harmoniemusik* with his period group Octophorus, and besides unearthing much lesser-known music made the first recording of Mozart's Concerto K. 622 on a Boehm-system basset clarinet in 1969. Hans Deinzer was a key member of Collegium Aureum, which had been founded in 1962 by the record label Harmonia Mundi to re-create original sound worlds. It maintained a historical perspective that allowed Deinzer to utilize generously mechanized instruments, not least for his first recording of the Mozart Concerto (1973) on a boxwood basset clarinet. Nor was small-scale phrasing much in evidence within the reverberant acoustic in which recordings of repertoire such as Beethoven's Septet and Schubert's Octet were made. In 1976 Neal Zaslaw observed, "whether because the instruments are played with modern technique … or because the recording engineer had in mind a "symphony" sound suited to later music, … the results hardly differ from more traditional recordings…. Clarity, lightness, brightness, leanness and intimacy … seldom emerge on these recordings."[33]

These remarks appeared in the article by Zaslaw that launched Christopher Hogwood's project to record the complete Mozart symphonies and Requiem on period instruments, for which Keith Puddy was principal clarinet. Only a few years earlier the second edition of Willi Apel's *Harvard Dictionary of Music* had defined performance practice as "the study of how early music, from the Middle Ages to Bach, was performed," noting that "in the period after Bach the problems of performance practice largely disappear, owing to the more specific directions for clearly indicating their intentions."[34] Hogwood and his Academy of Ancient Music had already begun to test that proposition during the 1970s with pioneering discs of Arne and the Stamitz concerto believed to be the work of Johann (with Hacker as soloist).

---

33 Neal Zaslaw, "Toward the Revival of the Classical Orchestra," *Proceedings of the Royal Musical Association* 103 (1976–77): 184.
34 Willi Apel, *Harvard Dictionary of Music*, 2nd ed. (Cambridge, MA, 1969), s.v. "Performance Practice," 658–59.

Zaslaw dismissed the notion of an unbroken tradition of performance practice as a myth, surveying instruments and playing techniques, interpretative problems, orchestral placement, concert rooms, standards, and personnel. For the Mozart project, the celebrated Mannheim orchestra was to be an inspiration as remembered in Burney's characterization as "… an army of generals, equally fit to plan a battle as to fight it." And the aesthetician Daniel Schubart had written of it in 1784, "Its *forte* is like thunder, its crescendo like a great waterfall, its diminuendo the splashing of a crystalline river disappearing into the distance, its *piano* a breath of spring."[35] After such a promise of historical riches, it was something of a shock in 1984 to read Eric van Tassel's review of Hogwood's complete Mozart set. He praised orchestral tone colors, intonation, and the vivid recording before continuing:

> the minimalist approach, which even in the last symphonies consists simply in getting all the details right, need not prevent our penetrating the surface of the music if we are willing to make some imaginative effort…. A performance not merely 'underinterpreted' but uninterpreted offers potentially an experience of unequalled authenticity, using the word in a sense as much existential as musicological. If the notes are all you hear … you have to become a participant: you are invited to complete a realisation of the music that begins in the playing.[36]

Ironically, Hogwood's baton-waving role, though an attractive marketing tool, was historically anachronistic.

Buried within the heated debate around interpretation was the evolving question of character and personality in so-called historical music making, reaching far beyond the simple argument that *any* decision on tempo or dynamics must constitute interpretation. Whatever the musical results, Hogwood's Mozart project was an inspiration to more orchestral players to enter the historical arena, and clarinetists were part of that new wave. They were given further impetus by Antony Pay's 1986 recording of Mozart's Clarinet Concerto, with Hogwood again in the historically unjustified role as conductor. Pay had commissioned an extended clarinet designed by Edward Planas and made by Daniel Bangham; his disc made a special impression not least because the modern basset clarinet was not as yet truly established.

---

35 *Ideen zu einer Ästhetik der Tonkunst*, 130, translated in Zaslaw, "Toward the Revival," 158.

36 Eric van Tassel, "Mozart Symphonies" (recording review), *Early Music* 12, no. 1 (1984): 125.

Shortly afterward Hogwood proved an important influence in America, recording with the Amadeus Winds the Serenades K. 375 and K. 388/384a (release date 1987) and the *Gran Partita* Serenade K. 361/370a (1990), though in strictly historical terms his role was again redundant. The ensemble's clarinetists were Lawrence McDonald and William McColl, playing respectively a copy by Eric Hoeprich of his five-key clarinet by August Grenser of Dresden and an original by Bühner and Keller of Strasbourg.

Since the early 1990s an upsurge in interest in the early clarinet has made it a popular subject for specialist study, and it is now routinely available as a principal subject in conservatories around the world. But only a few years before, it would have seemed inconceivable that there could be any advantage in resurrecting clarinets from pre-Boehm days. As late as 1980 the *New Grove* article "Performing Practice" contrived to perpetuate the myth that in contrast to pre-1750 repertoire, a "continuity of tradition" existed from the Classical period onward which marginalized the necessity for historical awareness: "there has been no severance of contact with post-Baroque music as a whole, nor with the instruments used in performing it."[37] Subsequent musical revelations proved this assertion untenable, as Hogwood's Mozart project was followed by Beethoven cycles, of which there would be as many as three by the end of the 1980s.

In 1982 The Hanover Band ventured an LP of Beethoven's First Symphony and First Piano Concerto for Nimbus, again with Keith Puddy as principal clarinet. The band claimed to present Beethoven's orchestral music "in a form he would recognise," with original sound, lower pitch, late eighteenth-century feeling for tempo, an intimate, chamber music approach, the open-textured articulation of that time, and the dramatic address to rhythmic accent. Only now was it possible to assemble specialist performers with the technical facility and stylistic knowledge that enabled them to play the instruments on their own terms. The liner notes were confident, the reviews broadly welcoming. *Early Music News* supplied the tagline "The most original Beethoven yet recorded," while in *Early Music* Eric van Tassel wrote of the promise of much new light and some indication of what would be possible in the future.[38]

As part of the Hanover Band's pioneering work from 1987, the present author experienced the real pressure to perform note-perfectly

---

37 "Performing Practice," *New Grove Dictionary* (London: Macmillan, 1980).

38 *Early Music News*, July 1982, p. 178; *Early Music* 11, no. 1 (1983): 125.

under studio conditions. Beethoven's "Pastoral" Symphony felt like a real challenge, but recording sessions were usually knife-edge and exciting. These were heady days for marketing and public relations. The conductor Roy Goodman had already exchanged his violin for high-voltage baton conducting, so that it was somewhat surprising to read in the liner notes that the band was directed either from the violin or the keyboard, "as is in keeping with the period and according to the repertoire."[39] But there was public hunger to be satisfied; the disc reached no. 13 on the United States Classical Billboard charts.

How "historical" were such projects? The orchestral conditions in Beethoven's Vienna were subject to scrutiny by Clive Brown in a 1988 article, in which he painted a picture of variable standards in an environment that was socially, politically and musically challenging.[40] The Hanover Band, Hogwood, and Norrington could all argue that their 1980s Beethoven cycles had made a selection of optimal conditions. Yet in 1991 Brown declared that the pedigree of many of the instruments was of doubtful authenticity. The commercially motivated rush to push period instrument performance ever more rapidly into the nineteenth century did not offer much hope for the consolidation of historical playing styles. Despite some revelations, he felt that there was "infinitely more to historically sensitive performance than merely employing the right equipment, and the public is in danger of being offered attractively packaged but unripe fruit."[41] Brown noted an uneasy synthesis between modern Baroque style applied to Beethoven and a modern approach applied to old instruments. Nevertheless, the agenda quickly moved on apace from Haydn to Mendelssohn, Berlioz, Schumann, Brahms, Verdi, and Debussy. This later orchestral repertoire established period clarinets as part of mainstream musical activity. Understandably, there was variable success in matching the design and nationality of clarinets to the repertoire in question, and not always a desire to do so.

---

39 Caroline Brown, liner notes to *Beethoven: Symphony no. 6, "Pastoral," and "Consecration of the House,"* Nimbus Records NI 5099, 1988.

40 Clive Brown, "The Orchestra in Beethoven's Vienna," *Early Music* 16, no. 1 (1988): 4–20. Brown taught at the Universities of Oxford and Leeds. His publications include a critical biography of Spohr, and he is currently engaged in research into nineteenth-century performing practice.

41 Clive Brown, "Historical Performance, Metronome Marks and Tempo in Beethoven's Symphonies," *Early Music* 19, no. 2 (May 1991): 248.

The explosion of activity in the early 1980s coincided with the arrival of the compact disc. The substantial catalogue of solo and chamber music on period clarinets was then driven largely by principal players associated with ensembles from around the world, of which several, such as the Concentus Musicus Wien (founded 1953), had roots in the Baroque repertoire. A huge variety of approaches to re-creating early music may be observed in the work of La Petite Bande (1972), the Academy of Ancient Music (1973), the English Baroque Soloists (1978), the London Classical Players (1978–96), Les Arts Florissants (1979), The Hanover Band (1980), Orchestra of the Eighteenth Century (1981), the Handel and Haydn Society of Boston (period instruments from 1986), the Orchestra of the Age of Enlightenment (1986), Anima Aeterna (1987), the Freiburg Baroque Orchestra (1987), the Orchestre Révolutionnaire et Romantique (1989), the Orchestre des Champs Elysées (1991), and Les Siècles (2003). The clarinetists within these groups have adopted a wide range of approaches in terms of equipment and style. For example, Eric Hoeprich began life as a recorder player and was greatly influenced by Frans Brüggen, co-founder and director of the Orchestra of the Eighteenth Century, of which Hoeprich is principal clarinet. The orchestra's live 1985 recording coupling Beethoven's First Symphony with Mozart's Symphony no. 40 promoted the distinctive features of the Dutch school of playing and came as something of a revelation in England and America. Hoeprich's first recording of Mozart's Clarinet Concerto (1988) belonged firmly to that same tradition, emphasizing the expressive power of the *messa di voce*. He has proved to be an influential teacher, especially through his work at the Paris Conservatoire and at the Royal Conservatoire in The Hague, where his pupils included such prominent figures as Lorenzo Coppola (Freiburg Baroque Orchestra) and Nicola Boud (Orchestre des Champs Elysées).

It was inevitable that Mozart should become a particular focus for period clarinetists. Since Stadler's basset clarinets do not survive, a generation of soloists in the 1980s (including Pay, Hoeprich, and the present author) commissioned their own re-creations, either extending the bore or opting for a design based on the basset horn. The first monograph devoted to the Concerto appeared in 1996, and in the same year Pamela Poulin published some important discoveries relating to the work.[42] She unearthed several of Stadler's concert programs

---

42 Colin Lawson, *Mozart: Clarinet Concerto*, Cambridge Music Handbooks (Cambridge: Cambridge University Press, 1996); Pamela Poulin,

and an advertisement in Riga containing an engraving of Stadler's extended instrument. This bears a strong resemblance to the clarinette d'amour, with a curved neck and bulbous bell. One of the few surviving letters written by Stadler mentions his interest in ordering "a new type of clarinet d'amour" from the instrument maker J. B. Tietzel in Bremen, whose instruments Stadler had seen and admired. Hoeprich's book, mentioned earlier, offers much advice on how to address Mozart's Concerto, including the complex challenge of reconstructing the text. Following Poulin's revelations, a large number of period clarinetists began to commission basset clarinets with bulb design. What for Stadler had been special was now standardized and ubiquitous. Mozart's 199-measure Allegro sketch K. 621b for basset horn in G was recorded by Gilles Thomé in 1999 and reveals something of the composer's original conception for the first movement of the Concerto, strikingly without orchestral bassoons.[43] Meanwhile, trios of period basset horns found widespread popularity, focusing repertoire around Mozart's so-called Divertimenti K. 439b. An especially important release was the Stadler Trio's *Mozart and Contemporaries* played on three original basset horns made by Theodor Lotz.[44] Discovered in Andrassy Castle in Krásna Hôrka in Slovakia, these instruments are numbered 1, 2, and 3, and therefore might be thought to offer important evidence of tuning and temperament, an under-researched topic beyond the world of historical keyboards.[45]

Of special relevance is Stadler's "Musick Plan" of 1799, a curriculum of music education designed by Stadler in response to a commission by the Hungarian Count Festetics. He advocated a six-year course in which all students would learn aspects of theory, composition, and performance—including piano, organ or figured bass, violin and wind instruments—to complement their principal study. All music students were to learn the art of singing, whatever the quality of their individual voices. Emphasizing the importance of a good general education, Stadler observed that anyone wanting to understand music must know

---

"Anton Stadler's Basset Clarinet: Recent Discoveries in Riga," *Journal of the American Musical Instrument Society* 22 (1996): 110–27.

43 *Wolfgang Amadeus Mozart – une soirée chez les Jacquin,* Zig Zag Territories, 1999, ZZT 990701 (1) & (2), 2000.

44 Glossa GCD920603, 1999.

45 However, the three instruments are reported to be remarkably similar in response, each with effective cross-fingerings in the lower register. See Eric Hoeprich, "A Trio of Basset Horns by Theodor Lotz," *Galpin Society Journal* 50 (1997): 228–36.

the whole of worldly wisdom and mathematics, poetry, rhetoric, art, and many languages. It is significant that more than two centuries later the appropriate breadth and depth of music education remain a heated topic for debate. Harald Strebel's monumental study (2016) of Anton Stadler provides a wealth of further documentary evidence relating to this major figure in the history of the clarinet.[46]

Alongside Mozart, Brahms has also proved a natural focus of attention for period clarinetists. Despite his greater proximity to our own times, the re-creation of a historical style of performance has proved elusive. Several conductors have essayed the symphonies and the *German Requiem*, and the Clarinet Quintet was recorded by Jean Veilhan as long ago as 1996. Since that time, Richard Mühlfeld's somewhat old-fashioned Baermann-system clarinets made in Munich circa 1875 by Georg Ottensteiner have been widely copied by such makers as Rudolf Tutz and Jochen Seggelke. It is of course highly significant that Mühlfeld continued to play boxwood instruments until his untimely death in 1907. Their mellow tone quality matches the less aggressive, more articulate sound of a string quartet playing with gut strings, or the more gentle colors of a late nineteenth-century piano. The extent to which the qualities of an instrument dictate a player's musical impulse remains a controversial issue, but Ottensteiner clarinets in boxwood do suggest a more vocal approach, and this significantly changes the perspective of the perennial argument with viola players as to which instrument better serves Brahms's two sonatas op. 120.

Significantly, Mühlfeld's famed vibrato has not been widely emulated on copies of his instruments, nor has the rhythmic flexibility exhibited in early recordings by clarinetists such as Charles Draper and Reginald Kell. Indeed, theory and practice appear especially at odds within this repertoire, notwithstanding the encouragement of such volumes as Robert Pascall's *Playing Brahms: A Study in 19th-Century Performance Practice* [47] and the collected essays in Musgrave and Sherman's *Performing Brahms: Early Evidence of Performance Practice.*[48] A more recent publication serves to add to the many observations in the commentaries

---

46 Harald Strebel, *Anton Stadler: Wirken und Lebensumfeld des "Mozart-Klarinettisten"* (Vienna: Hollitzer, 2016).

47 Robert Pascall, *Playing Brahms: A Study in 19th-Century Performance Practice* (Nottingham: Nottingham University Music Department, 1991).

48 *Performing Brahms: Early Evidence of Performance Style,* ed. Michael Musgrave and Bernard D. Sherman (Cambridge: Cambridge University Press, 2003).

to the performing editions by Bärenreiter. *Performance Practices in Johannes Brahms's Chamber Music* by Clive Brown, Neal Peres da Costa, and Kate Bennett Wadsworth provides wide-ranging background information on performance features in Brahms's time, drawing on tutors, reminiscences, and recordings.[49] The relationship of text and act is especially significant; as Musgrave has observed in his review, "few would dispute that modern Brahms playing is generally much more standardized in style than that represented in early recordings. In the age before widely available sound reproduction, individuality was more prized than the avoidance of technical flaws, which were soon forgotten in a live performance."[50] In relation to Brahms's clarinet chamber music as a whole, the natural flexibility exhibited by violinists and violists offers an in-house tutorial to complement the scholarly evidence.

While it is natural that Mozart and Brahms should have attracted particular attention, many other byways of clarinet repertoire have been illuminated in the age of recording. The 1980s saw the publication of the first book devoted entirely to the chalumeau, an instrument whose different sizes have found their way into the catalogues of the main manufacturers.[51] With specialist research into early eighteenth-century composers such as Fux, Caldara, and Conti, more pieces have been added to the list of known repertoire (see Albert Rice's chapter in this volume) and the chalumeau has achieved greater prominence in the studio. Among other chalumeau composers whose music is readily available to the curious listener are Fasch, Graupner, Handel, Hoffmeister, Telemann, and Vivaldi, as well as a host of lesser-known composers. There is a poignant enthusiasm for the instrument in Schubart's book on aesthetics, where he belatedly wrote in the mid-1780s that "its tone is so interesting, so individual and so endlessly pleasant that the whole world of music would suffer a grievous loss if the instrument ever fell into disuse."[52]

---

49   Clive Brown, Neal Peres Da Costa, and Kate Bennett Wadsworth, *Performance Practices in Johannes Brahms's Chamber Music* (Kassel: Bärenreiter, 2015).

50   Michael Musgrave, review of Brown, Peres Da Costa, and Wadsworth, *Performance Practices in Johannes Brahms's Chamber Music*, *Performance Practice Review* 21 (2017): 4.

51   Colin Lawson, *The Chalumeau in Eighteenth-Century Music* (Ann Arbor, MI: UMI Research Press, 1981).

52   Christian Friedrich Daniel Schubart, *Ideen zu einer Ästhetik der Tonkunst* [1784–85] (Vienna: J. V. Degen, 1806), 326.

The two-key Baroque clarinet has become more widely known through Rice's research, though the main focus of attention among period players is likely to remain Vivaldi's three concertos, Handel's *Ouverture* for two clarinets and horn, and the six concertos by Molter, notwithstanding the discovery of orchestral C and D clarinet parts by Caldara, Conti, Faber, Telemann, and Graupner, as well as later examples by Rameau in Paris and Arne in London. As the five-key classical instruments in C, B-flat, and A became established, the clarinet's cantabile qualities began to be exploited by the Mannheim school of Johann and Carl Stamitz. Around this time a greater security in the lowest register sounded the death-knell for the chalumeau as a separate entity during the 1770s. The discography of the period clarinet extends to concertos by Mahon, Hook (attrib.), Crusell, Weber, and even Spohr, and to chamber works ranging across *Harmoniemusik*, quartets and quintets for clarinet and strings, larger mixed ensembles, and duos with early piano. The character of small-scale classical repertoire, such as the sonatas by Devienne, Vanhal, Lefèvre, Mendelssohn, Danzi, and Weber, as well as Mozart's "Kegelstatt" Trio K. 498, especially suits the lighter tone of boxwood instruments. It is significant that although the Austro-German repertoire has tended to predominate, clarinetists and composers associated with the French Revolution have also found a place in the catalogue. Some recent recordings of the twelve sonatas from Lefèvre's tutor have preferred his accompaniment of a simple bass line (almost certainly intended for cello) to the once-popular yet over-burdensome keyboard reductions.[53]

Explorations of the nineteenth century have involved variants of the new thirteen-key B-flat clarinet presented by the clarinetist-inventor Iwan Müller in 1812 to a panel of judges at the Paris Conservatoire. He somewhat rashly claimed that it could play fluently in any tonality, and it was initially rejected on the grounds that its exclusive adoption would deprive composers of an important tonal resource provided by the sounds of the A, B-flat, and C clarinets then in use. Müller's invention remained hugely influential; original thirteen-key French instruments survive in some numbers and have recently been used for orchestral projects devoted to Berlioz, who memorably described the clarinet as the voice of heroic love. In England the much-loved Albert (or simple-system) clarinet based on Müller was overtaken by the Boehm system only during the interwar period; it has recently been

---

53 *J. X. Lefèvre: A Revolutionary Tutor,* with Colin Lawson (clarinet), Clarinet Classics CC0055, 2007, and CC0058, 2011.

revived on disc.[54] Some later projects purporting to re-create the sound world of Debussy and Ravel have brought early Boehm-system clarinets (sometimes in boxwood) back into use.[55]

Old Instruments, Modern Copies

We might ask ourselves what actually constitutes an early clarinet. As might be expected, old instruments survive in a variety of conditions, sometimes with virtually invisible problems relating to the bore and occasionally having been subject to later modification. For those with an interest in the physical characteristics of original instruments, a panoramic overview of some 800 early clarinets is provided by the *Catalogue of the Sir Nicholas Shackleton Collection* (Edinburgh, 2007), notably some important Viennese and French specimens.[56]

In contrast, copies bring an opportunity to choose both original and modern makers; there is the opportunity for more than a nod toward practical considerations, with the addition of anachronistic key-work, tweaking of intonation on the workbench (often via electronic tuning machines), and even a "normalizing" of the pitch to standardized historical pitches of a' = 415 (Baroque) or a' = 430 (Classical). This regularization has been ironic, given that Quantz in 1752 lamented the lack of a uniform pitch standard, which he reckoned was detrimental to his work as a flutist and to music in general. Significantly, a wind instrument manufacturer's advertisement in the *Wiener Zeitung* of February 25, 1789 contained a request that prospective foreign clients should specify the required pitch, "whether Viennese pitch, *Kammerton*, or even French pitch, or send him a tuning fork."[57] Equally unhistorical has been the tendency to copy a limited number of admittedly first-rate clarinets, for example by the Viennese maker Tauber (for Mozart) or Simiot (for French repertoire). Clarinets by the Dresden

---

54   *100 Years of the Simple-System Clarinet*, with Colin Lawson (clarinet), Clarinet Classics CC0044, 2002.

55   For example, recordings by the French period orchestra Les Siècles of Debussy's *La mer, Jeux*, and *Nocturnes*; Ravel's *Daphnis and Chloe*; and Stravinsky's *Rite of Spring* and *Firebird*.

56   Heike Fricke, *Catalogue of the Sir Nicholas Shackleton Collection* (Edinburgh: Edinburgh University Collection of Historic Musical Instruments, 2007).

57   Quoted in Richard Maunder, "Viennese Wind-Instrument Makers, 1700–1800," *Galpin Society Journal* 51 (1998): 185.

maker Heinrich Grenser, whose clients included the Swedish/Finn-ish virtuoso Bernhard Henrik Crusell, have proved popular models for the music of Weber and his contemporaries. Their design (incorporating as many as twelve keys) contrasts radically with the designs of earlier Classical clarinets in enabling greater volume within a more focused sound.

Listings of modern makers of copies have rarely been attempted, and in any case are destined to become quickly out of date in an ever-changing marketplace. But one such account from 1996 found a huge range of models available from some nine manufacturers, including such specialized projects as early bass clarinets and clarinettes d'amour.[58] In the intervening period a whole generation of player-makers has embraced the challenge of making early clarinets. The scale of current manufacturing operations can be quickly comprehended by reference to the catalogues of eminent makers such as Daniel Bangham (Cambridge, UK), Guy Cowley (Nottingham, UK), Stephen Fox (Richmond Hill, Ontario), Agnès Géroult (Paris), Peter van der Poel (Utrecht), Andreas Schöni (Bern), Schwenk & Seggelke (Bamberg), and Rudolf Tutz (Innsbruck).

Practical expediency has a significant effect on mouthpiece lay, design, and material, as well as reed type. The commercial German-cut reeds in general use are a convenience, yet their pedigree barely reflects the type of set-up that would have been known within Stadler's Vienna. The demands of recording and the exigencies of air travel can only partly justify such shortcuts in historical terms, given that a great deal of advice about reeds is contained within tutors for the clarinet. In relation to technique, there has also been a tendency to ignore uncomfortable evidence from primary sources; for example, the Baroque clarinet was originally played with the reed against the upper lip, the modern practice of reed-below becoming official policy at the Paris Conservatoire only in 1831. There has been little appetite to explore this technique, though the historical evidence has recently been thoroughly researched, notably by the scholar-performer Ingrid Pearson.[59]

---

58 Colin Lawson, "An Investigation of Clarinets and their Makers," *Early Music Today* 6 (Winter 1996): 20–23.

59 Ingrid E. Pearson, "Clarinet Embouchure in Theory and Practice: The Forgotten Art of Reed Above" (PhD diss., University of Sheffield, 2001); Ingrid Elizabeth Pearson, "Ferdinando Sebastiani, Gennaro Bosa and the Clarinet in Nineteenth-Century Naples," *Galpin Society Journal* 60 (2007): 112–15, 203–14.

Early nineteenth-century repertoire across Europe was doubtless played with radically differing embouchures and articulations, though this is yet to be reflected among today's performers. In terms of fingering, treatises and tutors are a useful guide to original practice, notwithstanding Fröhlich's observation that each instrument was different from the next and that it was up to the player to find his own solutions. There can be no doubt that almost every aspect of music making was far less standardized than we can nowadays imagine.

Historical Styles

Performance on a period clarinet can never be a guarantee of stylish interpretation, and today one often hears early instruments played with a direct transference of modern articulation and phrasing. In any event, clarinetists have something of a reputation among those schooled in the Baroque for lacking stylistic awareness, and it does take a special determination to become a truly articulate player and to match the nuance of an expressive violinist. Harnessed to an instinctive knowledge of stylistic parameters, early clarinets can facilitate exploration of the language of the slur and other expressive devices of earlier composers. This pursuit of different performance styles may involve a variety of instruments, but these are essentially the means to an end.

The *Méthode de clarinette* written for the Paris Conservatoire by Lefèvre in 1802 remains instructive and relevant. Indeed, it continued to be reprinted well into the twentieth century.[60] Its commissioners drew attention to the clarinet's ability to sing, reminding students that they should aim to move listeners, rather than merely surprise them. Lefèvre's text dilutes an old-style philosophical approach with sound practical advice, illustrations, and fingering charts. His practical applications include instruction on posture, holding the clarinet, and finger placement. He found good cane for reeds difficult to acquire, reckoning that cane tended to be cut too green or too dry, a problem that all modern clarinetists will recognize. Lefèvre's detailed list of the clarinet's out-of-tune notes, those needing correction by means of the embouchure, is important evidence in today's ongoing debate about intonation in the past. He seems all too realistic about the clarinet's shortcomings and perhaps over-optimistic about the manner in which they might be overcome. His comments contrast

---

60   e.g., A. Giampieri, *Metodo per clarinetto* (Milan: Ricordi, 1939).

radically with those of the Leipzig flutist Tromlitz, who a decade earlier was discussing different sizes of semitone within the scale and the use of unequal temperaments.[61]

In terms of articulation, Lefèvre describes a much smaller range of options than Tromlitz, while advising use of the tongue rather than the throat or chest, techniques that had previously been in vogue. Artistic aspects of clarinet playing attracted special attention, with the observation that clarinet playing can become monotonous without articulation and nuance.[62] It is not sufficient merely to read the music and play the notes, but the musical character must be assimilated. A prevalent uniformity of execution means that a certain coldness and monotony has often been attributed to the nature of the instrument, whereas in fact this is the responsibility of the player, whose armory must include a good knowledge of harmony to complement musical taste. Significantly, he regards an Adagio as the most difficult movement to execute, its character quite distinct from an Allegro; he recalls eighteenth-century sources in referring players to listen to the finest singers.

Like Lefèvre, his German contemporary J. G. H. Backofen (*Anweisung zur Clarinette*, 1803) placed a high priority on playing in tune, recommending the insertion of wax into tone holes to correct the intonation.[63] Hoeprich has remarked that Backofen shows numerous examples of difficult passages on the clarinet, which he states are nonetheless possible, whereas Lefèvre prefers to give examples of what is technically impossible. As already implied, these clarinet tutors can be supplemented by primary sources beyond the clarinet literature, which often point up broader stylistic ambiguities and controversies as well as possible solutions.

It need hardly be added that primary evidence must be read in the spirit of the time, and there is much that cannot be taken too literally. In 1811, when health was still a relatively fragile affair, Franz Joseph Fröhlich recommended for wind players a moderate lifestyle and the avoidance of anything that could damage the chest, such as running, horseback riding, and the excessive consumption of hot drinks. One should not practice after a meal, so the afternoon was

61 J. G. Tromlitz, *Ausführlicher und gründlicher Unterricht die Flöte zu spielen* (Leipzig: Böhme, 1791), trans. and ed. A. Powell as *The Virtuoso Flute-Player* (Cambridge: Cambridge University Press, 1991).

62 J. X. Lefèvre, *Méthode de clarinette* (Paris, 1802), facsimile (Geneva: Minkoff, 1974), 14.

63 J. G. H. Backofen, *Anweisung zur Clarinette* (Leipzig: Breitkopf & Härtel, 1803).

best avoided; furthermore, one should not drink immediately after practicing if the lungs are still warm, since this has been the cause of many early deaths. In the case of dry lips—very bad for the embouchure—the mouth should be rinsed with an alcoholic beverage to give one new strength.[64]

In assuming a good knowledge of harmony and the art of singing, writers of tutors and treatises were in fact expecting that performers would glean a great deal of interpretative information from the rhythm, melodic intervals, phrasing, and harmony notated in the score, and adapt their technique accordingly. For example, it was expected that dissonances would be stressed, with corresponding release at their resolution. This invitation to engage more intimately with the musical notation will surely be an important legacy of today's historical movement. Appropriate sound quality relates closely to such an outlook and ultimately justifies the constant effort of furnishing various clarinets with responsive reeds, as one constantly strives to adjust to their different techniques and fingerings. In some ways the present musical climate is calculated to defeat even the most dedicated player, who may be required to play clarinets from several historical periods in a single day. The realities of the profession incorporate a view of the past which has many worthwhile elements, but which is on the whole decidedly unhistorical.

A Personal Perspective

Individual experiences within historical performance have been less documented than the philosophical debate surrounding period performance. There have been exceptions, such as Sherman's *Inside Early Music*, which reports conversations with high-profile practitioners, mainly directors and conductors.[65] Occasional interviews with orchestral players have been revealing; for example, in discussing modified copies of natural trumpets Crispian Steele-Perkins memorably remarked on the necessity to own equipment "with which to earn a living in an environment where time is money and where there are

---

64 Franz Joseph Fröhlich, *Vollständige theoretisch-praktische Musikschule* (Bonn: Simrock, 1811), 15–16.
65 Bernard Sherman, *Inside Early Music* (New York: Oxford University Press, 2003).

monstrous egos to be satiated."[66] In addressing historical evidence, the art and craft of music making need to be kept in balance. For the present author it has felt important to assimilate historical evidence into articulation and phrasing, but also to prioritize sound quality, even when the means were not always strictly historical. C. P. E. Bach's remarks about moving an audience deserve special attention. And after all, Anton Stadler's clarinet was described as having so soft and lovely a sound that no one with a heart could resist it.[67] Two decades later, in 1808, the Paris maker Simiot directly anticipated Berlioz in observing: "The range, the variety and the quality of sound of the clarinet distinguish it from all the other winds; it has all the characteristics which composers desire, and can play equally well the hymn of the warrior or the song of the shepherd."[68] Yet the experience of the present author has been that no record producer and only one conductor have ever taken any interest in the pedigree of his clarinets, preferring to focus upon technical accuracy. Were they really concerned if mouthpieces were made of ebonite—a material shown at the Great Exhibition, well after Mozart's death? Yet this is stable material well able to withstand long airplane journeys. Moreover, audiences are likely to prefer instruments that work efficiently.

Directors themselves have taken radically different views of historical performance. For example, Trevor Pinnock clearly prioritizes sound and intonation, whereas Roger Norrington uses sound as a means to the language of gesture, shape, and form. These conductors' musical personalities have been well served and supported by producers and engineers of fine artistic judgment. But overall, no one has ever probed even the basic differences in national playing styles that would be taken for granted in Baroque repertoire. While leading the London Classical Players, Norrington wrote in one of his booklet notes that the earliest gramophone recordings are of limited help to anyone seeking a historical viewpoint. It was somehow reassuring that a mere dozen years later he could write, in relation to his latest crusade

---

66 Crispian Steele-Perkins, "The Trumpet," *Early Music Today* 8 (Spring 1998): 12.

67 J. F. Schink, *Litterarische Fragmente* (Graz: Widmanstättischen Schriften, 1785), 286.

68 Jacques François Simiot, in his *Tableau explicative des innovations et changements faits à la clarinette* (1808), quoted in Hoeprich, *The Clarinet*, 123.

against pervading orchestral vibrato, that most of today's musicians had no notion of what can be so simply revealed in a good gramophone collection.[69]

It is well to remember that Mozart and Beethoven had no experience of air travel or the microphone, nor for that matter would they have expected conductors to be part of their concerto performances. With the benefit of hindsight, we can be selective in how we use the music and the evidence. And surely musical notation is just the beginning; even a scholarly *Urtext* can only reveal a certain amount. Taruskin was right about historical performance being the most modern sound around, but Kenyon was also justified in observing how tradition has been literally reshaped by it. And in the last analysis, we might want to return to the question of whether there is indeed any *moral* obligation to follow a composer's earlier intentions, even where they can be discerned. While reflecting on such matters, we can be assured that the early clarinet has already been part of a transformation of musical life that has inspired a true conjunction of mind and spirit.

69 Roger Norrington, "The Sound Orchestras Make," *Early Music* 32, no. 1 (2004): 2–5. Cf. Norrington's liner notes to Brahms, Symphony no. 1, EMI CDC 7 54286 2, 1991.

10

THE CLARINET IN VERNACULAR MUSIC

S. Frederick Starr

For nearly two centuries the clarinet reigned as the premier wind instrument for vernacular music. So modestly did it play this role that the world came to recognize it only in the second third of the twentieth century. Only then did the Western public acknowledge its most popular and finest players as true virtuosi who equaled or surpassed in brilliance the finest "classical" clarinetists. But soon after attaining this high distinction, the clarinet slipped off its pedestal and receded to the status of a respected if limited voice in world vernacular music.

This may come as surprise to those who, like the present author, consider a fine performance of the Mozart or Brahms Clarinet Quintet as one of the highest achievements of our civilization. How can vernacular or popular musicians employ the same instrument in such radically different ways and still make great music? The secret is that the clarinet, a relative newcomer in comparison to the violin or trumpet, can express almost as broad a range of emotions as the human voice. Vernacular clarinetists on several continents have exploited this possibility.

From the time of its invention in the eighteenth century, the clarinet was acknowledged as a natural vehicle for folk music and light melodies. This is what prompted the clarinet-playing brothers Ludwig and Conrad Bänder of Kassel, Germany (1780s–1850s), to offer audiences on their concert tours "Variations on Tyrolean and Swiss Songs," which doubtless included yodeling,[1] as well as a potpourri of Russian folk songs. In the same spirit, Joseph Beer (1744–1812) offered the public a "French Royal Hunting Song," and Aloysius Beerhalter played his folksy "Im kuehlen Keller sitz' ich hier," (Here I sit in a cool basement) from the Singspiel *Die Kritikaster und der Trinker* (*The Cavalier and the Drinker*) on his basset horn.[2] Beerhalter, it turns out, was trained by a village musician, which doubtless gave his pieces an authenticity that a court musician would have struggled to achieve. An even earlier clarinetist with such training was Joseph Lacher (1739–1805) from near Augsburg, who was taught by his father, a proficient clarinetist in spite of the fact that he couldn't read music.[3] The sheer number of paintings and engravings of clarinet-playing village musicians from the Biedermeier era in Germany and the Austrian lands attests to how solidly the clarinet had established itself as a folk instrument. Schubert tapped into this popular association when he chose a clarinet to accompany the soprano in one of his last works (1828), *The Shepherd on the Rock* (*Der Hirt auf dem Felsen*).

It is curious that the oboe, the instrument the clarinet pushed aside in order to find a place in wind ensembles (*Harmoniemusik*), had few if any of these folkish connotations. This was due in part to the differing nature of the two instruments but also to the fact that the modern clarinet emerged as an instrument during the early Romantic era, when folkishness was all the rage. More than a century later, the popularity achieved by diverse "folk" clarinetists (real or supposed), whether klezmorim, practitioners of Balkan wedding music, or jazz, coincided once more with a period when Western popular culture as a whole eagerly looked downward in society, rather than upward, for inspiration. The cult that grew up around such otherwise dramatically different clarinetists as Ivo Papazov, Giora Feidman, or George Lewis, not to mention scores of other "vernacular" clarinets on four continents, is inconceivable without this folk perspective.

By what process did the clarinet attain so lofty a role in the world of vernacular music? Even though by the 1950s the diverse strands of development came into contact with and even influenced one another, no single strand connects the folksy clarinetists of the German world in the 1820s to the diverse vernacular idioms of the present. Rather, they followed what turned out to be three largely separate lines of

---

1   Pamela Weston, *More Clarinet Virtuosi of the Past* (London: the author, 1977), 33.
2   Weston, *More Clarinet Virtuosi*, 44–45.
3   Weston, *More Clarinet Virtuosi*, 150.

development that took place worlds apart from each other. The first of these traces to Eastern Europe and the Balkans; the second to French and Spanish colonies in the New World; and the third to North America. All three were initially colonial appendages of Europe, specifically of the Austrian and Russian Empires, of France and Spain, and of Great Britain. In other words, the spread of the clarinet as a vernacular instrument coincided with the expansion of Europe as a political and cultural zone.

The Austrian Clarinet Diaspora

The first of these developments took place largely within or near the borders of the multi-national Austrian (later Austro-Hungarian) Empire. It is worth noting that it did not take place elsewhere in the Germanic world, and especially not in northern Germany or Scandinavia, which remained wedded to the fiddle as their prime folk instrument. Curiously, this was due to the more precarious security situation in southeastern Europe. That vast territory had been assembled under Vienna's rule through a combination of dynastic marriages and wars. Like all the other empires that figure in this history, it depended for its maintenance and security on army garrisons spread across the territory, and on economic and cultural ties. Austria had maintained military bands since the late seventeenth century, but they gained new importance and popularity during the Napoleonic era. Instrument makers of the day focused on inventing new instruments for these ensembles, refining old ones, and producing inexpensive ones for popular use. As a result, piston cornets (*cornets à pistons*) came on the scene by the 1830s, as well as sections of clarinets with five or more keys. Both increased the ensembles' volume and flexibility of sound. During the peaceful decades that followed, garrison bands had little to do, and were regularly engaged on Sundays and holidays to serenade the local populace. Inevitably, that meant playing for dancing as well.[4]

With its territory secured, the Austrian Empire naturally extended Vienna's cultural and economic reach throughout Central Europe and the Balkans. This meant opening theaters and opera companies in all the major cities. Not only did these establishments maintain

---

4   For information on Austrian military bands, see Eugen Brixel, Gunther Martin, and Gottfried Pils, *Das ist Österreichs Militärmusik: Von der "Türkischen Musik" zu den Philharmonikern in Uniform* (Graz: Edition Kaleidoskop, 1982).

orchestras, but they hosted touring virtuosi, on clarinet as well as other instruments. Like the military bands, the smaller theater orchestras also made themselves available to play for dances. Between lessons offered by military clarinetists and theater clarinetists and the inspiration provided by touring virtuosi, aspiring clarinetists in cities like Budapest, Lemberg (today Lviv), Olmütz, Belgrade, Zagreb, and Sarajevo all had access to both instruction and inspiration.

The fact that both military bands and theater orchestras played for informal entertainments and especially dances is of great importance to the history of the clarinet as a vernacular instrument. To satisfy the public's desire for the most melodic pieces, they played popular operatic arias, folk melodies, and everything in between. To meet the dancers' demands they played grand promenades (i.e., marches), galops, waltzes, schottisches, and local folk dances. In so doing, they created an instrumental model that could be reproduced on a smaller scale in every village band and ensemble in the region. This opened major new vistas for clarinetists. Thanks to the mass production of inexpensive clarinets and, eventually, clarinets of ebonite, even a child of modest means could dream of becoming a clarinetist. Indeed, clarinets were being turned out by small shops in places like Brno, Lemberg, and Buda, and anyone who could read German could get tips from the many clarinet instruction books on the market. The contrasting sounds of its different registers gave it a broader emotional range than the oboe, while it clearly surpassed the flute in volume. By the mid-1800s, the instrumental culture that spread outward from Vienna had touched nearly every town and rural village across Central Europe and the Balkans. In the process the clarinet became increasingly popular and vernacular.

Musicologists would classify the small ensembles that emerged from this process as purveyors of *Gebrauchsmusik*, i.e., music for practical use. Such "practical use" meant weddings, saint's day parties, and even funerals. But their core function was to accompany dancing and drinking. While the link with dancing is obvious, it is worth pausing to note the specific connection between the vernacular clarinet and drinking. At one level, this may seem obvious, the inevitable result of its taking over at least some of the functions heretofore fulfilled by the violin or rustic bagpipe. In Moravia, for instance, dulcimer ensembles, which were often heard in inns, scrapped the flute for a clarinet, along with a violin or two.[5] In the Austrian world the link with drinking gained enormous visibility and symbolic meaning in 1886 when the two Schrammel brothers from Vienna added a bass guitar to their two violins, and also a high G clarinet.[6] Played by Georg Dänzer, this *picksüßes Hölzl* (sickly-sweet little stick) wove a soprano line above the violins and sometimes broke into a kind of obbligato. Brahms greatly admired the group. The Schrammel quartet had a large book of written music. But through years of playing together it acquired the ability to improvise arrangements of new and folk melodies, with Dänzer's clarinet dancing above the two harmonized violin lines.

Most village and town bands performed for dancers who expected the music to roll on and on without interruption. This required the musicians to repeat endlessly simple and popular melodies. If printed music was used at all it was soon discarded and the players began ornamenting and elaborating what they had memorized. It is this process that propelled the clarinet into the lead position in the hundreds of these ensembles that existed, for it was ideally suited both to present the melody and to ornament it. Because most such bands arose from long-settled and stable villages and towns, membership tended to stay constant over many years, if not decades. Even though the musicians were usually paid for their efforts, the group itself became a kind of social club. The clarinetist offered up his ornamentations, elaborations, and improvisations as much for his fellow musicians as for the drinkers or dancers. The goal for all such players was, and is, to dazzle fellow musicians and discerning members of the audience with their virtuosity and ability to touch the emotions, and thus to spread the clarinetists' fame.

It is a curious fact that whereas by the end of the nineteenth century most clarinetists in the Germanic world had shifted to the sophisticated twenty-one-key clarinet developed by Oskar Oehler (1859–1936), it was the simpler and in some respects less adroit fingering system adopted by Eugene Albert in Brussels that gained favor across the Balkans. Firms like Albert and Mahillon, also from Brussels, found a large market there and managed to dominate the field; their instruments

---

5   Lubomír Tyllner. "Dudy a nástrojové sestavy lidové hudby v Čechách 19. století" [The bagpipe and the composition of folk instrument ensembles in Bohemia during the nineteenth century], *Český lid: etnologický časopis* 79, no.1 (1992): 47–60.

6   On the Schrammels, see Kurt Dieman Dichtl-Jörgenreuth, *Schrammelmusik—Schrammelwelt: Eine österreichische Zeitgeschichte* (Vienna: Residenz Verlag, 1981).

are still valued and played today in vernacular music. Mouthpieces featured a narrow lay, which demanded very hard (and durable) reeds. The use of a double-lip embouchure, toughened through long hours of playing, assured both an open, unimpeded tone and the requisite volume. Although C instruments were sometimes used, by far the most common was the clarinet in B-flat.

Beginning in the second half of the nineteenth century and culminating in the early twentieth, every country in southeastern Europe and the Balkans developed its own type of small ensemble featuring the clarinet. In Hungary, for example, nationalists moved on from the clarinet in favor of a wooden instrument with a conical bore, the *tárogató*. Conceived as more authentically Hungarian than the clarinet, the *tárogató* is in fact a wooden straight soprano saxophone with a rather nasal tone.[7] Many Romanian players also switched to *tárogató*. Macedonians, Albanians, and Bulgarians stayed with the clarinet and soon developed phenomenal techniques. Best known today for the so-called Bulgarian "wedding bands" (every band in the region played for weddings), this genre of *svadbarska muzika* (wedding music) is as arresting for its asymmetrical meters and the unusual scales it employs as for the dizzying proficiency of its clarinetists. This music emerged in the late nineteenth century, but because of the communist domination of Eastern Europe down to 1989–90, the most brilliant exponents of the style—players like Tale Ognenovski from Macedonia and Selim Leskoviku from Albania—did not become known in the West until recent decades.[8]

Closely related to these Balkan clarinetists but nonetheless comprising a distinct school are the Greek clarinetists who perform with village ensembles and wedding bands in that country. Again, they use exclusively Albert-system instruments in B-flat and C, but unlike their Balkan brethren, they often practice circular breathing. It is likely that this derives from the *kaval*, the Turkish shepherd flute that was once ubiquitous in the lands where Greeks lived and which is always played with a continuous flow of air. Together with the insistent drumming, circular breathing imparts to the music a powerful forward propulsion. Although this folk idiom was doubtless fully formed before 1900, it remained largely unknown to the Western public until after World

---

7   On the *tárogató* see Eszter Fontana, "Tárogató," *Grove Music Online.*
8   For further reading, see Stephen Cottrell and Evangelia Mantzourani, "The Clarinet and Its Players in Eastern Europe and Greece," in *The Versatile Clarinet*, ed. Roger Heaton (New York: Routledge, 2006), 40–55.

War II. When it finally came to the attention of European and American audiences in the 1960s it caused a sensation.[9] The impact of Greek clarinetists like Petroloukas Chalkias and Vasilios Saleas was scarcely less electrifying than that of the best Balkan players, and eventually gave rise to new currents that made themselves felt far beyond folk music circles.

A final form of instrumental folk music from the Balkans that came to center on the clarinet is that of the klezmorim, the Ashkenazi Jewish version of the region's ubiquitous "wedding bands." Like the other groups in the region, klezmorim performed waltzes, galops, and other dances of the day. Likewise, they too included their own dances in the repertoire, in this case freylekhs, horas, and shers. Like its counterparts elsewhere the klezmer style came to center on the clarinet, but the Jewish ensemble was more likely than the others to include brass instruments, including baritone horns or cornets.[10] And like them, too, we know the original sounds only from recordings that were made many decades after the music was first played. This presents serious problems in the case of klezmer music because the earliest recordings all date from after the players' emigration to the United States, where they quickly fell under the strong influence of early American jazz. Peeling back the layers, one may safely assume that the clarinetist's early role was to play the melody in such a way as to leave space for the violinist to show his skills through ornamentation, and occasionally to show off alone. Only with the impact of jazz did the clarinet emerge as the dominant musical driver of klezmer bands. Nonetheless, the earliest recordings of clarinetists like Naftule Brandwein and Dave Tarras indicate a strong technique on the Albert clarinet.

Klezmer-type music extended far beyond the borders of the old Austrian Empire, penetrating deep into Romania, Ukraine, the so-called Pale of Jewish Settlement, and clear to the regional capital of Odessa. Leonid Utesov (1895–1982), later a popular bandleader in the USSR, grew up in Odessa's seamy Moldavanka Jewish quarter and recalled talented vernacular musicians who gained fame there

---

9   On Greek folk clarinetists consult the audio compact disc collection *Greek Clarinet Virtuosos: Authentic Recordings, 1928–1964,* Vintage Music, 2013.

10   On the transformation of klezmer music in the United States see Mark Slobin, ed., *American Klezmer: Its Roots and Offshoots* (Berkeley: University of California Press, 2002).

playing the popular music of the day.[11] The popularity of the clarinet as a vehicle for vernacular music even extended to Turkey. In this case, the advent of the clarinet can be dated quite precisely, to the decision by Sultan Mehmet II (r. 1808–39) to equip his army with European-style bands. In other words, the clarinet was again introduced "from the top down."

Sultan Mehmet had the misfortune to lose control over Greece during his tenure. Blaming the traditional Ottoman military corps, the Janissaries, for this misfortune, he disbanded them and set about building a modern, European-type army. This of course required marching bands, so he recruited Giuseppe Donizetti (1788–1856), elder brother of the opera composer Gaetano Donizetti, to staff and train them.[12] Donizetti hailed from Lombardy, which was then ruled by Austria, and he was therefore familiar with the same Austrian ensembles that had provided the model for army bands across the Balkans. Clarinets were central to Donizetti's plan. Soon he was importing crates of instruments and training whole ranks of clarinetists to staff bands across the Ottoman Empire. Later, as the first recruits retired and returned to their homes across the Empire, they introduced the clarinet to even the most remote districts of Turkey and the Middle East.

Mehmet's reign ended with his introducing a series of bold reforms to bring the Ottoman state into the modern world. For several decades everything European was considered desirable and worthy of emulation. This included the clarinet. But the Turks did not simply adopt the reigning B-flat or E-flat military clarinet; they made the unusual decision to favor the clarinet pitched in low G, an instrument found but rarely used in Europe. The added length gives it a dark tone, somewhat like a basset horn but with an edge due to the all-metal construction of the most popular models. These Turkish instruments, manufactured today in both metal and wood and sold very inexpensively, are arguably the first clarinets anywhere to be designed and marketed as folk instruments explicitly for the performance of vernacular music. They have the further distinction of being the only clarinets in the twentieth century to be designed specifically to have a warm, deep, and muted sound, even at the price of less brightness in the upper

---

11   Leonid Utesov, *S pesnei po zhizni* (Moscow: Iskusstvo, 1961), chap. 1; and Leonid Utesov, *Zapiski aktera: vospominaniia, vstrechi, razdumia* (Moscow and Leningrad, 1949), chap. 1.

12   On Giuseppe Donizetti's astonishing Ottoman career see the essays in Federico Spinelli, ed., *Giuseppe Donizetti Pascia: traiettorie musicale e storiche tra Italia e Turkia* (Bergamo: Fondazione Donizetti, 2010).

register. In recent years the Turkish clarinetist Hüsnü Şenlendirici has gained immense popularity in his own country and even some exposure abroad for his facile and heartfelt performances on the Turkish G clarinet. To date, the greatest foreign impact of Turkish clarinetists is in the Arab world rather than in the West.[13]

The Vernacular Clarinet in the Caribbean World and Mexico

Most books on clarinet history, including ones that are otherwise erudite and comprehensive, short-change or ignore Italy, Spain, and the New World. However, for the history of the clarinet as a vernacular instrument this leaves a major gap. For it was precisely in the French- and Spanish-speaking regions of the New World that important elements of that evolution occurred. Because these elements are both central to our story and generally neglected, we will focus on them more closely here.

Like the story of Austrian influence on the vernacular clarinet in southeastern Europe, the history of that instrument in the Americas is intimately tied up with empire. The narrative begins in North America, where the clarinet first appeared in the eighteenth century. Here the driving factor was above all the staffing of bands attached to military units sent by London and Versailles to their respective colonies in the New World. Then the story will shift to the Caribbean, specifically to the French colony of Saint-Domingue, arguably the richest spot on earth through much of the eighteenth century. Military bands were a factor here, but the most transformative developments took place in the civilian sector, specifically in local theaters. Then the focus will move to the Spanish colony of Cuba, which played a central part in defining the role of the clarinet in twentieth-century popular music, and finally to the former Spanish colony of Mexico, which developed a strong band tradition that gave prominence to the clarinet.

Both Portugal and Spain boasted talented locally born clarinetists by the 1790s.[14] Indeed, Madrid maintained no fewer than twelve venues that regularly employed clarinetists.[15] By the early nineteenth

---

13 An accessible overview of this subject is Boja Kragulj, "The Clarinet as a Defining Instrument of Turkish Musical Culture," *The Clarinet* 39, no. 3 (June 2012): 59–61.
14 Weston, *More Clarinet Virtuosi*, 273.
15 Weston, *More Clarinet Virtuosi*, 306–7.

century Spain had its own touring virtuosi, and decades later, it had its own "Romero system" clarinet, invented by Antonio Romero y Andía (1815–85).[16] Translations of Klosé (*Méthode complète de clarinette*, 1843) were supplemented by Romero's *Metodo completo de clarinete* (Madrid, 1860). Moreover, there were opera houses, theaters, and military garrisons with their own bands in many cities in Brazil, Peru, Venezuela, etc., just as there were in Austria's imperial holdings in southeastern Europe.[17] All these establishments maintained clarinetists on their staffs, men like Gaspar Campos, originally from Barcelona, who played in the orchestra at the São João Theater in Rio de Janeiro throughout the period 1820–50. But in none of these places did local conditions create the kinds of folk societies that would develop their own distinctive vernacular music employing European-type instruments, and specifically the clarinet.

France was a latecomer to imperial expansion in the Caribbean, gaining control over the western side of Hispaniola only in 1659. Nor did it seriously begin developing the place until the early eighteenth century. But the discovery that both coffee and sugar grew more bountifully there than anywhere else, and that the island supported indigo and cotton as well, made the island fabulously rich, and truly the "Pearl of the Antilles." This bounty attracted not only aristocratic investors but also French ne'er-do-wells, both of whom were beholden to the labor of a large enslaved population recently brought from Africa. A significant mulatto population soon emerged as well. No sooner were they emancipated than they, too, bought land and slaves, to the point that by 1789 free people of color owned a third of the island's land and slaves.[18] To keep order, the King of France maintained several regiments on the island, each of which had its own band, replete with newly minted clarinets.

During the mild winters, whites and free people of color congregated in cities like Port au Prince, Cap-François (Cap Haitien), Jacmel, Gonâve, Jeremie, Les Cayes, and Grande Rivière. With plenty of money

---

16 Weston, *More Clarinet Virtuosi*, 186–87.

17 The impact of military bands on local music making worldwide is discussed in Suzel Ana Reily and Katherine Brucker, eds., *Brass Bands of the World: Militarism, Colonial Legacies, and Local Music Making* (London: Routledge, 2013).

18 Although there exist many modern studies, the classic source on Saint-Domingue in these years remains Louis Elie Moreau de Saint-Méry, *Description topographique, physique, civile, politique et historique de la partie française de l'isle de Saint-Domingue*, 2 vols. (Philadelphia, 1797).

and ample time during the off-season, they built theaters and imported actors, singers, and instrumentalists to staff them. The most renowned stars of the French opera stage found it advantageous to tour there, as did famous instrumentalists. Small orchestras of eight to fifteen musicians were essential for the operatic performances and also for plays. These ensembles included Frenchmen and also free people of color who had received instrumental training. At first flutes were the lead woodwinds, but by the 1780s the clarinet had triumphed. Indeed, we know the names of two clarinetists who played with the ensemble at the Comédie theater in Port-au-Prince during that decade: Messrs. Barbier and Lewis.[19]

Repeating the practice we observed in southeastern Europe, all the various musical ensembles on Saint-Domingue regularly played for dances. Most active in this area were the theater orchestras. Because seating in the performance halls was on the flat ground, orchestra musicians had simply to turn their chairs to face the audience as dancing commenced. These post-performance dances at the theaters of Saint-Domingue germinated what became the dominant form of vernacular music in the Caribbean and eventually in much of the Americas a whole. The absolute rage among French dancers from Versailles to Saint-Domingue in the years 1770–90 was what they called the contredanse, a corrupted form of the English term "country dance."

In fact, the two versions of this popular dance were strikingly different. Whereas the English country dance placed men and women in two files facing each other, the French version organized the dancers into groups of two couples each. This simple AB structure called for the men to introduce the dance with the A strain, with much swagger, and the women then to add an element of lilting grace during the B strain, after which the process was repeated. Also, thanks to the influence of African dances, the West Indian version as a whole was far more sensuous, and involved closer contact between partners.[20] As befitted a rough colonial outpost where money and booze flowed, the music for these contredanses was louder and more raucous than would have been the case back home in France. In the days before the *cornet à pistons*, clarinets were perfectly suited to carrying the melody in the A strain, leaving the violins to take the lead in the softer "B" strain. The rhythm, too, was bouncier, thanks to the incorporation of drums derived from African prototypes. But whereas authentic African

---

19 Weston, *More Clarinet Virtuosi*, 40, 166.
20 Described in detail by L. E. Moreau de Saint-Méry, *La danse* (Philadelphia, 1796).

polyrhythms were (and are) endlessly complex, for these dances the dominant rhythm was reduced to a simple ♫♩♫♩ pattern. The two chief variants of this five-beat syncopation came to be known through their Spanish names as *tresillo* and *cinquillo*. Originating in after-theater dances on Saint-Domingue under the ancien régime, the contredanse spread rapidly throughout the Caribbean and then beyond.[21] The product of true cultural merging, it transformed both of its constituent elements—the European and African—in ways that appealed to the entire population of much of the New World. In North America, the simple syncopation that originated on Saint-Domingue found expression a century later, first in ragtime and then in jazz and rock music.

If Saint-Domingue's theater orchestras dominated the first phase of the development of this new vernacular music, the second phase was dominated by Spanish military and social bands in the city of Santiago on the eastern tip of Cuba. The French Revolution had fatally impacted the fragile social order in Saint-Domingue. A massive slave rebellion in the years 1790–1804 resulted in the death or expulsion of nearly all the white population and a significant part of the free mulatto slaveholders as well. While many sought refuge in Jamaica, Philadelphia, Charleston, and New Orleans, most simply sailed across the Windward Passage to nearby Santiago de Cuba. Thousands of whites, free mulattoes, and their slaves transferred their life and boisterous culture to this easternmost city of Cuba. Soon they had established their own French theater and were convening regularly at the all-French Venus Café.[22]

One of the French musicians who settled in Santiago was the clarinetist Monsieur Dubois, who played at local pleasure gardens. He and other émigrés introduced local Spaniards to the syncopations demanded by the French-speaking immigrants from Saint-Domingue.[23] No Spaniard was quicker to grasp the potential of the new syncopated dance form than Juan Casamitjana, a Catalan who directed the garrison band of the Regimento de Cataluna beginning in 1836. Equipped with the new piston cornets and a small section of B-flat clarinets, Casamitjana's band was soon charming audiences at the Venus Café with its leader's arrangements of French tunes from Saint-Domingue and also the great local hit, "El Cocoye," later picked up by the composer

21 This thesis was first advanced by Alejo Carpentier, *La música en Cuba*, 3rd ed. (Havana: Editorial Letras Cubanas, 1988), chap. 6.
22 Carpentier, *La música en Cuba*, 114–16.
23 Carpentier, *La música en Cuba*, 115.

Gottschalk from New Orleans.[24] Meanwhile, black musicians manned
the local police band, which included seven clarinets, six fifes, an oboe,
bassoon, serpent, and drums. By the 1820s the first syncopated Spanish
contredanses, now *contradanzas*, had been published in Santiago for
piano. Instrumental versions soon followed.[25]

By the 1840s the new *contradanza* had won the hearts of dancers in
Cuba's capital, Havana, and such nearby cities as Matanzas. With the
new rhythms and dances came the musicians who could play them.
Many were Afro-Cubans who had gained their freedom and now
worked as professional musicians. Their ensembles, which at first were
dubbed simply *charangas francesas*, or "French bands," and then came
to be known as *orquestas típicas*, invariably featured "one or two clarinets, two or three violins, two horns, a bass viol, and a large drum that
was called a *tambura*."[26] Over time this format was reduced to a pair of
clarinets, a cornet, a single violin, ophicleide or trombone, bass, and
tambura. Barely had the new dance taken root in Havana than a group
of talented composers led by the Cuban Manuel Saumell Robredo
(1818–74) and his New Orleans–born friend Louis Moreau Gottschalk
(1828–69) began turning out yet more gracefully syncopated compositions for dancing.[27]

It is worth stepping back for a moment to take note of the remarkable parallels between the rise of vernacular dances and the music that
accompanied them in southeastern Europe and the Balkans, and in
the New World. Both showed the influence of elite fashions but were
thoroughly transformed by popular taste as expressed through boisterous dances. Rooted initially in formal compositions played by military bands and theater orchestras, the music in both settings quickly
evolved to suit the needs of revelers and dancers. Small groups of six
to eight musicians arose, with the clarinet emerging as the most important instrument. At times its role was to play a harmonized second part
to the lead cornet or violin; at others it played the lead itself; and at

24 Carpentier, *La música en Cuba*, 133; Zoila Lapíque Becali, *Música
    colonial cubana* (Havana: Editorial Letras Cubanas, 1979), 71.
25 Carpentier, *La música en Cuba*, 120, 133.
26 Laureano Fuentes Matons, "Les artes en Santiago de Cuba," in
    Evolucion de la cultura cubana (1601–1927), ed. Jose Manuel Carbonell
    (Havana: El Siglo XX, 1928), 109.
27 S. Frederick Starr, *Bamboula! The Life and Times of Louis Moreau
    Gottschalk* (New York: Oxford University Press, 1995), 184ff.; also
    Solomon Gaoles Mikowski, "The Nineteenth Century Cuban Danza
    and Its Composers" (PhD diss., Columbia University, 1973).

still others it would weave an obbligato above and around the melody. This role arose from the nature of the clarinet itself, not just from its low cost and the ease with which one could start playing it, but from its commanding but nuanced tone and the infinite flexibility afforded by the addition of new keys by the 1840s. Both the violin and flute could dance around a melody with equal ease, but they were less audible; the new cornets were more audible, but their players had yet to attain the bravura technique that came later. Only the clarinet provided the right combination of assets, as musicians worldwide were quick to discover.

Many hugely popular ensembles arose in Havana to play *contradanzas* and, later, *danzas* for adoring audiences. The presence in Havana's Italian opera orchestra and military ensembles of a series of talented Spanish clarinetists like Pedro Broca y Casanovas (1794–1836) ensured that all the city's rising clarinetists, whatever their color, received good technical instruction. Of the ensembles of mid-century, none attracted a larger number of dancers than La Orquesta Típica and La Flor de Cuba, the latter a band of Afro-Cuban musicians which flourished for more than a decade around 1850. With two B-flat clarinets, cornet, trombone, bass, and tambura, the band could produce more than enough decibels to be audible throughout large outdoor dance halls like the Tivoli, while the syncopated pounding of the tambura (which had evolved into a kettledrum) ensured that dancers could follow the beat. Since both photographs of this ensemble and the instruments of several of its members are preserved in the Museo de la Música in Havana, it is possible to speak with some certainty of the clarinets that were used, which were fifteen-key Albert-system instruments. The wooden mouthpieces are smooth and intact, implying a double-lip embouchure, while the small gaps between reed and mouthpiece indicate that the clarinetists played on hard reeds.

During the second half of the nineteenth century the still rather formalized *contradanza* gave way first to the *danza*, a formal partner dance, and then to the raucous *danzón*, followed in the twentieth century by the *son*, rumba, and a proliferation of new dances, ever more sensuous. Interestingly, the bands that played these new styles maintained basically the same instrumentation as La Flor de Cuba for half a century, notwithstanding the ever-shifting fashions on the dance floor. The suave black cornetist Miguel Faílde (1852–1921) from the city of Matanzas, who in 1878 introduced the sensuous *danzón*,[28] reduced the

---

28 Osvaldo Castillo Failde, *Miguel Faílde, creador musical del danzón* (Havana: Editora del Consejo Nacional de Cultura, 1964).

canonic number of horns to three (clarinet, cornet and trombone), but a second clarinet remained common.[29] Among the many Cuban groups that recorded *danzóns, sons,* and rumbas around the year 1906 were the Orquesta Enrique Peña, Orquesta Valdez, and Orquesta Babuca, in all of which the clarinet is audibly present. Retrogression also occurred, however, as when some *danzón* ensembles dropped the clarinet and reverted to the violin and flute. The rhythm grew ever more emphatically syncopated, with the *cinquillo* or so-called "habanera" rhythm being only one of several variants that were prevalent. And throughout the period clarinetists rose steadily in their visibility and popularity.

Among players of that era, the absolute star was José Urfé González (1879–1957), whose career began as a second clarinetist, after which he rose to become the star clarinetist in his own band and then the composer of such popular tunes as "Mariposa" and "Aurora."[30] The clarinetist Urfé gave the *danzón* its definitive musical form and, in his highly syncopated composition of 1910, "El bombín de Barreto," introduced new elements from another Cuban dance, the *son.* Urfé made several recordings beginning in 1915, which show him to have been a melodic player, but with a commanding rhythmic sense. Urfé brought the clarinet to the peak of its popularity in the Caribbean world, but even during his lifetime the trumpet was rising to the fore as players encountered early jazz recordings and especially the virtuosity of Louis Armstrong. Within a generation the clarinet had been consigned to those few ensembles that harkened back to the less frenetic world of the nineteenth century.

The mention of jazz calls to mind one of the most intriguing questions in the history of the clarinet, namely, what were the sources of the virtuosic performance styles and techniques that became a hallmark of that music during the period spanning roughly 1915–55? We shall address this issue shortly, but only after reviewing two more countries where the clarinet gained a large following in vernacular music: Mexico and the United States. Along with developments in Europe and the Caribbean, the role of the clarinet in both Mexico and in the United States as a whole facilitated and shaped the rise of the clarinet as a jazz instrument.

---

29 Argeliers León, *Del canto y el tiempo* (Havana: Editorial Pueblo y Educación, 1974), 246.

30 Radames Giro, *Diccionario enciclopedico de la música en Cuba,* 4 vols. (Havana: Editorial Letras Cubanas, 2007), 4:225.

The path traced by the vernacular clarinet through southeastern Europe and the Caribbean was linear and depended on only two institutional and social settings. The patronage of public institutions—military bands, opera houses, and theaters—constituted the first of these. Not only did they provide employment for many clarinetists, but they also spread geographically with the expansion of European empires, bringing formal European music and the techniques for producing it into regions where they had scarcely existed earlier. The second setting was created by the universal human desire for revelry. As ordinary men and women gathered to dance and drink, they seized on whatever would enrich the occasion, with music at the top of the list. Preferences in food and drink tend everywhere to be deeply local and resistant to change, whereas music, while also rooted, tends to be more open to new styles and fashions.

Turning to vernacular music in Mexico, or at least that part of it that involved the clarinet, we find three quite different geographical settings. The first comprised those ports along Mexico's eastern coast that traded with Cuba; the second was defined in terms of the national capital in Mexico City and the changing governments that ruled there; and the third was the broad zone across central and northern Mexico where German immigrants settled in the nineteenth century. Each embraced the clarinet, but each did so differently.

For centuries, the Mexican cities of Veracruz, Tampico, and Campeche and the smaller ports along the Caribbean and Gulf of Mexico all traded with Cuba, and especially Havana. It is therefore no surprise that the influence of Cuban tastes in everything from food and dress to dance and popular music should have been felt there. Beginning in the mid-nineteenth century the people of Veracruz, the largest port, embraced the Cuban *contradanza* and *danza*, as well as the music that went with them. Both white and black Cubans emigrated in some numbers to Mexico's coastal towns during the late nineteenth century and brought with them their music and dances, including the *danzón*, habanera, *criolla*, rumba, and *son*. The large and popular Veracruz Orquesta de Severiano y Albertico featured clarinets, as did many smaller *danzón* and *son* groups. Beginning in the 1920s travelling ensembles and recordings by coastal groups brought this music to other parts of the country. But with the rise of the *son jorocho*, the clarinets were abandoned in favor of plucked instruments and vocals.[31]

---

31 An excellent overview of the *danzón* and its history is Alejandro L. Madrid and Robin D. Moore, *Danzón: Circum-Caribbean Dialogues in Music and Dance* (New York: Oxford University Press, 2013). Of

The second and more important locus of clarinet playing in nine-teenth-century Mexico was the capital. Plagued since its 1821 independence by poor governance and an invasion from the United States, Mexico by the 1860s was in a desperate state. Dependent on foreign loans which were now coming due, and with the country's powerful landed interests unwilling to bail out the treasury, the government suspended further interest payments in the fall of 1861. Spain, Britain, and France seized the opportunity to launch a joint invasion. When the first two powers then dropped out, the ruler of France's Second Empire, Napoleon III, was left in control. More interested in Mexico's silver than in ruling the country, he supported the choice of a Habsburg prince from Austria, Maximilian I, as Mexico's emperor. Maximilian's empire lasted only to 1867, when he was executed by forces loyal to Benito Juárez, who had served briefly as president prior to the European invasion and who subsequently waged a fierce guerilla war against Maximilian. Juárez went on to rule a proudly and narrowly nationalistic Mexico down to his death in 1872.

How, one might well ask, does all this relate to the vernacular clarinet? In fact, both the European invasion and the Mexican counter-attack directly affected Mexican instrumental music. The 1860s were arguably the high point of the nineteenth-century military band. In every major city in Europe and America well-rehearsed ensembles seized on the slightest pretext to parade down the main street. In their resplendent uniforms and with a high-stepping drum major leading them, they blasted out stirring new marches and patriotic airs. What young person would not be awestruck by the drum major, cornetists, bass drummer, or clarinetists? No other setting presented the now refined and serviceable B-flat and E-flat clarinets in a more flattering light or did more to spread their popularity.

Mexicans were thunderstruck by the esprit and brio of the imported bands and wasted no time in forming their own along similar lines. Scarcely an army unit in the country was without its bands, and town bands soon followed. Local composers pumped out bold patriotic marches to match the snappy new uniforms that local tailors had sewn for them. And it was all in the service of the new patriotism that surged when Juárez defeated Maximilian and reclaimed the Mexican

---

special relevance to this essay are chaps. 2 ("Danzón as a Performance Complex") and 4 ("The Danzón and Musical Dialogues with Early Jazz").

presidency. Bands symbolized the new unity of army and nation.[32] The Mexican band movement soared to a new level in 1891 when Genaro Codina (1852–1901) from the old silver town of Zacatecas composed the "Marcha di Zacatecas" for that city's municipal band. Popularized by his friend, the bandmaster Fernando Villalpando (1844–1902), the sprightly "Zacatecas" became Mexico's second national anthem and was soon being performed across the Americas and in Europe. The lyrical trio afforded clarinetists the chance to play Codina's obbligato (which anticipated Sousa's famous piccolo obbligato in "Stars and Stripes Forever") or to improvise their own, which many did. Scores of Mexican bands gave weekly performances of the most popular new marches and soon committed them to memory. For dancers at Sunday concerts on town squares they also played schottisches and waltzes, among which "Sobre las olas" (Over the waves) by the conservatory drop-out Juventino Rosas (1868–1894) gained phenomenal popularity that extended even to Europe. This lilting waltz became a favorite solo for vernacular clarinetists across Mexico and Central America. Half a century later it was reborn in the United States as "The Loveliest Night of the Year."

It is not possible to speak of a distinct Mexican school of clarinet playing, or of a Mexican vernacular style on that instrument. But the high competence of scores of Mexican clarinetists, and the fact that so many of them picked up money by giving lessons, ensured that the boom that occurred in the generation after 1870 would continue. Nearly all Mexican clarinetists played simple Albert-system instruments imported from Belgium, France, or England. Reed-on-top mouthpieces were common but not universal, and larger ensembles regularly employed E-flat clarinets as well as the standard B-flat instruments.

While all this was going on, Mexico gained a further current or school of vernacular clarinet, as tens of thousands of Germans flooded into Mexico during the half century preceding World War I. Including Catholics and Mennonites, these newcomers settled in Veracruz, Mexico City, Chiapas, and as far north as Austin County, Texas. They brought with them the rich tradition of village-based amateur bands that had existed in the land of their birth. Not only did such "oompah" bands thrive in the Mexican countryside, but Mexicans formed their own groups in imitation of the immigrants. By the turn of the last century the marches and local airs that formed the repertoire of

---

32 Charles V. Heath details this phenomenon in his *The Inevitable Bandstand: The State Band of Oaxaca and the Politics of Sound* (Lincoln, NE: University of Nebraska Press, 2015).

these Mexican bands and the spunky rhythms they devised for village dances (called "Banda," "Ranchero," and "Norteño"), gave these rustic ensembles a distinctive and very Mexican voice that was enhanced by their clarinetists' increasingly florid performances.

The Vernacular Clarinet in the United States and New Orleans

Bearing in mind the development of the clarinet as a vehicle for vernacular music in both the Caribbean world and Mexico, let us turn now to the later fate of the vernacular clarinet in the United States. This reverses the assumed natural order of things, which would normally begin with the clarinet in North America and then explore the manner in which vernacular performance styles there, especially jazz, came to influence the rest of the Americas. To justify this reversed order of influence and to defend the seminal role of Saint-Domingue, Cuba and, to a lesser extent Mexico in shaping the vernacular clarinet in the New World is the task to which we must now turn.

As in southeastern Europe, the Caribbean, and Mexico, military bands in America played the central role in the dissemination of the clarinet as a popular instrument. Both British and American armies brought bands with them, and when Versailles or London failed to pay for them, officers themselves often covered the costs, on the grounds that bands benefited morale. Jane Ellsworth has shown how the clarinet edged out the oboe in North American military bands, as it had in Europe.[33] Again as in southeastern Europe, local craftsmen in Philadelphia and Boston, and also in small towns like Utica, New York, and Winchester, New Hampshire, began turning out high-quality clarinets that competed successfully against London-made instruments from the shops of Goulding, Metzler, and Astor. Around 1803 there appeared a teaching manual that enabled its readers to improve their playing skills on their own: *A New and Complete Preceptor for the Clarinet* by George Blake.[34]

---

33 On all aspects of the early clarinet in America through 1820 see Jane Elizabeth Ellsworth's authoritative "The Clarinet in Early America, 1758–1820" (PhD diss., Ohio State University, 2004).

34 George Blake, *A New and Complete Preceptor for the Clarinet* (Philadelphia: G. E. Blake, ca. 1803). See Ellsworth, "The Clarinet in Early America," 138 and 140–42.

Parallel with these developments, German immigrants had long since employed the clarinet to accompany congregational hymn singing in Lutheran services in Pennsylvania. Also in the late eighteenth century, congregations of Moravian Brethren in North Carolina and Pennsylvania were using locally made clarinets in both religious and secular settings. One Moravian composer, David Moritz Michael (1751–1827), penned wind music for many liturgical events and even a suite of secular music to accompany a boating picnic along the Lehigh River in Pennsylvania, for which he assigned the lead role to two clarinets.[35] But in spite of these strong forays into the Protestant world, the clarinet played at best a supporting role in religious music, one that was definitely secondary to the "church bass," a kind of large cello, and the serpent horn.

Notwithstanding advances in a few spheres, the clarinet made slow progress in America during the early Republic. Whether at rustic coaching stations in the countryside or in the refined ballrooms of New York or Virginia it was the fiddle, not the clarinet, which produced the music. Clarinetists were simply unable to produce the ceaseless flow of sound and the relentless propulsion that the popular Irish and British dances required and which a good fiddle player could turn out, nor could they compete with the mass popularity of touring fiddlers like Ole Bull from Norway. Reflecting this reality, popular genre painters like William Sidney Mount of Long Island (1807–58) and George Caleb Bingham (see *The Jolly Flatboatmen*, 1846) depict cloggers and dancers at rustic hoe-downs accompanied by fiddles, not clarinets. Nor did the clarinet become an instrument for expressing the tender yearnings that flowed during the Romantic era. While the immensely popular Pittsburgh-born composer Stephen Foster (1826–64) included clarinet in the popular quadrilles he scored for dancing, he himself played the flute, not the clarinet.

Despite these constraints, American clarinetists found their true calling with the rise of so-called "clarinet bands" and other mixed wind bands in the 1820s and the "saxhorn bands" or "brass bands" in the 1840s. The first phase was typified by the Boston Brigade Band, founded in 1820, and James Kendall's Boston Band, founded in 1829.[36] The latter phase began when American brass players adopted

---

35 David Moritz Michael, *The Water Journey*" (*Wasserfahrt*) with Pacific Classical Winds, New World Records 80490-2, 1996, audio compact disc.

36 For these bands, see Jane Ellsworth's comprehensive study "James Kendall and Mixed Wind Bands in Antebellum Boston," MS, courtesy

the new *cornet à pistons* from France, and when such American makers as the New Englanders Isaac Fiske and E. G. Wright began providing them with quality horns of their own. The saxhorn's gentle tone created an opening for the clarinet. As a result, even towns as small as Wellington, Ohio, boasted their "saxhorn band," replete with clarinets. American clarinetists remained loyal to their old five-key instruments that were still being produced in some quantity, but in the 1840s began to embrace clarinets with more keys, a process that was to culminate in the adoption of Albert-system clarinets (mainly from Paris and London makers) after the Civil War.

The American Civil War did more to promote amateur performance on both clarinets and brass instruments than any other event in the nineteenth century. Both the Federal and Confederate armies formed scores of bands and equipped them with horns and uniforms. Private publishers rushed out new collections of sheet music for these ensembles. Curiously, besides marches, it was operatic transcriptions from the works of Donizetti, Verdi, and Bellini that formed the backbone of the Civil War repertoire. The lyrical sound of the clarinet, which nicely matched the round and gentle sound of the early small-bore brass horns, imparted to such performances a sweetness that was out of step with the martial environment and hence all the more appreciated.

In its constantly evolving forms, the clarinet figured prominently in both military and civic bands throughout the band era that extended from the 1850s to around 1920. Such ensembles became the premier locus for the emergence of the clarinet as a vernacular instrument in North America. The scale and depth of the musical and institutional infrastructure that supported the vernacular clarinet in the brass band era can scarcely be overstated. Town councils across the country committed funds to construct bandstands to serve as focal points of community life.[37] Businessmen from coast to coast formed and equipped factory bands. The appearance of an English edition of Hyacinthe Klosé's 1843 *Méthode complète de clarinette* in 1873, as well as numerous American publications, enabled teachers and students in the most remote locales to improve their skills. The principal American manufacturers published newspapers for woodwind and brass players. Amateur players across the country addressed

of the author.

37 S. Frederick Starr, ed., *The Oberlin Book of Bandstands* (Washington, DC: Preservation Press, 1987).

letters to these news sheets highlighting inadequacies in the instruments and reeds and proposing improvements.

Specialized publishers of band music responded to local demand by issuing collections of marches, hymns, quick-steps, one-steps, and waltzes that could be performed by amateur groups. By the 1880s these collections included pieces in the new syncopated ragtime style that was exciting dancers from coast to coast. Chief among such publishers was C. L. Barnhouse, a self-taught cornet player who settled in Oskaloosa, Iowa, and in 1886 began issuing works by a range of American composers specializing in music for town bands. His arrangements, which could be performed by large ensembles or a mere handful of players, assumed and reinforced a high level of musical literacy among the general populace. Other popular tunes were issued in formats that facilitated home performance by players gathered around the upright piano. Since these latter editions never included clarinet parts, many domestic players purchased C clarinets so that they could read violin parts without transposing.

This, then, was the booming world of vernacular music in late nineteenth-century America, in which clarinets and clarinetists played an increasingly significant a role. That world had many local variations. Regional differences were shaped in part by the national backgrounds of local musicians, with strongly Germanic ensembles in cities like Cincinnati, Chicago, and St. Louis; Italian and Portuguese bands in many cities along the Atlantic coast; Scandinavian groups in the upper Midwest; and Irish bands popping up almost everywhere. They were shaped also by strong personalities like the Yankee musician George Edward Ives (1845–94), leader of the town band in Danbury, Connecticut, whose fascination with the sometimes undisciplined braying of vernacular musicians in small-town America inspired his son Charles to become one of the most innovative composers of the twentieth century.

Nowhere did the interplay of strong national traditions and powerful personalities give rise to a more distinctive vernacular band tradition than in New Orleans, and nowhere else did a local band tradition produce a richer school of clarinet playing. Indeed, the New Orleans school of clarinet playing eventually exerted a powerful influence on players far beyond the boundaries of its locality, enriching the emotional range and expressiveness of the vernacular clarinet everywhere.

Thanks to acoustic recordings, the distinctive voice of the New Orleans clarinet had become nationally audible by 1917–19, but its history traces back at least half a century before that year. It was the product of a complex interweaving of numerous distinct musical streams, several of which were so thoroughly assimilated into the whole that it is easy to ignore them or take them for granted. But each was essential. Of these, the American band tradition was of prime importance. Old local military units like the Washington Artillery maintained bands even before the Civil War, as did the garrison at the Jackson Barracks, established in 1838. It was quite common for as many as ten local bands to step out in parade for national holidays or Mardi Gras.[38] The capture of New Orleans by Admiral David Farragut of the United States Navy in 1863 shifted the focus from military to civilian bands, with independent groups like Jacques' Band performing at formal events, serenades, and dances throughout the rest of the Civil War and thereafter. Suburban parks like West End, Milneburg, and Spanish Fort offered venues for brass bands to perform, as did neighborhood institutions like the Crystal Ballroom downtown. Even though these were racially segregated, the musicians had ample opportunities to hear one another, not only at open air neighborhood picnics but at parades and civic events. White and black bands, as well as bands formed by Creoles of color, played the same type of instrument, ordered their music from the same publishing houses, and sent off for the same mass-produced uniforms and caps emblazoned with their names.

Most players were small tradesmen, with a sprinkling of more menial jobs among them. Nearly all were musically literate, though, and could read their assigned parts. However, limited repertoires meant that many musicians learned their parts by heart, which invited ornamentation and even improvisation. Bands were used to sell products, accompany early silent films, and drum up audiences for prize fights. Bands from all groups also accompanied hearses to the suburban cemeteries, and at gravesides played the same hymns from band books issued by C. L. Barnhouse and other firms. On national holidays all the bands also turned out for street parades, as they did for Mardi Gras. Such events invited showing off, which manifested itself both musically and kinetically. Black bands especially engaged in such

---

38 On the context for nineteenth-century New Orleans band music, see Henry A. Kmen, *Music in New Orleans: The Formative Years, 1791–1841* (Baton Rouge: Louisiana State University Press, 1966), chap. 10; and John H. Baron, *Concert Life in Nineteenth Century New Orleans: A Comprehensive Reference* (Baton Rouge: Louisiana State University Press, 2013).

swagger, egged on no doubt by the crowds of young people who fell in behind them in a "second line."

Moderating such manifestations was the reality that most bands of all types played mainly for dancing. New Orleanians rich and poor had always been dance-crazy, which generated a steady demand for bands that could play the latest national hits and lay down a solid beat for each new dance fad as it appeared. Playing for dancing forced clarinetists to think both horizontally and vertically, riding solidly on the beat and at the same time putting forth a continuous yet rhythmic lyrical flow. And since dancers were concerned more with the overall beat and "sound" than with an endlessly repeated melody, the situation naturally invited ornamentation and improvisation. It also defined the repertoire in terms of popular hits that were best suited to each dance.

To this point there is surprisingly little to differentiate the vernacular music scene in New Orleans from what existed in many other American cities. But New Orleans was different, not least in its national and racial diversity. The uppermost (fifth) gallery at the French Opera House was open to anyone who could spare a few cents, white or black, young or old. An Alabaman who visited New Orleans in 1847 recalled hearing a black man on the street who was humming an aria from a recent opera.[39] The clarinet ranked second to the piano as a solo instrument, and as early as 1810 no fewer than twenty-two clarinet solos were performed with local orchestras.[40] Clarinetists from the several orchestras regularly gave lessons to young people of all races and backgrounds who could pay for them. The best-known of these pedagogues were French or Belgian and used Albert clarinets with as few as nine keys to inculcate the French style, with a bright tone produced by a double-lip embouchure and a hard reed. At least one of the opera orchestra's clarinetists performed with "Papa Jack" Laine's brass band, a pioneering group that flavored more traditional band music with jazz after 1900.[41]

Another point of differentiation between most American town bandsmen and their counterparts in New Orleans is that, beginning with the appearance of the Mexican Eighth Cavalry Band at the Cotton Centennial Exposition in 1876, New Orleans clarinetists were regularly exposed to visiting players from Mexico. The scholar Jack Stewart, himself a reed player, has discovered reports on Mexican

39   Albert J. Pickett, *Eight Days in New Orleans in February, 1847* (Montgomery, AL, 1847), 47.

40   Kmen, *Music in New Orleans*, 217.

41   From Jack Stewart's unpublished MS on Laine, courtesy of the author.

bands of all sizes and styles in New Orleans at the turn of the last century.[42] Several Mexican professional clarinetists from this era stayed in town and gave lessons, further raising skill levels. Nor were the style and bravado of the Mexican bands lost on the more committed amateur players of New Orleans, both white and black, who readily concluded that to play the clarinet (or cornet, the other "signature" horn) and be a bandsman was a high calling indeed. New Orleanian bandsmen were also quick to enrich their repertoire with tunes like "Zacatecas" and "Sobre las olas."

A further stream of influence arose from the wave of Italian immigrants who arrived in New Orleans beginning in the 1870s and included a large cadre of musicians, including clarinetists. Nearly all came from just two towns near Palermo in Sicily, Contessa Entellina and Aruburesche, both with a population even today of under 3,000. In spite of living close to each other, a gulf separated these two Sicilian villages. While the Contessa Entellina folk were all Catholics, the Aruberesche townspeople, who were descended from immigrants from Albania, adhered to the Byzantine rite. The rivalry between them continued in Louisiana, with the result that there were two churches, two benevolent societies, and, inevitably, two bands that competed to have the most splendid uniforms and to play with the most brio. Every bandsman in New Orleans stood in awe whenever one of these ensembles passed on the street.

The Sicilian clarinetists brought with them high technical mastery and a distinctive role in the band. Guided by Roman Ferdinando Sebastiani's 1855 *Método per clarinetto* and more local self-study guides such as Gaetano Labanchi's *Método progressivo per il clarinetto* (Naples, 1868) and Emanuele Krakamps's *Metodo practico per clarinetto* (Palermo, 1870), these players generated a distinct Sicilian school of popular clarinet playing.[43] They strove for a light, singing tone and therefore adhered to the reed-on-top method. Their repertoire featured stirring marches by Verdi and his Italian followers, who assigned the clarinet the role of a bel canto singer, dancing above and around the melody. No sooner did New Orleans's homegrown players hear it than they incorporated it into their own playing. In the same years other Italian clarinetists were showing up in South America. But the only places on that continent where the clarinet figured prominently in popular

---

42 Jack Stewart, "The Mexican Band Legend: Myth, Reality, Musical Impact," *The Jazz Archivist* 6, no. 2 (December 1991): 1–9.

43 Eric Hoeprich, *The Clarinet* (New Haven, CT: Yale University Press, 2008), 201.

music was, and is, Brazil, where it is often employed in the *choro*. Even there the Italians did not influence the locals to the same extent as in New Orleans.

The final influence that caused New Orleans clarinetists to blaze a distinctive path arose from their contact with the school of syncopated dance music that had arisen over the previous century in Havana and other Caribbean port cities. We have traced the origins of this unique beat to Saint-Domingue and followed its evolution through the *contradanza, danza, danzón*, and *son*. Equally important, we saw how musicians responded to evolving fashions in dance by devising small ensembles in which two clarinets and a cornet or two passed the melody between them, the clarinets playing an obbligato whenever the brasses took the lead. The once-dominant violin slipped into a decidedly secondary role.

We do not know the precise paths by which this arrangement reached New Orleans, but we can be sure it was borne by the many passenger ships plying between the Crescent City, Havana, and such Mexican ports as Veracruz and Tampico. One New Orleans band of the 1920s, the Owls, even played a piece that it called "Tampeekoe." As a result of this interaction, the composer W. T. Francis could observe that "You can listen in New Orleans to the music of the Spanish nations, which in many cases is inexpressibly beautiful."[44] The Cubans' instrumental lineup and syncopated beat set the standard for early New Orleans bands after 1880. Frontally posed photographs of several early Louisiana bands are indistinguishable from photos of the Flor de Cuba from the 1850s or Miguel Fialde's band from the 1880s. Typical of these is the 1896 photograph of the John Robichaux Orchestra, with two cornets, trombone, string bass, drums, two violins, and a clarinetist posted prominently front and center.[45] Because the first recording of a New Orleans band was issued only in 1917, it is impossible to know what the earlier bands sounded like. But research by the late Lawrence Gushee confirms that by 1900 the important early impact in New Orleans of syncopated music from Cuba was overwhelmed by syncopated ragtime music from the United States itself.[46] Beginning with

---

44 Quoted in Jack Stewart, "The Mexican Band Legend, Part 2," *Jazz Archivist* 9, no. 1 (May 1994): 9.

45 Reproduced in John McClusker, "The Onward Brass Band and the Spanish-American War," *Jazz Archivist* 13 (1998–89): 25.

46 Lawrence Gushee, "The Nineteenth Century Origins of Jazz," *Black Music Research Journal* 14, no. 1 (Spring 1994): 1–24. From the large literature on the history of early New Orleans jazz, a concise overview

the publication of William H. Krell's "Mississippi Rag" in 1897, American publishers flooded the market with ragtime dance music with much the same syncopations as those that came earlier from Cuba and had been issued in profusion during the 1880s and 1890s by Junius Hart in New Orleans. Of course, the similarity is not accidental, as Caribbean rhythms had been well known in North America since the time New Orleans-born Louis Moreau Gottschalk incorporated them in compositions as early as 1849.[47]

The simple twelve-bar blues form also came to infuse New Orleans's musical life and American band music in general, beginning about 1905 and culminating in the publication by W. C. Handy of his "Memphis Blues" in 1912. Originating in the countryside as a vocal form with guitar accompaniment, blues were far removed from what either black or white bandsmen played at the time. But New Orleans bands, which had doubtless been exposed to sung blues, quickly assimilated them, both from the local popular culture and from voluminous blues publications being issued by music publishers in New York's emerging Tin Pan Alley. With their bent notes and semitones, blues posed a challenge to clarinetists, who were quick to address it through shifts in the embouchure rather than attempting to finger semitone "blue" notes.

Over time New Orleans clarinetists assimilated this yeasty amalgam of models and influences and evolved innovative new techniques and performance styles embodying them. Many have praised the so-called New Orleans school of clarinet playing. Beginning in the early 1920s when recordings made it widely known, it has been characterized as a kind of folk style created by brilliant but semi-literate musicians who achieved what they did because they were untutored in the classic elements of clarinet performance, and were certainly not music readers. Nothing could be further from the truth. Whether white, black, Creoles of color, Hispanics or Sicilians, New Orleans clarinetists were good music readers, were familiar with the march and dance repertoires, and through years of practice had mastered

of the subject is Jeff Taylor, "The Early Origins of Jazz," in *The Oxford Companion to Jazz,* ed. Bill Kirchner (New York: Oxford University Press, 2000), 39–52. Some useful clarinet-related readings are Michael Ullman, "The Clarinet in Jazz," in Kirchner, *The Oxford Companion to Jazz,* 583–96; Chris Tyle, "The Albert System Clarinet in Early Jazz," *The Clarinet* 28, no. 1 (December 2000): 74–75; and Chris Heaton, "Jazz Clarinet Performance," in Heaton, *The Versatile Clarinet,* 51–74.
47 Starr, *Bamboula!,* 73ff.

the role of their instrument in both those repertoires. Far from being self-taught primitives, they all took music lessons from some of the imported teachers mentioned above, or from a variety of other local pedagogues. The few who didn't were quickly made to understand that reading music was essential.

Among local teachers, none did more to nurture early jazz clarinetists than Mexican-born Lorenzo Tio (1867–1908), who came to New Orleans with his brother Louis "Papa" Tio (1862–1922) in 1890 and was the father of Lorenzo Tio, Jr. (1893–1933).[48] The family hailed originally from Louisiana but spent several decades in musically rich Veracruz before returning to their home state. Not only did the Tios themselves constitute a clarinet dynasty, but their students Achille Baquet, Louis "Big Eye" Nelson Delisle, Sidney Bechet, Barney Bigard, Johnny Dodds, Omer Simeon, Louis Cottrell, Jr., Jimmie Noone, and Albert Nicholas were all to become leading jazz clarinetists. Alone among the Tios, Lorenzo Jr. actually came to play jazz. But the Tios' contribution was less the advancement of jazz clarinet per se than the inculcation of classical technique and musical knowledge into a host of eager students who went on to pioneer a new vernacular social music.

The teachers of several other major early players are not known. Alcide Nunez (1884–1934), descended from immigrants from the Canary Islands and the equal of the other pioneer jazz clarinetists of the period 1912–24, had a very solid technique but the name of his teacher is not recorded. The same cannot be said of Leon Roppolo (1902–43), whose 1923 recordings with the New Orleans Rhythm Kings anticipated many elements of the later Swing style. Roppolo's father and grandfather both played the clarinet, as did several cousins, bringing the family total of clarinetists to eight. He also came by his bel canto style naturally, as his sister Lillian was a soprano with the New York City Opera.[49]

Alongside the myth that early jazz clarinetists were untutored folk, musicians without formal training and unable to read music, there exists a second myth, namely, that there existed in New Orleans not one but two schools of clarinet playing. The first group supposedly comprised "Downtown" players from the Creole wards, Catholics who had French names and were descended from families who had been

---

48 Charles E. Kinzer, "The Tios of New Orleans and Their Pedagogical Influence on the Early Jazz Clarinet Style," *Black Music Research Journal* 16, no. 2 (Autumn 1996): 279–302.

49 The author is indebted to the historian Jack Stewart for information on the Roppolo family.

"free peoples of color" before the Civil War. These players are thought to have been schooled readers who boasted classical techniques. The second group is said to have been comprised of young *déclassé* black players from "Uptown," who were unschooled, could not read music, and played a rougher style more infused with the blues.[50] This myth, too, is utterly baseless. Because Johnny Dodds (1892–1940) played a simpler, more declarative style, and recorded many soulful blues, he is seen as the epitomizing the "Uptown" style. But this great clarinetist grew up not in the Uptown section, but in coastal Mississippi; he came from a family that was half Creole, and himself spoke French; moreover, he was a fluent reader, could orchestrate for small band, and told his son, John Jr., that he had succeeded only thanks to his early training and because of his years of practicing scales and long tones. His other son, Rudy Dodds, recalls his father sitting for long hours before his method book and practicing.[51] There is indeed a difference between Dodds's style and, say, Omer Simeon's. Simeon ornamented the melody and even wove dazzling countermelodies of his own. Dodds, with extensive band experience, improvised parts that were more linear and were clearly voiced so as to resemble the supporting clarinet parts in a band. To be sure, this "uptown" player could and did play blues, but so could Simeon, Noone, or the other so-called Creole players. The real division between them is not between being sophisticated vs. primitive, formal vs. blues-tinged, but between Dodds, who adhered to elements of American band scoring, and Simeon, who was ten years younger and was free of that constraining influence.

It is important to note that down to the mid-1920s nearly all New Orleans players used hard reeds on rather closed mouthpieces and employed a double-lip embouchure. The thirteen-key Albert-system instrument was standard among them, but Roppolo, whose style was in certain respects highly advanced, performed on an old Buffet clarinet with only twelve keys and two rings.[52] Dodds, whose playing is sometimes described as "elemental," favored a very up-to-date Buffet instrument with an unusual articulation mechanism between the register key

---

50   On the Uptown–Downtown thesis see Samuel B. Charters, *Jazz: New Orleans 1885-1957: An Index to the Negro Musicians of New Orleans* (Belleville, NJ, 1958), 5–13.

51   Interviews by the author with Rudolph Dodds in New Orleans, 1982, and with John Dodds, Jr., in Chicago, 1983.

52   The Roppolo clarinet passed from George Brunies to the author, who donated it to The Historic New Orleans Collection.

and the ring on the left forefinger.[53] Most New Orleans players stayed
with their Albert-system Buffets down to the end of their lives. While
it might have been advantageous to switch to the Boehm system, with
its more convenient fingerings, these players preferred the large bore
of the Albert system instruments, which produced a fatter, woodier
sound. When Leblanc began producing a Boehm-system horn with a
larger bore, many opted for it.

Golden Age: The Virtuoso Vernacular
Clarinet in the Twentieth Century

The jazz clarinet, and the vernacular clarinet more generally, were
utterly transformed in the twentieth century by two new technologies.
The first of these was acoustical recording, which was first applied to
Cuban vernacular music by 1897, to klezmer music in the 1910s, to
Balkan players in 1928, and to jazz in 1917.[54] Clarinetists responded
to the new technology in one of three ways. Most continued to play
exactly as they had before, which failed to fit the new format. Others
tried to attract attention through tricks and gimmicks. The clarinetist Larry Shields's imitation of a rooster call on the 1917 recording
of "Barnyard Blues" exemplified this trend, as did the howling and
moaning by several early players from the Balkans. One who put
eccentric sounds to truly artistic uses was Pee Wee Russell (1906–69),
one of the most original vernacular clarinetists anywhere. A third and
more serious minority addressed the problem posed by the ten-inch
shellac record's duration of three minutes by devising carefully for-
mulated solos, which they presented as spontaneous improvisations.
Gunther Schuller has pointed out how many jazz improvisers developed a signature solo on a given piece and then repeated it thereafter.[55] In the end, the best musicians grasped the fact that the brevity

---

53 Possession of the author, gift of John Dodds, Jr., of Chicago, 1983.
54 For Cuban music, see http://esquinarumbera.blogspot.com/2011/05/
    filiberto-sanchez-first-to-record-rumba.html; for klezmer see https://
    www.amazon.com/Yikhes-Early-Klezmer-Recordings-1911-1939/dp/
    B00000AU55; and for Greek music see https://www.amazon.com/
    Greek-Clarinet-Virtuosos-Authentic-Recordings/dp/B00IAC13TW.
55 Gunther Schuller, "Sonny Rollins and the Challenge of Thematic
    Improvisation," in *Musings: The Musical Worlds of Gunther Schuller* (New
    York: Oxford University Press, 1986), 86–97.

of 78 rpm recordings placed a premium on virtuosity and flash, and responded accordingly.

The second transformative invention was electronic sound amplification. For decades, the clarinet had been fighting a losing battle with brass instruments, which were being re-engineered to produce ever more volume. Narrow-bore brasses with funnel-shaped mouthpieces were replaced with large-bore instruments with hemispherical cup mouthpieces, and mellow cornets with brassy trumpets. Confronted by this onslaught of decibels, the best that vernacular clarinetists could do was to replace their traditional straight wooden bells with saxophone-like metal bells that several manufacturers put on the market to project the sound outward—at a predictable price in intonation. As the brasses grew yet more powerful, bands began to favor the saxophone, which gradually supplanted the clarinet in all areas of ensemble jazz except solos. Only the mass-production of simple public address systems changed this situation for the better.

Electronic amplification began appearing in private entertainment halls at the end of the 1920s. Thanks to electric microphones and speakers, clarinetists no longer had to fight to be audible. The immediate response of all but the oldest players was to switch to more open mouthpieces and softer reeds. Many players who earlier rejected Boehm instruments for their slightly narrower bore and supposedly smaller sound, now embraced them for what was thought to be their more precise intonation. And the entire chalumeau register, which except in Turkey had never figured in vernacular music, now came gloriously to the fore, as clarinetists learned to place the middle joint of their horn rather than the bell near the microphone. This gave vernacular players the possibility of transmitting the most intimate sounds and nuances to large audiences. True, with only a few notable exceptions (e.g., Duke Ellington's "Creole Love Call"), this did not lead to the creation of whole sections of clarinets in jazz bands. But it did thrust the best clarinet soloists into the limelight. Also, the release of a Vitaphone recording by the Philadelphia Orchestra in 1925 marked the debut of electrical recording. Nuances of tone and expression could now be permanently recorded. By 1929 the new technology was being widely applied to vernacular music, including jazz.

Nothing in the entire history of the vernacular clarinet did more than amplification and electric recording to transform its fate worldwide. Everywhere they spread, the combination of these technologies facilitated the rise of extraordinary performers, with jazz clarinetists leading the way. Four players who gained great distinction during those

years were Omer Simeon (1902–59), Barney Bigard (1906–80), Benny
Goodman (1909–77), and Artie Shaw 1910–2004).[56] Simeon and
Bigard were both New Orleanians who continued with Albert-system
clarinets, but Goodman and Shaw made their career on Boehm-system
instruments. All four had solid traditional training: Bigard, who went
to Straight College in New Orleans, had studied with Lorenzo Tio, Jr.,
as did Simeon, albeit briefly. Goodman and Shaw (born Arshawsky)
both came from East European Jewish families, and Goodman especially had direct contact with the Jewish band tradition in his native
Chicago. Goodman also studied under Franz Schoepp of the Chicago
Symphony Orchestra, but early came to admire the style of Leon Roppolo and the technique of Omer Simeon, who was by then in Chicago.

While Bigard plied the chalumeau register with success, Goodman
and especially Shaw mastered the clarinet's top register, with Shaw
using it extensively. Bigard shone in solos with Duke Ellington's large
ensemble, while Shaw was at his best with his own big band. Goodman, arguably the most accomplished all-around clarinetist of the
twentieth century, was equally brilliant sailing deftly above his big band
on pieces like "Sing, sing, sing," or playing lyrical ballads like "After
you've gone" with his trio. Both Goodman and Shaw also played classical music and commissioned major composers to write for them, while
Shaw published a two-part study called *Jazz Technic* that included four-
teen clarinet etudes. Simeon remains the least-documented of these
four masters, but his trio recording of Jelly Roll Morton's "Shreveport
Stomp," with its clean articulation and forward thrust, rises so far
above the vernacular that it can be considered a true masterpiece of
red hot chamber music. The only other jazz clarinetist of the era who
was capable of such driving virtuosity was Jimmy Noone, as displayed in
his fiercely intense rendition of "I know that you know."

During the decades after these American virtuosi extended the
clarinet's expressive possibilities, vernacular clarinetists in the Balkans,
Greece, Turkey, and Jewish Eastern Europe followed suit. All extended
the instrument's virtuosic potential through emotionally intense solos
packed into the brief span of a disc recording. It is no exaggeration
to say that the vernacular clarinet reached its apogee thanks to non-
distorting amplification and acoustically precise electric recording,
as well as to the continuing time compression imposed by seven- and

---

56   Interestingly, all of these clarinetists have been the subjects of academic biographies, and two of them, Bigard (*With Louis and the Duke*,
1988) and Shaw (*The Trouble with Cinderella*, 1992), penned their own
autobiographies.

twelve-inch records. Among the earliest "eastern" players to record were the klezmorim Naftule Brandwein (1889–1963) and Dave Tarras (1897–1987), both of whom recorded extensively after emigrating to the United States in the 1920s. Communist controls prevented Bulgarian players from entering the world mainstream, but Ivo Papazov (b. 1952) quickly made up for lost time beginning in the 1970s. Bulgaria's most renowned "wedding clarinetist," Papazov follows Goodman and Shaw in playing a Boehm-system instrument with a very soft reed. Greek, Albanian, and Turkish clarinetists use similar mouthpieces and reeds, although most still adhere mainly to seventeen-key Albert-system instruments, which they find comfortable for the modified Phrygian mode of their music. All of these players who emerged after the mid-century staked their claim on the basis of sheer virtuosity.

A Gentle Afterlife

In terms of the public's enthusiasm, the vernacular clarinet everywhere reached its apogee in the period 1930–70. During those decades, the top virtuoso players were highly visible stars in many countries, and the brilliance of their technique won them followings that crossed national and cultural borders. This trend has continued in a muted form to the present, but since 1980 new players have emerged in many countries who use the vernacular clarinet quite differently from the virtuosi of the preceding decades. Whereas the old virtuosi specialized in playing intensely and "hot," the new players were more often than not cool, even soulful. In jazz, the understated bop of Alvin Baptiste, Don Byron, Joe Lovano, and Anat Cohen, and above all Jimmy Giuffre's solo meditations, were all at a lower temperature than the previous generation. The analogous figure in the world of klezmer music is Giora Feidman (b. 1936), a former classical player who plays with a slow, broad vibrato and bends notes both upward and downward to produce lyrical and very soulful performances. Like many of the "eastern" clarinetists of recent vintage, Feidman has a complete control of vibrato, which enables him to switch easily from a vibrato rising above the note to one that sinks below it, with results that touch the emotions. While the wailing clarinets and frenetic tempi of Bulgarian and Greek wedding music continue, the biggest innovators in recent decades may be the Turks. Using their distinctive Albert-system instruments pitched in low G and employing the bent tones and slow, diverse vibratos used by Feidman, the Turkish masters Hüsnü Şenlendirici and Mustafa Kandıralı have developed a melancholy style that is all their own.

At the dawn of the twenty-first century, the vernacular clarinet encountered an entirely new type of competitor, and one which threatened its very existence. Now inexpensive electronic synthesizers can produce sounds that roughly approximate any instrument, including the clarinet. The ability of these instruments to change timbre, add or subtract vibrato, and play any of thousands of stored pieces has made them attractive alternatives to live musicians everywhere. That they can be used also to transcribe and notate the most complex recorded improvisations by the likes of Benny Goodman or Ivo Papazov is a secondary advantage useful only to clarinetists and musicologists. The number of vernacular musicians of all types who can make a living from their music diminished everywhere, and by the end of the twentieth century pessimists foretold the end of live music at informal and popular small-scale gatherings worldwide.

But this grim prognosis is turning out to have been wrong. Even a listener who is musically illiterate can appreciate the spontaneity of a vernacular performer who is subject to different moods ranging from ardent excitement to deep melancholia. An unschooled dancer senses when a vernacular player is "on" and able to transform the evening for everyone on the dance floor. Technique and timbre may be musical terms, but ordinary people everywhere respond with visceral intensity to what they prefer in these qualities, especially in vernacular music. It is beyond doubt that such realities will help sustain the vernacular clarinet in the future.

Beyond this is the sheer fascination of producing attractive sounds by blowing across the end of a fragile reed connected to a tube. This elemental joy, first discovered by ancient peoples thousands of years ago, will not disappear from the world. It will continue to be rediscovered by musicians of every generation. They will put it to different uses, and will cause the physical clarinet to evolve further, as has happened throughout the past two and a half centuries. By this process, live vernacular music brought into being by talented and inventive clarinetists is almost certain to remain part of our life and culture for years to come.

CONTRIBUTORS

JANE ELLSWORTH is both a musicologist and a professional clarinetist. She is professor of music history at Eastern Washington University and the author of *A Dictionary for the Modern Clarinetist* (2015) as well as a forthcoming monograph on the clarinet in eighteenth- and nineteenth-century America. She is also a bass clarinetist with the Spokane Symphony.

ERIC HOEPRICH specializes in performing on historical clarinets in music from the Baroque to Brahms. He is a founding member of the Orchestra of the 18th Century, based in Amsterdam, and teaches at the Royal Conservatory in The Hague as well as at the Royal Academy (London), Indiana University, and the Paris Conservatory. His monograph, *The Clarinet*, was published in 2008.

COLIN LAWSON is director of the Royal College of Music, London, where he holds a Personal Chair in Historical Performance. He has an international profile as a performer and has played principal clarinet in many leading period orchestras, with which he has recorded extensively and toured worldwide; his solo appearances include New York's Lincoln Center and Carnegie Hall. Lawson has published widely on performance practice and the history of the clarinet. He is coeditor of *The Cambridge History of Musical Performance* (2012) and *The Cambridge Encyclopedia of Historical Performance in Music* (2018), which was awarded the C. B. Oldman Prize in 2019.

INGRID E. PEARSON has an extensive profile as a clarinetist in the arenas of historical and contemporary performance. She has recorded for DG Archiv and performed with major UK period ensembles. Activities on modern clarinet include an exploration of 19-tone equally-tempered microtonality and chamber music by twentieth-century émigré composers. Pearson's publications encompass iconography, musical listening, organology, and woodwind performance practices as well as aspects of teaching and learning in the conservatory environment. Pearson has been a member of the professoriate at London's Royal College of Music since 2005.

ALBERT R. RICE is a clarinetist, appraiser of musical instruments, and retired museum curator and librarian. His publications include *The Baroque Clarinet and Chalumeau*, *The Clarinet in the Classical Period*, *From the*

Clarinet d'Amour to the Contra Bass, The Note for Clarinetists: A Guide to the Repertoire, and *Four Centuries of Musical Instruments: The Marlowe A. Sigal Collection.*

JULIAN RUSHTON is emeritus professor of music at the University of Leeds, having previously taught at the Universities of East Anglia and Cambridge. He has published widely on various topics including opera (Gluck, Mozart, Berlioz and others) while also playing the clarinet. He was president of the Royal Musical Association (1994–99), past director of the International Musicological Society, and chairman of the editorial committee of *Musica Britannica* (1993–2020).

DAVID E. SCHNEIDER is the Andrew W. Mellon Professor of Music and European Studies at Amherst College where he has taught music history, theory, and chamber music since 1997. In a former life he was artistic director of the Buckley Chamber Players, played clarinet and bass clarinet under Kent Nagano in the Berkeley Symphony, and toured Europe and the Soviet Union as soloist in the Copland Clarinet Concerto. He is the author of *Bartók, Hungary, and the Renewal of Tradition* (2006).

S. FREDERICK STARR is a clarinetist (Albert system) and co-founder of the Louisiana Repertory Jazz Ensemble of New Orleans, which for forty years has travelled, performed, and recorded across America, Europe, and Asia. He is also chairman of the Central Asia-Caucasus Institute at the American Foreign Policy Council and has served as president of Oberlin College and the Aspen Institute and as vice-president of Tulane University. He is the author of *Bamboula!*, a biography of the New Orleans-born Louis Moreau Gottschalk, and of *Red and Hot: The Fate of Jazz in the USSR.*

MARIE SUMNER LOTT is associate professor of music history at Georgia State University in Atlanta. She is the author of *The Social Worlds of Nineteenth-Century Chamber Music: Composers, Consumers, Communities* (University of Illinois Press, 2015). She has also published articles and book chapters on the music of Carl Czerny, Louise Farrenc, Robert and Clara Schumann, and Johannes Brahms. Her current project, *Imagining the Middle Ages in Nineteenth-Century Music*, focuses on Romantic Medievalism in the works of Brahms.

INDEX

An italicized page number indicates a figure, example, or table.

Eastman Studies in Music

Ralph P. Locke, Senior Editor
Eastman School of Music

A complete list of titles in the Eastman Studies in Music series
may be found on our website, www.urpress.com.

www.ingramcontent.com/pod-product-compliance
Lightning Source LLC
Chambersburg PA
CBHW071008140426
42814CB00004BA/167